Daniel Farson was a friend and neighbour of Henry Williamson for a quarter of a century. After a cosmopolitan career as parliamentary correspondent, photographer, sailor, television interviewer, and publican he retired to the West Country in 1964 to concentrate on writing. He has had 21 books published including the bestselling *Jack the Ripper* and, most recently, *A Traveller in Turkey* and *Swandsdowne*, a novel. He has also written several plays for television and contributes regularly to numerous magazines and newspapers.

HENRY
WILLIAMSON

Henry Williamson as a young soldier in 1915.

HENRY WILLIAMSON
A Portrait

DANIEL FARSON

Robinson Publishing
London

Robinson Publishing
11 Shepherd House
5 Shepherd Street
London W1Y 7LD

First published in 1982 by Michael Joseph Ltd.
Published in 1986 by Robinson Publishing

Cover photograph courtesy P. Thurston/Sunday Telegraph

British Library Cataloguing in Publication Data
Farson, Daniel
Henry Williamson: a portrait.
1. Williamson, Henry —— Biography   2. Authors
English —— 20th century —— Biography
I. Title
828′.91208   PR6045.155Z/
ISBN 0-948164-27-1

Printed in England by Richard Clay (The Chaucer Press) Ltd.

Title page and end-of-text illustration: Henry Williamson's owl sketch,
his characteristic signature.

Half title illustrations: Part One, lino-cut by William Kermode from *The
Patriot's Progress* (Geoffrey Bles, 1930); Part Two, extract from Henry
Williamson's inscription to Edward Stokes on his personal copy of
The Peregrine's Saga.

Contents

Acknowledgements

I should like to thank all the people who have helped me so generously in preparing this book, including those who wrote to me after publication of my book on North Devon, *A Window on the Sea*, offering further information concerning Henry Williamson with the hope that this book would be written.

My special thanks to John Hanson for providing me with copies of the Williamson letters in his collection, which were indispensable; also to Mary and George Heath for making their unique collection of Williamson books and documents so available (at the time of writing, Mary Heath is Membership Secretary of the Henry Williamson Society, c/o Longclose, Langtree, North Devon); to Betty and Amanda Allsop, for their advice, and for access to the notes made by the late Kenneth Allsop; Father Brocard Sewell, for loaning me his paper on *The Old Soldier*; David Cobham, for inviting me to a private screening of his film, *Tarka the Otter*; Barbara Rogers of Appledore, who lent me books and listened uncomplainingly; Harry Stevenson Balfour, of Crowberry Cottage, Georgeham; Jim Ashford, of the Rock Inn, Georgeham, described as the 'Upper House' in the Village Books; Frank Swinnerton, for his annotated copy of *The Labouring Life*; Sir Angus Wilson; Frederic Raphael; J. C. Trewin; Barry Driscoll; Brian Kingshott; Sir Maurice Renshaw; the Hon. Lady Mosley; Colin Wilson, for his unfailing assistance; Ronald Creasy; Frederick Rendle; Constable and Co. Ltd, for permission to reproduce extracts from *Katherine Mansfield and Other Literary Studies* by John Middleton Murry; Victor Gollancz Ltd, for permission to reproduce extracts from Ian Niall's biography of C. F. Tunnicliffe, *Portrait of a Country Artist*; The Bodley Head for permission to reproduce two illustrations by C. F. Tunnicliffe from *Tarka the Otter*; Macdonald Ltd for permission to reproduce one lino-cut by William Kermode from

Acknowledgements

The Patriot's Progress; the Equerry to Her Majesty Queen Elizabeth II, for replying to my correspondence so patiently; the Chief Constable of Norfolk, for the trouble he went to on my behalf; Lord Buxton of Stiffkey, Norfolk; Eric Hiscock; Christine (née) Duffield; Eve Elwin, widow of Malcolm Elwin, who encouraged Macdonald to publish 'A Chronicle of Ancient Sunlight'; Commander Stokes and his sister, 'Queenie', and Mr and Mrs Peter Gibbs, for their reminiscences of Henry at Georgeham in the early 1920s; the *Daily Telegraph* Colour Library for their generous assistance and kind permission to reproduce, on the jacket and in the text, photographs of Henry by P. Thurston and David Steen; A. C. Littlejohns (photographer) of Bideford; Derrick Ireland for invaluable bibliographical guidance; Peter Bradshaw for his wise advice and constant encouragement.

My indebtedness, as always, to the efficiency of the London Library, and particular thanks to Victor Bonham Carter and Mark Le Fanu of the Society of Authors.

I should like to express my appreciation to Richard and Anne Williamson, executors of the Williamson Literary Estate. They were not able to grant me access to the Henry Williamson papers, but gave generous permission for this book to be written. The Williamson family have donated the Williamson manuscripts to the nation, and their own collection of papers and letters will form the basis of the definitive biography, to be written by Richard Williamson, which is being looked forward to eagerly by admirers of his father's genius, including myself. Indeed, my thanks go to the entire Williamson family — to his daughter, Margaret; his son, Harry, who has made me welcome always at Ox's Cross; and especially to Mrs Loetitia Williamson, who kindly invited me to visit her in Norfolk. There are aspects of Henry's personal life which the family felt should be treated only in the full biography: any omissions should be seen in that light.

Henry Williamson was a complex man. I hope they will feel that I have been true to him.

Daniel Farson, 1981

Publisher's Note
Dates of first publication of Henry Williamson's works have been given in brackets in the text, on first mention of each title.

Dedicated to Mary and George Heath
of Torridge Books, Langtree, North
Devon, with gratitude for their
constant encouragement

Preface

HOW FORTUNATE I AM in having my book on Henry Williamson reproduced in paperback for this gives me the chance to produce futher evidence which arrived too late for the first edition.

Henry's second wife, Christine, sent me the photograph which is reproduced here as the frontispiece. Henry was nineteen and a tommy on leave. The date was 1915. For me this portrait is the key to so much that came later. I have seen a photograph of him as a young officer taken a couple of years later, but that is a smiling, studio mask compared to the dazed young soldier devoid of vanity and still vulnerable. This is the beginning of the brutal transition from boy to man, forged in the trenches of the First World War.

Henry's boyhood had been happier than he realised, as it often is, though I received some perceptive 'jottings' from F.A. Swann who was a fellow pupil at Colfe's and remembered Henry as 'unusual', even then. He described Henry as, 'Slight, thin-faced with sharp features, dark hair and large dark eyes. He tended to speak in short bursts when excited. I think he knew we called him "Mad Williamson" – hence his character Willie Maddison? His imaginative powers were well-developed, manifesting themselves in frequent departures from the strict truth. A slight clue to the future Henry may lie in his announcing the time and venue of a "fearful fight" with some boy or other. These "fearful fights" never came off, and we learned to discount the exciting promises. Wishful thinking by Henry?'

Another correspondent was kind enough to send me an article which I had overlooked. Always a first-rate journalist, Henry described that halcyon summer in 1914 when he left school, bought a greenheart fly rod in a pawnshop for eighteen pence, a pair of grey flannel trousers and a Donegal tweed jacket at 3s 6d and 12s 6d respectively, and set out for North Devon with a return excursion ticket costing 9s 6d. 'This left a credit of 8s 3d in my Post Office Savings Book.'

The train journey from Waterloo was a glorious adventure then, as strange as travelling abroad with porters wearing red ties, speaking in 'burring voices' at the railway stops where the platforms were alive with rambler roses and beds of wall-flower. After twelve hours he reached his destination (I assume the station was Braunton) to be met by a 2-wheel cart drawn by a plump Exmoor pony and a cider-drinking driver, sent by Henry's aunt.

His holiday was unsullied, full of 'the wide and shining days' as he crossed the empty sands where the only prints were those of gulls or his own tracks, and strode across the moors: 'Twelve, fifteen, once nearly thirty miles in one day, to Ex-moor and back, my face dark brown, my bony limbs all sinew. I fished in the brook, using a dark hawthorn fly, and caught my first trout. And on the last day visited my near and familiar sands and headland and to all I said Goodbye, I shall return . . .'

For most of his generation, life could seldom have seemed so secure yet so promising. There was no hint of imperman-ence and distant rumblings in far off places like Sarejevo were inconsequential. British sterling was inviolate, her navy irre-sistible.

Back in London, Henry reported to his sunless office working there from 10.00 to 4.00 in the regulation uniform of black short jacket, striped trousers and umbrella. When he heard that the staff received an extra fortnight's leave for the annual camp, he joined the Territorials and was issued with a rifle. 'Life wasn't bad.'

In his spare time he explored the unspoilt countryside of north-west Kent only four miles from London Bridge, travelling to the woods on his bike. Finding two young kestrels he tamed them in twelve hours, and sometimes they sat on his shoulders when he climbed to the local sports ground at the top of the hill at Blackheath where music was played on Thursday nights and 'thin, ragged children, dirty and wild' streamed up from the Thames. At dusk the crowds watched the fireworks sent heavenwards from the Crystal Palace, with moans of wonder and delight. The summer was burning itself out and in only weeks to come Henry was to watch the illuminations of the German flares across the trenches.

'It was a strange day,' he remembered, when he bought a paper announcing RUSSIA ORDERS MOBILISATION, on August 3rd. Asquith gave his guarantee to Belgium and the Germans failed to reply – 'wild cheers arose on every side'. Going home, his father said 'Well, old man, we are at war,' and the next day Henry received his call-up papers from the London Regiment, to which the Territorials were attached. Henry describes the poignant close to that summer of extreme innocence: 'My mother helped me to put on my khaki uniform, and after many attempts to roll my puttees, I set out across the Hill. My kestrels followed, wheeling, and coming down to cry to me. They flew as far as the row of elms on the crest. There they perched and watched me going away. I heard their wistful cries as I went through the gates at the end of the Hill. I never saw them again. The last summer of my boyhood had come to its end.'

My certainty that Henry's development was arrested by the horror of the trench warfare awaiting him is stronger than ever, though no wound was visible. Again, I feel it is time to forgive any man his politics if they are forged through such an experience. The frontispiece of young Henry, as wistful as his kestrels, conveys his first doubt and disillusionment, and the animal hurt in his eyes not fully understanding 'Why?'

D. F. 1986

4 Capstone Place, Ilfracombe, Wednesday 9th
April, 1975. Time, 10.55 a.m. Condition —
Pallid, burnt out (feeling) as 1 December
approaches. A failure, henceforward. Sitting in
this little room with tall windows facing north,
and east. And that is all.

Dear Dan

The flow has stopped. It was drying up after my 15th volume of
The Gale of the World, 15th, &, ultimate volume of *A Chronicle of Ancient
Sunlight*, dedicated to Kenneth Allsop. (As a 16 year old, bicycled
from Hertfordshire to Devon to call on the author: & years later
'couldn't take' *The Gale*. (Masefield's opinion — 'You have written
more classics in the English language than any man now living.'
(Well, well . . .

Dan, *in confidence*; I feel I am only litter left. Litter on tables
here — scattered — HERE I CHANGE MY MIND, from Sloth & near-
despair to start again. And I pick up, from the round mahogany table
(all a-litter) your letter. With your help, dear neighbour, I feel I could
start again — a fresh start.

David Cobham, bless him and his dear companion-wife, gave me a
chance on film.

Now the son of dear Negley Farson offers a new hope. Thank you,
Dan! (I changed my mind over your dinner party: & glad I was to find
such a cheery atmosphere.)

(I did hope that 1 December would be kept dark: but what's the
odds? *Times*, and *Telegraph* keep tabs on such items. But it's rather like
prophesying one's own doom — but no! Heart & lungs etc. are sound.

I've never done a *complete* interview — it's all been the other way!
And never embarrassed by any questions. Or the other way round.
(I first broadcast from Savoy Hill in the late twenties, questioned by
my old friend John Heygate.

Heigh Ho! I'm in a blue-red dressing gown, in my sitting room
facing Capstone Place, very grand and tall — & reflecting the southern
sunlight.

TIME 11.22 am. TIRED. Done no journalism for nearly a year. Ditto
broadcasting. It will be fun to see the Savage Club again, after 1½
years; ditto Nat-Liberal Club.

Blessing upon you, Dan'l Farson! And many thanks!
Yours, Henry

Introduction

THIS WAS THE LAST LETTER I received from Henry Williamson. It was written in the year of his eightieth birthday when he looked forward to honours that were, in the event, to be denied him. I find it poignant now: those wistful expectations, the harking back to Masefield (sometimes confused with Hardy), the bitter realization that he was a writer with little left to write. My suggestion of a television programme to celebrate his birthday on 1 December 1975 was more of a lifeline than I knew.

Henry visited me constantly that year, either from the Hut in the field known as Ox's Cross, above Georgeham, or from the cottage he had bought in Ilfracombe. I was living in the grey-stone house left me by my parents above the three-mile stretch of sand along Woolacombe Bay. It was there on the beach one brilliant spring morning in 1968 that I met Henry shortly after he had finished writing *The Gale of the World* (1969), the last of the fifteen volumes that comprise 'A Chronicle of Ancient Sunlight'. This sequence is one of the literary achievements of the century, yet he had doubts that morning, wondering whether he should have conceived the 'Chronicle' as an autobiography rather than fiction. What an admission, I thought with shocked admiration, after so many years of irretrievable effort. I doubt if Henry had lost

1

confidence in himself; but he knew that he was unfashionable with the critics, and was shrewd enough to realize that
this final volume would prove the most unacceptable of all,
even to our mutual friend, Kenneth Allsop, to whom it was
dedicated. When it was published in 1969 Ken told me that
he found it impossible to send the praise Henry was waiting
for; while neighbours of mine implored me not to read the
book because it pilloried my father, Negley Farson, portrayed as the boorish Osgood Nilsson. For a time this did
cause a rift between us, but it had been forgotten by 1975 and
during that year he came down to see me most days of the
week, navigating his MG down the narrow roads as if it
were a tank, resenting any vehicle coming from the opposite
direction. When the retired colonel, who lived in the house
beyond mine, complained that Henry left his car sprawled
across the lane, Henry was indignant: 'I was going to give
him a biff, but thought he'd biff me back.' Sometimes he
would walk from Ox's Cross; once he said that he had
walked all the way from Ilfracombe, and I had no reason to
disbelieve him for his stamina was remarkable, but he gasped
as he sat down: 'I do hope you've got wood for the coffin.'

Henry looked magnificent during his final year in North
Devon. Ellen Terry compared Henry Irving in his old age to
'some beautiful grey tree that I have seen in Savannah'.
Henry, too, had a lean, tree-like strength, wind-swept and
knotted, but unlike the bent beeches at Ox's Cross he
remained upright with the bearing of an old soldier. His hair
was white, but abundant, and though his eyes were watery
they were riveting — he expected you to look at him when
he was talking. Sometimes they flared with anger. He had
never taken kindly to fools, but by 1975 fools were sometimes impatient with the solitary old man in the grey raincoat
sitting in the corner of the pub cupping his hands together
as he imitated the call of the cuckoo. He was neither
mellow nor tamed, and his energy was still prodigious, but

he was becoming forgetful, his mind turning constantly to his experiences in the Great War like a needle stuck in the groove of a record.

Henry was frequently alone by then, which explains his visits to me, in search of company. One evening he arrived ebulliently declaring that it was time he dropped in, and I did not have the heart to point out that he had been to see me only that morning. He greeted food with surprise, as if unused to it. 'Is this sugared tea?' he asked me. 'It's very nice.' He was grateful when there was something interesting to eat instead of his usual diet of pub pasties. 'I feel rather wan,' he admitted; 'I have gone down ten pounds.' Once, when I saw him huddled in his raincoat, I asked if he were cold. He shook his head: 'I don't feel anything. I don't expect I'd feel it if you hit me.' He made an effort to be agreeable, stroking my dog instead of kicking her aside, as he had done once to her great-grandmother when he was reading aloud, but he ruffled her fur the wrong way as he murmured, 'Poor doggy-poggy, poor little man', while she regarded him white-eyed and askance.

One night, after a surfeit of Henry, I took *Life in a Devon Village* (1945, a miscellany of his country tales) from my bedside shelf and was saddened by the passage in 'The First Day of Spring' which referred to a lonely, boring old man whom nobody wants to talk to — 'Little sharp-nosed man, lonely hedge peerer, I thought, come you out of the darkness and I will listen to you' — and wished then that I had been more compassionate myself. In no way was he pathetic, but there was a hint of vulnerability which I ignored. Regrettably, I saw so much of Henry that I took him for granted. It is only in writing this book, and for me it has been worth it for this alone, that I realize what an extraordinary man he was: difficult and complex, a man of such extremes that no single phrase, not even a single book, can tell the whole truth about him.

3

Edward Seago painted a portrait of Henry when they were neighbours in Norfolk during the Second World War, and expressed the hope that one day someone would do so 'in the written word'. He added the perceptive warning: 'Whoever it is will have a difficult task, for Henry Williamson will not be captured easily on paper. I think his biographer will find that he is writing the life of more than one man, and it will not be easy to keep them from getting muddled. But if he fails to do so the portrait will lose by it.' A daunting challenge.

To start with, I had to decide on the book I did not wish to attempt. This is not the definitive biography, for that will be written by his son Richard with his unique access to the vast documentation his father left behind him. Neither am I attempting a purely literary assessment. Nor is this intended as one of those books so popular today which denigrate famous men and slip too easily into newspaper serialization by concentrating on the nastier and more salacious aspects of a man's life, distorting the final balance by eclipsing the talent which gave pleasure for years and would continue to do so if allowed. (Reading a recent life of Somerset Maugham, I barely recognized the courteous, decorous gentleman who befriended me first when I was a boy in America. He had been transformed into a sensual monster, as if his malevolence were all that mattered.) Henry could be cruel to those he loved, but that was not the whole truth. You may well ask, what is this book about and what is the point of writing it? It is an apology for failing to recognize his true value when he was alive; a personal appreciation, to compensate. Fortunately, by the time I finished this book, I understood Henry Williamson better and liked him more.

Although he was best known for *Tarka the Otter* (1927), Williamson's importance in English literature goes beyond

4

one book, classic though it is and part of the pleasure of growing up. The four books comprising 'The Flax of Dream' (published individually in 1921, 1922, 1924 and 1928) evoke the innocence of the English countryside in North Devon as it never will be again; while the fifteen volumes of 'A Chronicle of Ancient Sunlight' (also published individually, between 1951 and 1969) are his life's work and vindication. They have been compared to Dickens and Proust, even to Tolstoy, but they are pure Williamson. These startling comparisons only prove their range; and it seems extraordinary that they are out of print although they are being advertised for and change hands for considerable sums of money. Their time will come, and with it Henry's.

Why was he neglected at the end? When Anthony Powell concluded 'A Dance to the Music of Time', his achievement was celebrated in every posh Sunday paper. When Sir Victor Pritchett reached his eightieth birthday, this was hailed as a triumphant occasion. Henry's birthday passed unnoticed. He was hurt, in spite of that deprecating, 'I did hope that 1 December would be kept dark: but what's the odds?' In *Cakes and Ale* (1930), Somerset Maugham described such a literary occasion as it ought to be, when homage was paid to Edward Driffield, a character based on Thomas Hardy: '... it was a thoroughly representative gathering — science, politics, art, the world; I think you'd have to go a long way to find gathered together such a collection of distinguished people as got out from that train at Blackstable. It was awfully moving when the PM presented the old man with the Order of Merit.' The people who got out of the train at Barnstaple were Henry's sons, and they took him to dinner at the Imperial Hotel. He valued that, but he deserved the OM.

Why, then, did a man whose books portray our countryside with such rare tenderness go to his death unhonoured? He offended. Henry Williamson was a supporter of Sir

5

Oswald Mosley and an admirer of Hitler. The English may give knighthoods to Soviet spies, but they draw the line at Fascists. Wodehouse was pardoned for his Berlin bumblings; Chaplin was excused his voluntary exile because he was a clown. Henry Williamson was never forgiven, because of his constancy.

Now that he is dead people come to visit me simply because I knew him, and I have noticed that they are not concerned with his private life or his politics, but accept Henry Williamson as one of the last true literary figures in England. Ironically, as I hope to show, I believe he was also a patriot. He deplored the last war because he loved this country and believed that the British and Germans should never fight one another again. This was consistent with his experiences in the First World War, the Christmas truce in particular. Everything stemmed from that.

PART ONE

Experience of war

ONE

'A beautiful war'

HENRY WILLIAMSON WAS READY and restless for war when
he joined up in 1914, after a childhood which he described
as deeply unhappy. This may not have been the whole truth,
for he always knew how to magnify a grievance. But that
was his claim.

He was born on 1 December 1895 at 66 Bradfield Road,
Brockley, on the edge of an expanding London. A small, thin
child with abnormally brown eyes, he was timid and wild
and thought himself loveless. Describing his 'nervous self'
arriving at school in a cousin's reach-me-down Eton jacket,
trousers and hobnailed boots, Henry admitted that he
exuded a mask of vulnerability — 'an irritating timidity and
inability to be as other boys'. This made him a target for the
school bullies who held his head under water while he was
learning the breaststroke at the Ladywell Baths, which
increased his nervousness. At the age of sixteen he was
ashamed of his small body, high voice and staring eyes,
which like his mother's filled easily with tears, to his father's
'exasperation and complaint'. But when he said of himself
that he was a coward and the 'worst boy' at school, it was
false modesty. Perhaps there were moments of misery, there
usually are at school, but a few years later he was able to look
back 'with affection' on his fellow pupils, 'including the

9

hundred or so of my generation who were killed in the 1914–18 war'.

At home Henry was cared for by a devoted mother and nanny. At school he had the freedom to escape every Wednesday and Saturday afternoon and bicycle to the Holme Park Woods in Kent, owned by the Dowager Countess of Derby, where he had permission to roam in search of wild animals and birds' eggs. He went to Brighton, Norfolk and the West Country on holiday. His one deprivation was the lack of a close relationship with his father, and he yearned for this so acutely that it may explain his lifelong search for 'the perfect companion'. Henry's first wife, Loetitia, told me that William Leopold Williamson was 'a difficult man, a perfectionist like Henry himself'; but, as Henry came to realize later, his father suppressed a warmer spirit in order to cope with his responsibilities, enduring the dull drudgery of his job as a bank clerk. Too dutiful for happiness, he was unable to release the love his son craved. 'A child lacking love forms itself alone,' Henry wrote later. 'It will live mainly in a world of fantasy.' Unfortunately, Henry's fantasies were seen by his father as wild inventions to avoid the truth, and his anger on such occasions made his son shrink from him. 'It is mainly true to say that many a small boy suffered malformation of the spirit in the first place through chronic fear in his father's home ...' This helps to explain why in so many ways Henry remained the perennial schoolboy.

One of the difficulties in writing about Henry Williamson is that he recorded so many versions of the truth himself — in conversation, letters, broadcasts and books. This was not necessarily wilful contradiction, he was simply recalling the truth as he saw it at the time.

Paradoxically, he was often closer to the truth in his fiction than his fact. *Donkey Boy* (1952, the second volume in 'A Chronicle of Ancient Sunlight'), gives a vivid description of his parents and a rich evocation of his childhood, through Phillip Maddison his declared doppel-gänger. The portrayal of his father as Richard Maddison is not unforgiving, but shows a cold, pedantic man with all the bigotry of the middle class at the turn of the century. We know, from the first volume (*The Dark Lantern*, 1951), of Richard's hopes that came to nothing, of his bad luck, and his marriage to the delightful Hetty who disappoints and irritates him with her constant anxiety to please. It is a riveting study of a narrow man who, in the first chapter, cleans the furniture with carbolic after a visit from his brother-in-law whom he suspects is a carrier of syphilis. The household exudes a gentility which Henry must have detested as he grew up under the influence of its inverted snobbery; in later years he exhibited a tendency to show off in front of titled people as if he felt himself inferior.

It is risky to interpret any passage as strictly true, especially where details are concerned, for it ignores the power of Henry's imagination, but sometimes an emotion shines through so brightly that it is hard not to accept it as autobiographical. Henry may have welcomed the guise of fiction when describing the inability of the father, Richard, to embrace the son, Phillip, and the son's rejection too. Lying joyfully in his parents' bed one Sunday morning, Phillip pushes his father away instinctively, although 'the child did love the father'. In his turn, Richard resisted the impulse to include 'the child too warmly in his affection, and so the child never merged as it were into the father, to draw the vital warmth, to become one flesh, the basis of natural feeling'. This was 'sealed off, and the son became, at an early age, as aggrieved in spirit as was the father'.

Writing about Phillip, Henry provides the key to his own character:

Lacking the father-hero vision on which to grow spiritually sound, he made his own wilderness vision later, through poetic feeling. It was not the war which deranged him; but the early pattern, 'poor twisted boy', ever seeking what was lacking in him, restless, escapist, hurrying to find over the next hill what he had not found in life — serenity through love.

The pattern had been set and the war forged it.

A difficult father, a difficult son. It is probable that William Williamson breathed an equal sigh of relief when Henry left to join the war in the summer of 1914.

Henry enlisted in the 1st Battalion of the London Rifle Brigade — 'next door to the London Scottish who went over a few days before we did and copped a hell of a packet' — and sailed from Southampton for France on 4 November after a day's leave in London. More than fifty years later, when we met in North Devon, he told me of his experiences and, typical of Henry, his versions varied. He claimed he was sixteen and a half when he joined up, but he was nineteen on 1 December 1914. Sometimes, remembering a British Tommy who comforted a German soldier, he would be that Tommy, sometimes not. None of this matters. As an artist, Henry was permitted to turn an incident to his advantage. As a participant, too. From such a distance the details of his recollections were blurred, and I can only navigate my way through the discrepancies as best I can; but the crucial images were etched indelibly upon his mind.

When they sailed for France, the night was cold and they slept on the rusty deck open to the rain, though they had blankets and sails to cover them. As they entered Le Havre, a pilot boat came out to greet them and when someone yelled out, 'Give them that song, they've never heard it over here,' the soldiers burst into 'Tipperary' which had just become popular. They were kept waiting at the dock for so long that

Henry collected money for bottles of red wine from a shop a few hundred yards away. When he returned with his purchase he was stopped by an officious lance-corporal who asked what he was doing.

'I'm shopping for the commanding officer of the battalion,' Henry replied blandly. 'Would you like a bottle?'

The lance-corporal refused indignantly, saying, 'I'm not going to be caught.' But he let Henry through.

Forty-eight hours later as they marched towards the front they halted at a convent which had been placed at their disposal. As dusk fell Henry climbed a nearby hill and listened to the soft 'boom boom' of the guns in the distance: 'How thrilling it was! Then I went back and slept on the wooden floor with two or three blankets. A week later we were in the trenches. It was lovely. Pheasants were crowing.' This is typical of his curious, vague ambivalence to war.

From the outset he left the trenches at night to wander near the German lines. This was not bravado, simply that the trenches were knee-deep in water and he wanted to keep dry. Near the enemy lines he was disturbed by the sound of young German voices, once even the poignant cry of, 'Mütter, Mütter'. One incident made a lasting impression and I heard him recount it many times:

> One of our chaps was hit in the ankle when he was out on patrol in No Man's Land at eleven at night. He hung there, draped over the barbed wire. I got on to the parapet, I'm not boasting, and shouted out 'I'm coming to the rescue of my comrade'. The firing ceased and a German officer helped me remove him, saluted and turned away. *That was a bloody miracle!* But it happened again and again, so we all thought they were very decent fellows and the propaganda back home was so much bunk.

The overwhelming experience for him, however, was the Christmas truce in 1914. It was the most redeeming moment of the war, and no sensitive man could have emerged unchanged. In Henry's case, it altered the course of his life.

Henry had been sent straight up the line because of the threat of a German attack. 'I didn't mind a bit, nor did the fellows.' There was an attack and about a week later, as he was walking the two-and-a-half miles back from the little dug-out, he 'suddenly remembered that it was Christmas Day and decided to get some food'. As he looked towards No Man's Land, he realized that something extraordinary had happened — a state of truce had been declared spontaneously between the opposing forces:

> There, on the one side, were all the Germans in field-grey, together with our chaps, all talking and exchanging photographs. A nice German had one of Princess Mary [the late Princess Royal, Countess of Harewood] — 'Ah, schöne, schöne prinzessin!' I wanted to get right behind their lines but a German officer came up to me and asked 'What do you do?' 'Admiring your beautiful field fortifications,' I told him. And he smiled and saluted and I went back and told my 2nd lieutenant, who ordered me not to do it again.

The friendship grew throughout that Christmas Day as the enemies played football and swapped photographs, cognac and cigarettes, and spoke in scraps of each other's language: 'After the war we'll come back, comrade.' One German soldier sang 'Heilige Nacht' incessantly, and Henry echoed the words years later in a voice surprisingly high and pure. The fraternization continued until dusk, when the officers gave the signal for the men to withdraw to their separate lines. A few hours later, shots were fired into the air and the slaughter recommenced. But the moment of mutual sympathy continued, for many British soldiers now realized that, like themselves, the Germans were only doing their duty.

'Did it have a deep effect on you?' I asked Henry.

'Oh yes, oh yes,' he replied very softly. 'Very deep, and I always felt an admiration for the Germans afterwards, for they were very decent fellows.' His voice lowered as if we had just entered a cathedral.

'Did it underline the futility of war?'

'The effect on me was — there must be fair-dos all round, and then we will have peace because we cannot go on murdering and killing...'

The Christmas truce marked Henry for life. His discovery that the 'ordinary' German soldier was much like himself coloured his whole approach to Germany and shaped his attitude towards Hitler and the Nazis in the 1930s.

Another wartime experience of deep significance to him was his first offensive in 1915:

> The night turning into a total brilliance as a battery of howitzer opened up on our left and 2,000 guns fired at once. It was 5.30 am by my wristlet watch — zero hour — and as soon as the barrage began, all the nightingales came out, you could hear them singing like hell. Tremendous exhilaration, like the end of Wagner's *The Ring*. Partridges flying from gunfire; larks in the sky. The guns, the lights, the great roar. It wasn't fear, it was magnificent.

Less exhilarating was the cold, which terminated his first spell at the front. He nearly lost his toes through 'frost feet' but was spared amputation:

> There was our wood and the German trenches a hundred yards away and my feet were terrible. They were frozen and I felt 'I've got to walk about' and I did, and came back to the dug-out and lit a candle, but it was no

15

good. Four or five days later they were like big tomatoes, also the boots I was wearing were one size too
small and bunched up my toes. I was very lucky, they
might have had to come off if I had left them one more
day. They've been painful ever since. I came away very
quickly when the doctors saw them.

Writing of this for the Colfe's School magazine, *Colfensia*, as
an old buff, he did not show off or exaggerate: '17 March
1915: ... I was invalided home about two months ago, but
am now cured, although, of course, I am not now very
strong; my nerves are a bit "joggy" too.' He went on to
describe his first spell at the front. It is his first published
work and shows his natural talent:

The first time we went in the trenches we were mixed
up with regulars, being, of course, rather nerve-shaken.
But the feeling of nervousness soon left us, and we set to
work to pump the trenches ... 2 feet deep in mud and
water, and the harder we pumped, the deeper grew the
water (or so it seemed to us). In the trenches we do one
hour 'on' sentry, and one 'off'. This is through the hours
of darkness. During one hour 'off' we pump, dig, fix up
wire in front, fetch rations and numerous other jobs ...
After three or four days of this the strain is rather acute.
The fact of no sleep, and legs, and, in fact, all the body
wet through, does not help to improve the situation.
Now and then we get a shell or two over, and when
very lucky an attack. We are literally overjoyed when
they attack us, for it means a great shooting practice.
They attack shoulder to shoulder and *march* on our
trenches. When (and *if*) they get within twenty yards
they open fanwise, and some sections lie down to allow
a clear pattern for the Maxim fire. But, generally, they
get to the barbed-wire entanglements, and there they
stop. It is a fine sound to hear thousands of rifles and

machine-guns all cracking at once, and now and then a 'rafale' of several batteries of French 75 m.m. guns.

To the headmaster, Henry wrote:

> The chief trouble is the mud. We sleep on mud, we get mud on our rifles, on our clothes, in our hair, in our food.
>
> We are men who live in the moment only; we cannot tell when a bullet will find us or a shell hasten our end, but for the moment the room is warm, the roof over our head keeps out the rain, we are happy and contented. Three weeks later, another week of wet and mud. Thus our life goes on.
>
> The past appears to have belonged to another world. We hope and pray that it will come again, and know inwardly that, if we are spared, the day is not so very far away when having done our duty to our country, we shall look back on the days of fighting as but a memory, and not a very pleasant one.

It was not to be so simple.

Transferred from the London Rifle Brigade to the 10th Battalion Regiment, he received his commission as a 2nd lieutenant on 13 June 1915 and returned to the front to find that the yellow clay of winter had been replaced by the aggravations of a summer made 'wretched with the blue-bottles eating up their dead'. He was promoted to full lieutenant on 1 July 1917 but was sent back to England shortly afterwards suffering from shock and dysentery. 'I was very thin and the doctors could see I had had my fill. I was sent up north somewhere, Manchester, I think, and we were taken up by the gentry, in our little blue jackets — really very nice.' (This referred to the 'hospital blue' worn by convalescing servicemen.) When he recovered he was sent to Folkestone where he was put in charge of 'a lot of irregulars, though I never went near them'.

When I knew him, Henry had obliterated the brutality from his mind, remembering only the finer qualities of war. 'Here and there we found some mercy and kindness, and that is what made the war generally, apart from the physical wounds, rather a nice one.'

'Rather a nice one!' Seeing my astonishment, he commented:

'It wasn't such a bad war really.' And then to confound me further, he murmured, 'Beautiful'.

Although Henry was able to say this to me years later, the artist in him would not accept such a travesty of the truth when the memory was still fresh. In 1928, the year before publication of Robert Graves's *Goodbye To All That*, an Australian painter, William Kermode, asked Henry to write the captions for his lino-cuts of the war. Characteristically, Henry reversed the rôles, producing a complete book with the lino-cuts serving as illustrations. After certain vicissitudes with the long-suffering publisher, Geoffrey Bles, *The Patriot's Progress* was published in April 1930. This is one of Henry's most unusual books, with a hard edge to his writing, justifying Arnold Bennett's claim that 'of its kind [it] has never been surpassed'. Henry claimed that he descibed the war with greater objectivity in the 'Chronicle', but it is precisely the lack of objectivity which makes *The Patriot's Progress* so powerful that you feel scorched by its anger.

After the jaunty beginning, with John Bullock hurrying to enlist in case he misses the fun, the reader gradually senses the horror of life in the trenches:

The long bright shafts of whitish light smacked the air, the shells screamed away just over their helmets. Each narrow light-blast was like concentrated moonlight. Surely the Germans would see them. His mind flung about in a panic. Stop firing, for Christ's sake. Blinding light, pas-aa-ang of shell screaming eastwards . . . as in a dream wherein terrible bright-bright-bright-bright-ness screeched itself into sudden smothering darkness.

The pace becomes surrealist as his friend Ginger is killed: 'Blood ran down from a hole in his right temple. The back of his head was open like an egg, hairy with thick blood and broken-sploshed grey brains. He snored and gurgled and twitched. Blood trickled from his ears and mouth; he kicked, blew blood bubbles from his nostrils. They heaved him over the parados when dead.' Now, facing death himself, Bullock thinks of home: 'He had a glimpse of a tablecloth, plates, a loaf, a whiskey bottle and mug, a magazine; wildly he imagined himself sitting there in paradise. Perhaps never see home any more, mother's face, hearing his death. O why, why was the War? Death was darkness, good-bye for ever. FOREVER. He couldn't go over the top. No, no. *Over the top* was terrible. DEATH. He couldn't.'

Then there is the silence of the white wards as he lies wounded: '... the swish of felt slippers, the terrible white walls and crying, the strange white sheets and beds in a row'.

At last the park bench in England, where the Toff and a boy with a flag notice his amputated leg and stop, condescendingly. '"We'll see that England doesn't forget you fellows," says the Toff. "We are England," said John Bullock with a slow smile. The old gentleman could not look at him in the eyes; and the little boy ceased to wave his flag, and stared sorrowfully at the poor man.... Here ends The Patriot's Progress.' A moving ending to a vivid portrayal of the horrors of trench warfare, quite at variance with Henry's romantic memories years later.

Ambivalent though his attitudes were, one thing is certain: after 1918, he missed the companionship of his fellow soldiers, realizing (as many do in wartime) that, searing though it was, he had shared an extraordinary and in some ways noble

19

experience which could never be recovered. If we imagine the enclosed comradeship of the trenches — which could never be fully understood by men who were not there — is it any wonder that this was the aspect of war which Henry chose to remember?

If Henry had been ready for war, he was not prepared for peace. Safely back in England, though the war still blundered on, Henry looked back, both appalled and fascinated. A friend from that period, Frederick Rendle, remembers his erratic behaviour in Folkestone, where he was in charge of the 'Irregulars'. Once he saw Henry seize several deck chairs and hurl them over the cliff from the Lees 'Angered, I seem to recollect, by the absurdity of his experiences at the front'. He believed that Henry had been invalided home due to shell shock, and though this may have been true in a general rather than a literal sense, Henry was probably suffering from a sense of anti-climax, as if his survival were both a miracle and a bad joke. But Henry was also deep in the grip of another strong emotion: he was in love. The girl was Evelyn (sometimes Eveline) Fairfax, romanticized in *The Dream of Fair Women* (1924, the third volume of 'The Flax of Dream') and in his memory. He mentioned her to me after I had the impertinence to ask him: 'Who were the women you have loved in your life?' This merited a snort of indignation: 'Does a gentleman tell? It's a question of form; you don't go and shout out, "I've just screwed Alice!"' Then he laughed. 'A famous lover is a lot of old rubbish — but who was that woman in Folkestone after the war?' As he remembered her he smiled with pleasure: 'Oh, she was a lovely girl, only eighteen, a great friend of Lord Somebody-or-other — was it Longford? — whom she met coming over on the boat from South Africa. It was wonderful . . .'

'Were you in love with her?'

'Oh yes. I was very happy. Walking hand in hand along the parade...'

The zest of the youthful affair was fun while it lasted, but Evelyn was unable to choose between her admirers, and Henry was not heart-broken by her ultimate rejection. 'I had been cast off from a disastrous love affair which had begun as a pleasant philander and ended in a conviction of my own utter sincerity and non-appreciation.'

Henry was looking back romantically to a first love; but Frederick Rendle remembers her as 'a red-headed houri, older than he was, and a great anxiety to her husband. She must have been startled to be so idealized. In later years she was thrown out of Kenya on the Governor's orders.'

Henry found the distraction he needed in the writing of his first novel, *The Beautiful Years* (1921, the first volume of 'The Flax of Dream'), which he started while awaiting demobilization, withdrawing from the regimental mess dinners into his hut and locking the door in case he was seen by his fellow officers. It was about this time, 1919, that he chanced on a copy of Richard Jefferies's *The Story of My Heart* (1883) in a second-hand bookshop in Folkestone: the rare occasion when a book can influence a lifetime. Writing in *The Pathway* (1928, and the last of the four novels of 'The Flax of Dream') he said:

> All the stored up impressions of my boyhood seemed to return, with a mysterious spirit that brought tears to my eyes many times. I stood there more than an hour, so rapt was I in the pages, which were a revelation to me of my own self, which had been smothered all through the hectic days of the war. Indeed, for some time afterwards... I thought that Jefferies was with me, and of me. I grew and grew in spiritual strength; and I realized that all the world was built up of thought; mostly mediocre and selfish thought. Change thought and you can change the world.

21

Exactly fifty years later, he told Roy Plomley that this was the one book he would take to a desert island: 'Brave and lovely and beautiful, it is part of the soul of man'.

After the Armistice and his demobilization, Henry returned home to Blackheath armed with his inspiration: 'I was burning inwardly with a belief that I had discovered mystically the source of the Mind of Man; and I felt, but never dared to say except in wild outbursts in my father's home, that I had the power to reveal everything through the written word.' It is possible to feel sympathy for his father, who was dismayed by the outbursts which smacked so dangerously of arrogance. It pained him to see his son idle, by his standards, when he should have been poised on the threshold of a stable career; he was unimpressed by all the protestations about literature, which he saw as a devious excuse to loaf.

But Henry's objective was no longer in doubt, as he revealed in his contribution to *The Book of Fleet Street* (ed. Michael Pope, 1930): 'I left the army, in September 1919, without the least intention of doing any work for my living, except by writing, my own kind of writing. Nothing could dispel my confidence; but many people tried to shake it.'

The determination not to take a job was fortified by the few hundred pounds given by a grateful government as 'blood money' on his demobilization. Henry commented that this was generous, considering 'the very good time' he had enjoyed; but when the money ran out he was forced into Fleet Street, not as a writer but as a salesman for the Classified Advertising Department of *The Times*. For someone who intended to change the course of the world, it must have been a wearisome delay as he trudged around the suburbs trying to canvas adverts from estate agents: Willesden, Harpenden, Ongar and Balls Pond — the very names sound like a dirge. At night he wrote *The Beautiful Years* in his bedroom with the stars shining above the elm trees outside, his tame owl perched on the back of his chair. He had reached that exhilarating stage where the book writes itself, 'flowing like sap from the roots of my being, the scenes creating themselves. Not in those days the tortured and blackened pages of the later books.' When it was finished the euphoria faded: 'I was certainly rootless and without hope; ... I was drinking far too much for one with a weak stomach, and sleeping insufficiently, "living on my nerves".'

In 1920 he gained an unlikely job in Fleet Street, as a 'motoring correspondent', and contributed notes to the *Weekly* at four guineas a time. When he needed ideas he became a 'fake merchant', as he described himself, inventing a story about a peregrine falcon which attacked the pigeons perched on St Paul's: 'It swished down at about a hundred miles an hour — I've dived in a Sopwith Camel and know what speed is — and, zooming up on its back, struck a pigeon on the breast with its talons.' 'Put that on page one!' cried the editor, or so Henry claimed. But on 16 September 1920 he was sacked in the name of economy. 'Good!' he exclaimed, 'now I shall begin to write.' His father was appalled, being a man who relied on routine and reported for work promptly each morning while his son lingered in bed. Emerging in the evening, Henry walked across the fields of Blackheath, talked to strangers in pubs, or went to Covent Garden to look down from the gallery as Thomas Beecham conducted such operas as *Mignon*. When his father announced that Marie Lloyd was 'not quite nice', Henry hurried off to see her at a music hall. He welcomed the darkness, like the owl which became his symbol. 'My "mind fire" burned only at night; the stars were my companions when the carters and labourers of the public bars had gone home after closing time.' Usually he returned home, crawling drunkenly through his bedroom window, at two in the morning.

There were bitter arguments with his father who accused him of using the house as an hotel. But their disagreements went wider than this and on one occasion, when Henry defended the bravery of the German soldier, his father (whose mother, interestingly, was Bavarian) shouted 'Traitor!', a taunt which pursued Henry for the rest of his life. At last they reached breaking point late one night:

'I don't know if you are ill,' cried his father, 'but you're killing yourself and you're killing me. You've got to leave home.'

'Yes, father,' Henry replied meekly, and it is easy to imagine how irritating this must have been.

His gentle, devoted mother tried to intervene: 'Oh no, not so late at night.'

'Yes,' replied her husband. 'He's kept me awake long enough. It's no good, I'm sending him away.'

'Yes, father.'

In *The Sun in the Sands* (1945, Henry's fictional account of his first few years after leaving London), there is another version. The straight-laced father refers to his son Phillip Maddison's suicide attempt as the final outrage — 'You have had two jobs and lost them both. And now that incident with the loaded revolver a week ago, when you threatened to kill yourself, has decided what has been in my mind for a long time now...' — and he orders him to leave. This was obviously based on Henry's own experience. Whether or not he threatened suicide at that time cannot be certain; but as we shall see later, his friend 'Queenie', who knew him as a girl in Georgeham, says that he did so subsequently.

This confrontation with his father was final. Collecting a friend (the Swinburnian poet whom he called 'Julian Warbeck' in his novels), Henry left London on his beloved Norton motorbike and headed for North Devon.

TWO

Dog days in Devon

W HEN HENRY CAME to Georgeham in 1921, the main disruption came from his own motorbike. He rented a labourer's
dwelling known as Skirr Cottage, below St George's Church,
beside the stream next to the graveyard where he is buried
today. The cost of £5 a year was paid for with the occasional
'snippet' sold to the *Daily Express* for one-and-a-half guineas.
It was a simple place at the end of a row of similar cottages,
with two small lime-washed bedrooms and a downstairs
room, about twelve feet square, with a stone floor, an open
hearth, and a battered black kitchen range at the back
which belched out blue wood smoke. A fastidious visitor
remembers it as 'a hovel, a ghastly place, no water, no heat,
no light, and no drains! Just a sort of roof over his head.' But
to Henry the cottage was home and the stream made it
idyllic: 'Even in the hot summer the water runs; I have made
a pool of stones where the swallows and martins can go for
the mud to build their homes. Beautiful it is to see, in the
shadows of the trees, these birds alighting softly on a
boulder, or by the pool's edge . . . . They are timid, restless
things, rising into the air at the slightest noise . . . . They soon
came to know me and minded not my presence.'

He surrounded himself with animals: the spaniel pup
named Billjohn; a black and white kitten; various birds

including a razorbill found on the shore, its feathers clogged with oil; and a white owl which rested in the tattered thatch above. Sometimes the animals would accompany him to the corner of Putsborough Sands a few miles away (also known as Vention after the 'invention' of the lime-kiln built on the edge of the shore). He swam and rested in the sun and tried to forget the past. But though these halcyon days were the perfect antidote to war, he yearned for what he had lost — a yearning which was shortly to find expression through Willie Maddison in the *The Dream of Fair Women*:

> Never again to have such friendships? Or to see the white flares beyond the parapet at night and hear the mournful wailing of gas horns over the wastes of the Somme battlefields? Gone, gone forever. His heart ached: the splendid, bitter days of the war dimmed as he lay on the beach of shells, among the dried weed and black brittle cases of the dogfish eggs cast up during old storms, and corks and rusty tins, and all the littered drift of the sea. He wandered, the twilight tracts of the lost generation, a dead man with dead men, with aching breast, for he was living.

Devon was not a chance destination. He had spent several holidays there while at school, staying with the postmistress in the Post Office opposite Skirr Cottage. A few weeks before the outbreak of war he had gone to Georgeham on a 9s. 6d. return ticket from Waterloo. As he was leaving he shouted 'Goodbye, heather! I'm coming back.' He also spent a leave there in 1916, after the Battle of the Somme, and had carved his initials on a rock at Vention. He felt he belonged to the West Country and liked to claim that his mother's family had been living on the edge of Exmoor at Knowstowe since 1015, before the arrival of the Normans. Then they were called Shapcote; but during the eighteenth century the family home was sold and they moved to Exeter where

Sarah Shapcote married an Irish naval captain, Thomas William Leaver. Leaver was his mother's maiden name and Henry William Williamson rejoiced in this ancestry: 'It was a good feeling that one had roots in Devon.'

It was a happy choice, for he arrived in Devon when it was still unspoilt and he was able to explore the countryside before it was overwhelmed by cars. Ham, as he named Georgeham in his novels, lay within walking distance of the savage coastline beyond Morte: the sweep of Woolacombe Bay; the powerful, jutting arm of Baggy Point, with the cliffs and caves at the end; Croyde Bay; and then the stretching miles of Saunton Sands up to the estuary of the rivers Taw and Torridge which swept out to sea over Bideford Bar.

Even today it remains an exhilarating landscape. The undulating dunes of the Burrows, which lie between Saunton Sands and the Great Field of Braunton, look arid from a distance but are rich with wild flowers when you descend into the valleys — yellow, poppy-like blooms on tall stems, blue viper's bugloss, and small wild orchids in the springtime after rain. These dunes are so immense that a dog was once lost there, revolving in circles, until it was spotted by a helicopter. I am delighted when I lose my way, after so many years, and am forced to climb to the highest point to find my bearings. It is a daring landscape that never disappoints, used by Gabriel Pascal for the Egyptian desert in his film *Caesar and Cleopatra*, and for Paradise in *A Matter of Life and Death*. With typically British compromise, the Burrows are now both a nature reserve and a training ground for amphibious manoeuvres, but it seems to work. You can walk for hours in the winter without seeing another person; in summer it is different, but visitors usually make for Crow Point beside the sea, and the dunes are spared.

Admittedly, there are many more visitors now than there were when Henry first discovered the Burrows. They come in their hundreds, through the toll gate outside Braunton at Vellator (once a small port for coasters bringing coal up the 'pill' from South Wales), and on past the marshes with the massive nests of swans who are increasingly harassed today and sometimes killed. It is pointless regretting the influx of people into places you have loved, but it is hard to resist when you have known better days. Henry deplored what he considered to be an 'invasion', in an article for *The Sunday Times* in 1962: 'The enemy is the motor-car. Later in the summer thousands of motor-cars will find their way, as they have in the past few years, and once again the beautiful wild place, beautiful despite its war-wounds [his reference to a road made by the American army], will be an area of litter, broken or abandoned milk-bottles, tents, haphazard sanitation.' He asked wistfully, 'Must Nature die, always, where man goes on wheels?' but even when he wrote that, the Burrows were unspoilt compared to nowadays. Will today's landscape seem wild in another twenty years' time? I expect so, but a saturation point can be reached when it is spoilt forever.

All things are relative, but it seems incredible today that Henry could visit Vention in the late 1920s and complain: 'On some days of August we passed as many as three or four cars standing in the rocky gateway near the top of the steep lane leading down to the old lime-burners' cottages. And on the sands themselves, often a dozen people besides myself were bathing. The place was spoiled.' A dozen people! In August! Today there is a shimmering stain of cars in the field, now effectively a car-park, beside the lane.

Henry had no idea how lucky he was to know North Devon in gentler times. He thought it indecent if he walked less than fifteen miles a day, and he grew to know the land 'intensely'. The summers were hotter then (no longer can there be any doubt of that), and he climbed the sandhills barefoot in the June sunshine: 'Pouring down with sudden heat when the sea-clouds thin away up the valley, the loose slops of sand spilling under the tread. Their crests held by marram grass, these hills rise, range upon range, to the remote murmur of the sea. As one trudges on, the heat feels to be Arabian, the eyelids narrow in the glare, the soles of the feet burn. But no giving in!'

Every day, on every walk, Henry gleaned material for his books; but in those early days he was scarcely known as a writer. It is a shock to realize that (although they were successfully reprinted years later), in their first editions only 750 copies of *The Beautiful Years* were printed, and 500 of *The Lone Swallows* (1922, a collection of essays of boyhood and youth) — of which only 140 were sold, at 8s. 6d., and the rest remaindered at 6d. each. How different from today's television dramas, which might be viewed by millions; but how much better for a young writer learning his craft.

One person who never lost faith in Henry, was Henry himself; but the villagers of Georgeham, like the reading public, were unimpressed. They became positively suspicious when he announced that he was going to use *them* as characters for his novels. He changed the names for his landscape — Georgeham becoming Ham, Croyde became Cryde, Braunton Branton — but, although the landmarks were often identical, it is not simply a matter of superimposing a negative on a print to see if they fit. That was not his objective, and he shifted his terrain whenever it suited his story. The shifting of people was trickier, as he explained in his preface to the American edition of *The Village Book* (stories of village life, first published in Britain in 1930):

Have I, for example, written truly about the character called the Rector? I call him an imaginary character, because I have manipulated him, for the purpose of fiction, while writing the various stories in which he appears. Therefore the character is Williamson-rector;

the Rector is not, by reason of manipulation, a truthful portrait of any living man. At the same time, it would be contemptible and dishonest to deny that the character is based upon the incumbent of the village where I lived for several years. It is based upon the late Rector of the village; and other characters are based on living people too.

In fact, the Rector took such offence at his portrayal that he preached a sermon from the pulpit aimed indirectly at Henry and his stories of Ham.

Henry was an outsider, even to other outsiders who found his behaviour both headstrong and aloof. When three ladies complained to the committee of the local tennis club that he was not a suitable companion for their sons, and certainly not for their daughters, he was expelled from the club. He was hurt by their rejection: 'When I didn't defend myself against the wild rumours and exaggerations made into charges of immoral behaviour brought by three ladies of the middle-class residing in Braunton, I injured my powers of living and writing.' Henry wanted to be accepted; but a big fish causes a ripple if he turns round in a small pool, and Henry thrashed the water.

Unless you have lived in such a small, rather isolated, Devon community you cannot truly understand the kind of suspicion that was directed against Henry. Beneath the apple-cheeked façade there is a hardness that an outsider would find difficult to penetrate. Even if the outsider conforms he is barely tolerated. Henry and his sense of humour were alien and misunderstood. In *The Sun in the Sands*, he curses himself for his stupidity in going to a fancy-dress dance, a mistake that made him 'shy of local society for ever afterwards':

How many times I writhed in bed at night, remembering my sudden idiotic appearance at that dance in

30

home-made costume assembled from pyjamas, riding boots, leather jerkin, with my face white-washed and burnt-cork black circles round my eyes, a baby's woollen cap on my head stuck with two turkey feathers, and carrying in my mouth a moth-eaten lambskin tied with rope in the shape of a mouse! Village boys cheered as I arrived on my Norton. Quickly up the wooden steps to the Dance Room I ran: it was an interval between dances: uttering a great screech, I announced myself as a Barn Owl. My joke or fancy at the Fancy Dress Dance fell flat and lifeless as a slab of wet putty. An old lady with white hair and a baby's complexion said, in my hearing, *Why was that drunken outsider invited, I wonder?* The room revolved about me: I felt the shock right through me. Desperately I thought of the Spartan boy and the fox, and stood in mock ease and interest by the doorway. I heard one of my new acquaintances saying to a friend a few minutes later, *My dear, he's quite harmless, only a little queer from the War. At least an original costume don't you think? Pyjamas are hardly original surely? Well, it's all fun. Oh, how do you do Mr Williamson! So you're an owl, are you? Well, you are certainly original!*

Henry was blessed with the ability to mock himself, but even this was taken literally and used against him. Fifteen years later, after he had moved from Georgeham, he discovered another reason for 'the jeers and derision of some of the cottage neighbours' — greed: 'Tidden you, y'know, tidden your books, 'tes the people you wrote about, visitors come to see, some people says my children'll be famous when'm old people ... 'tes us here who ought to have the money you've made out of they books ...'

It would be wrong, however, to suggest that he was friendless during the years at Skirr Cottage. 'Julian Warbeck' had left after a flurry of drunken debts and arguments;

but visitors came to stay, such as Frederick Rendle, his friend from Folkestone, who came in 1922:

> I recollect having a very pleasant few days with him; among the events being driven in his motor-cycle side car to an Otter Hunt Ball in a nearby town and getting rather tiddly with him in the local pub. The housekeeping was done by another red-headed good-looking lass [the other, of course, being Evelyn Fairfax whom Rendle had known in the Folkestone days], the daughter of the postman, who came in each day. Henry certainly knew how to charm them!

Above all, there were two households who cared for him and provided the sympathy he needed: the Stokes family and the Gibbs family. Mrs Stokes was recently widowed when she moved to Georgeham in the spring of 1922 and rented Stone Cottage; she lived there with her son, Edward, and two daughters whom Henry portrayed, affectionately in *The Sun in the Sands* as 'Annabelle' and 'Queenie'.

Henry had an exceptional affinity with children, and a notable preference for girls. Amanda Allsop (daughter of the late Kenneth Allsop), who was 'engaged' to him when she was seven, wonders if this was part of his search for 'Barleybright', the perfect companion: 'and, perhaps, little girls were less likely to upset his dream than really down-to-earth grown-up women.' When she was a child, Amanda told her mother that Henry was not like other men because he was kind; and she remembers, too, that if she and her brother did anything wrong it was always Fabian who was blamed and punished, 'as if I had no volition. Whatever Henry felt in his dreams about children, he seemed to treat little boys at least as an annoyance. I think he *must* have liked girls better.'

Edward Stokes proved an exception; he was granted equal favour with his sisters. Henry met Edward when he and his sister 'Annabelle' were filling baskets with primroses from a bank behind a hazel hedge on the way to Croyde. Their singing was interrupted by the appearance of a tall man dressed as a tramp, with black hair and neat moustache, carrying a 'thumb stick' of freshly cut hazel, with a bouncing brown-and-white spaniel beside him. 'Hullo, songsters!' was his greeting, followed by the less friendly question: 'Do you really have to murder those beautiful flowers?'

Many years later, Edward, now Commander Stokes, remembers the friendship. He thought him mad at the time:

But quite nice mad. He had a thin, rather reedy tenor voice and, as he peered through the hedge, we could see he was remarkably good-looking in an emaciated sort of way.

'Where do you live? We've not met before, have we?' He pushed his way through the hedge. His interest was obviously in 'Annabelle', then sixteen and promising considerable beauty.

'We've just moved into Stone Cottage,' we told him. The dog, tail wagging and tongue quivering, jumped up at 'Annabelle', upsetting some of the flowers.

'Down, Beel! I'm sorry, but he knows you shouldn't be picking them.'

'Tripe!' I cut in, but was ignored.

'What's your name?'

'What's yours?'

'Henry Williamson.'

This in a voice that clearly implied we ought to have recognized him, but, since ignorant children that we were, we hadn't, we would of course know the name. We didn't, but didn't say so. We had never heard of him. Neither had anyone else for that matter. Having made his dramatic entry into our lives, he departed, shouting instructions to Bill [Billjohn the dog] as he went, leaving us somewhat bewildered yet highly amused.

One day, brother and sister saw the inside of Skirr Cottage when they went to apologize for shattering one of Henry's windows. 'Annabelle' had seen his face at an upstairs window and thrown him an apple which missed and broke the pane:

The one downstairs room, into which the front and only door opened directly, was low and dark and stone floored. There was a bleak looking table strewn with paper, and an upright chair, against the front window, just inside the door. A couple of disreputable and disintegrating armchairs sprawled against opposite walls. In one, Bill lay curled up, apparently fast asleep. In the other, a fluffy black-and-white cat suckled and washed four newly born kittens, purring loudly the while as if to say, 'Look what I've done'. On the grimy top of the black kitchen range, a kettle boiled merrily. Down the stairs, as we closed the door, Henry appeared, bent double to avoid hitting his head on the ceiling.

We were duly invited to take tea and Henry explained to us that he was an author. Not only that, he made it quite clear that he considered he was a very great author. Richard Jefferies was, we learned, his idol and it was his ambition to emulate him. We ate some of his cake and learned later that by doing so we had denied him food for at least a day. He was penniless but confident, charming and stimulating. Definitely a man after my own heart, for he was a lover of nature; of wild life in every form.

He told us some of his experiences as a very young soldier at the front in Flanders. It was the first time I even began to realize just how appalling that war had been. He painted a picture of dirt and squalor and paralysing fear; something very different from the stories of valour and heroism and final victory which I had been brought up on.

When they told their mother of their new friend, she was suspicious, 'imagining "Annabelle" being picked up by some undesirable roué'; but once Mrs Stokes had met Henry, he entered their lives as part of the family. Mrs Stokes corrected his proofs, while her mother mended his clothes, and soon he was eating most of his meals with them as well. After dinner he would sing while 'Queenie' played the piano: 'He had a beautiful, though untrained tenor voice,' she remembers. 'We spent much time at the piano, myself playing and HW singing "Now Sleeps the Crimson Petal" and "I must go down to the seas again". Happy days!'

There were times during their explorations of the countryside — to see the buzzards' nests at the end of Baggy Point, for instance — when Mrs Stokes expressed a mild concern: 'Do you think it's wise, dears, sleeping on the haystack with Henry, instead of here at home? What will the villagers think?' Edward did not have the faintest idea what she was talking about. As for the villagers, it had nothing to do with them:

> 'Annabelle' and I had him as our constant companion and friend. He was twenty-five at this time but he understood the young. Never talked down to us. Never took advantage of our tender years. I don't think Mother ever really trusted him. Maybe she was a little jealous of close friendship. Until she died some forty years later, she always referred to him as 'that ass Henry'.

> 'Queenie' treated him with a jaunty irreverence that amused him. She liked him but saw through his tendency to glamorize: 'He was such a congenital liar!' She says that he

was 'heartily disliked' by all except a few close friends like themselves. Because of his compulsion to exaggerate, she was unable to take him seriously, even when he presented her with a copy of *The Beautiful Years* with the solemn assurance: 'I shall be famous one day and then you will be able to sell it for a large sum.' 'Oh, don't be such a ninny, Henry,' she laughed. (Sixty years later, 'quite a nice copy' of this first edition was advertised at £65, even without an inscription.)

In *The Sun in the Sands*, he compared 'Queenie' to the cool little flower of Speedwell; but 'Annabelle' he loved, or so he claimed in this uneasy blend of 'novel autobiography' (as it was listed by the publishers on the back of the jacket):

> Once, after a day's hunting, I had walked upstairs to wash, and had opened my bathroom door, surprised to find Annabelle in the bath. I saw a sponge upheld, and the loveliest face and shoulders and arms over the rim of the bath; and the pink-petal breasts, sleek with water; her hair in a dark knot. Annabelle's even white teeth and smile, her shout of GET OUT! and the sponge hurled with a watery splosh at my apologetic and precipitantly retiring self. Downstairs I paced about alone, thinking of her young beauty, her apple-blossom loveliness. Dinner that evening was great fun, and there was much laughter, and Queenie saying continually, *Oh, you are an ass, Willie!*, while Annabelle was silent, her brown eyes smouldering and abstract.

Perhaps 'Annabelle' represented the ideal companion he was searching for, the companion whom he mentioned to me rather dramatically, shortly after our own first meeting: 'I know what will happen. I shall die, and feel a salt tear go "plop" on top of my coffin, and I'll rise up and there she'll be — the perfect companion I've been looking for. Too late! And I'll sink back into my grave.' A startling remark to make to a boy in his teens; but the search was an obsession and constant source of dissatisfaction for Henry — even if he knew in his heart that the ideal companion was unattainable.

With 'Annabelle', he experienced young, unrequited love vicariously through his fiction : 'Yet though I knew myself to be hopelessly in love with Annabelle, the mocker, my longing was still for what my mind saw as a mother-maiden, whose arms would fold around me, and by whose cherishing I would lose the fatigue of the past and the present.' He ends that same chapter from *The Sun in the Sands* with a contented resignation for a love that might have been:

> A cock crowed from the farmyard opposite. Then a throaty, bubbling cry from the churchyard opposite, *skirr-rr-rr*. My lovely owls were still for me! By God, I would write again, I would avoid all human contacts in the future, lest I betray what the white owls symbolized! I would live only for my writing! Annabelle, good-bye, darling Annabelle, oh beauty of life and sun and dream. I sighed deeply, and slept.

Today, the real 'Annabelle' remembers him as 'very beautiful, wild, lonely and lovely'.

Her small brother, Edward, with none of the nonsense of love to cloud their relationship, may have come closer to Henry in reality. Edward appeared as 'a rude little schoolboy on an Exmoor pony' in the story called 'Redeye' in *The Peregrine's Saga and Other Stories* (1923, dedicated to his mother). Commander Stokes still has the copy with the tender inscription on the fly-leaf beside Henry's drawing of a tall, lugubrious owl. It is a marvellous thing to have written to a boy:

10 Dec 1923 Skerr Cottage [usually called Skirr]

Dear Edward, Since you have been with me in friendship to so many places in our beloved land where the doings of the small ones are herein chronicled with what art and patience to labour I possess, it is natural I should want to give you a presentation copy. You at least know how lovely it is to see Mewlibry soaring his winged arcs above the headland, where the stonechat watches on the withered bramble-spray and the seal fishes in the sea below. You have slept with me on a haystack, and watched the Swan burning over the hills, in the pale and luminous sky. We have made our fires in the spinney, and we have seen the stars wavering watery and winking blue and red in the heat arising. The night, the floating spark, the damp larch branches, the immense and mysterious darkness which the heart of man can never know! A little of the glamour I have tried to put into this book: when you think of me forget that I am lank and unprepossessing, and remember only the strange spirits of the birds, the trees, the stars, and that lovely spirit in men's hearts.

Always your friend.   Henry Williamson.

Together, the three children and Henry formed the Owl Club, swearing 'eternal friendship in nature'. The owl had long been a favourite of Henry's. He had an owl emblem painted on his Norton, possibly in honour of the half-tamed owl he had had at Blackheath; whilst at Skirr Cottage, two barn owls nested under the thatch, snoring, hissing, flying out through the trees of the churchyard in the late afternoon. The Owl Club met in a ruined cottage at the top of the hill, in the lane that led from Georgeham to Ox's Cross. The windows were glassless and the room upstairs, where the mice scattered at their arrival, was littered with the droppings and the regurgitated fur and bone pellets of owls. When the weather was fine, the club held banquets near the beech spinney at Ox's Cross, frying sausages, bacon, tomatoes, fish, or anything that was available. There were always two fires: one for cooking on, the other to keep warm by. When the meal was over, the Owl Club and their guests would lie back and gaze at the sparks as they flew upwards, and listen to Henry's favourite records which he played on his portable, hand-wound gramophone: Debussy's 'Prélude à l'après-midi d'un faune', Rimsky Korsakov's 'Hymn to the Sun', and excerpts from Wagner's *Tristan and Isolde* — the extent of his collection. They talked on subjects ranging from motor-cycles to ghosts, from birth to the battlefields of France. Many years later, Commander Stokes returned to Ox's Cross with his wife. New trees had risen in the spinney and, to his surprise, he noticed two or three shacks in a clearing. As they approached, an old grey-haired man came up to them, exclaiming furiously, 'Who the hell are you? This is private property.' Commander Stokes stood his ground silently. Then a burst of recognition: 'Edward!' The Owl Club had met again, after thirty-five years.

The other household which befriended Henry in George-ham was the Gibbs family. Peter Gibbs, who was a boy at the time, reveals that his father, Dr Stanley Gibbs, often invited Henry to meals. 'He saw that this obviously very sensitive chap was in need of help and friendship and companionship, and food. We frequently found him starving. As he was too proud a man to accept charity, father deliberately included him in the family.'

Henry had a lean and hungry look anyhow, but he must have bared his ribs most effectively if he appeared to be starving. When I asked Peter Gibbs if Henry really was that hungry, with so many friends anxious to feed him, he explained that food was not something which Henry thought of: 'When he was writing a book he forgot about food altogether.'

Presenting a copy of *The Lone Swallows* to Dr Gibbs in 1922 Henry showed that he did not forget the kindness he received, for he inscribed it 'To my kind friends'. Years later, he told Peter that he had never forgotten the generosity of his parents to 'a shell-shocked young man in his early twenties'.

Peter Gibbs remembers Henry thus:

[He was] a bit of an oddity, in a shocking condition mentally. My father had been through the war himself and felt a special sympathy for the shocked ex-soldier, looking after him in a personal if not a strictly professional capacity. His shell-shocked condition was mental rather than physical; undoubtedly that was the trouble. In ordinary circumstances he could hardly bear to speak of the war, equally he could never get it out of his mind.

Another reason for Henry to be grateful to Dr Gibbs was the introduction to his brother-in-law, Dr Elliston Wright, who had written *Braunton – A Few Nature Notes with Lists of Flora Macro Lepidoptera and Birds Known to Occur in the District* (1932, published at his own expense). With his expert knowledge he encouraged Henry's interest in Braunton Burrows. Henry sent a copy of the ponderously titled book to a former fellow-officer with a note: 'The silly ass paid for it, wouldn't let me bother to get it done by a London publisher. Illustrations are his own, don't you think they are fine? Especially the coloured caterpillars. This fellow, who is a great wild primitive sort of Celt, very jolly and boasts he's never worn a boiled shirt in his life, would make a fine trio on the burrows one day.'

Peter Gibbs's wife also remembers Henry. While she would agree that he did have a lean and hungry look about him, her description is rather more romantic: 'Oh, very attractive I'd say, to a mere woman! Shy, very dark, very pronounced features. Personally, I only saw the fiery side of him if someone roused him on a particular subject. Not angry looks, but such piercing eyes, and a beautiful speaking voice.' Introducing the subject of Henry's meeting with his first wife, Loetitia Hibbert, in 1925, Mrs Gibbs said that she was out of his class, 'though he was gradually being drawn into that circle because of his writing. But normally she would not have met him socially'.

Dark-haired and radiant, Loetitia was nicknamed 'Gypsy', which was so apt a description that she has been called it ever since, even by Henry and their children. She is a cousin of Sir Francis Chichester, the navigator, and her father was a well-known sportsman, the oldest member of the Cheriton Otter Hunt, the prototype for Uncle Sufford Chychester in *The Pathway*, in which Gypsy featured as the heroine, Mary Ogilvie.

When I spoke to her in Norfolk after Henry's death, she told me: 'We met at an otter hunt, and when he exclaimed "This is just like *Bevis*!" he was astonished to find that I almost knew it by heart.' (*Bevis*, by Richard Jefferies, based on his childhood, was a particular favourite of Henry's.)

When I mentioned that at the time Henry and his work were quite unknown, she corrected me:

'No, he was not totally unknown. He had just written an article for the *Saturday Evening Post*, receiving £500 — and that's what we married on.'

Their wedding took place on Wednesday 6 May 1925 at Landcross Parish Church, near Loetitia's home, and an escort of Girl Guides lined the aisle as a guard of honour. The best man was Richard de la Mare. Henry was described by the *Bideford Gazette* as 'an author of note who wrote "The Lone Swallows"', while Loetitia was referred to as 'the only daughter of Mr C. C. Hibbert of South Close, and a cousin to Lady Ashcombe'. It was reported that after changing from her bridal dress of white georgette into a tweed coat and skirt and brown hat, Mrs Williamson left with her husband for their honeymoon in France.

Eight months later, shortly before the birth of their first son, Henry summed up married life with devastating

41

candour: 'Not altogether had they been happy months,' he revealed, 'in part for causes which probably go back to my childhood; and also for differences in mind or nature. Loetitia was serene, because not quickly imaginative: I was too often agitated because vividly imaginative.' When I met Loetitia Williamson, the quality that impressed me, apart from her serenity, was the composure of a woman with an imagination quick enough to appreciate the best in people and wise enough to tolerate the worst. It is hard to believe that the unhappiness came from her.

To a certain extent the artist needs to be selfish in his battle to make time for himself. If he cannot be bothered with the mundane necessities of life, then others must buy the loaf of bread for him. He has to live with the fact that he may seem egotistical, even cruel, when all he wants is to concentrate on his work. For Henry, the combination of guilt and frustration — for he was seldom satisfied with his work — must have seemed intolerable. He lashed out at anyone who came between him and his work, punishing those who loved him, and characteristically exaggerated his unhappiness as if to justify his ruthless behaviour. Hence the reference to 'causes which go back to childhood'; and he found further excuse in his experience of the Great War: 'My mind, new-made with meditations arising from the battlefields, was striving always to dissolve the crystallized thought of the Pre-War minds about me. It took a World War to crack the crystals of the European consciousness; but hard, selfish, unimaginative fragments were lacerating to youth, which dreamed of fairer things.'

Fine-sounding phrases, which concealed an inability on Henry's part to count his blessings. Perhaps it was more than the selfishness of the artist; but whatever it was that gnawed at Henry's mind, it began to mar the life around him. 'I have a dog inside me,' he once said, 'who warns me when an evil spirit is about.' That dog was barking at itself.

THREE

An otter cub 'brown as a bulrush'

NOT LONG AFTER HENRY settled at Skirr Cottage, an unexpected visitor led him to the source of inspiration for what was to become his most famous book. A stranger knocked at his door to ask his advice about some abandoned otter cubs. As the man had been wounded in the war he was made doubly welcome.

Henry had glimpsed his first otter in the summer of 1912 during a cycling tour of the Norfolk coast. Searching for nests in the reeds, he had noticed a small brown seal-like face, but had kept still and allowed the otter to escape. In the winter of 1916/1917, he saw his second otter in an abandoned German emplacement. Four years later, the stranger introduced Henry to a cub of his own.

He told Henry that he had seen the corpse of an otter bitch strung up outside a farmhouse door, in the tradition of the warning 'vermin pole'. The farmer had shot it the night before beside a stream and, when asked why, had replied: 'What good be it, anyway?'

'But here's the point,' the man explained to Henry: 'there's a litter of cubs somewhere by the riverside.' He thought he knew where to find them, in a drain running down from the marsh. Would Henry help him dig the cubs out? 'Rather!'

Henry's dog, Billjohn, leapt about in gleeful anticipation as they set off in the stranger's horse and cart on an hour's journey through remote, deep-set lanes. After exploring the marshland, Henry fetched a pick from the cart and broke open the old, choked drain. One of the abandoned cubs was dead, the other lukewarm. Henry lifted the tiny survivor in his cupped hands, and the puzzled dog nuzzled it enquiringly (it was the size of a rat, yet did not bite him; looked like a small rabbit, but did not struggle to escape). The men fed it, through a fountain-pen filler, with cow's milk mixed with warm water; then they wrapped it in cotton-wool and hoped for the best. The stranger took the cub away with him for the night, while Henry returned home to bacon and eggs beside a fire of teak from a recent wreck. There he sat reading by the light of his oil lamp and the blue salt flames, in his favourite chair, with his cat curled against him and his exhausted spaniel stretched out at his feet.

The next morning, while Henry was working on *Dandelion Days* (1922, later extensively revised), the stranger reappeared. He had brought the cub with him and did not think it could survive. Henry's cat expressed slight interest in the listless object, sniffing it suspiciously and then racing upstairs to tend her small kitten, which was scarcely any younger. Henry followed, removed the kitten, rubbed the cub against its fur: 'Thereafter the otter cub was fed and washed and enjoyed equally with her own kitten until it was strong enough to go back to its owner.' The otter still belonged to the stranger, who had sworn Henry to secrecy over the whole affair.

As it grew even larger than the mother cat, Henry watched the cub's progress with pleasure. It had short fur 'as brown as a bulrush', with a long, low body which seemed to glide over the ground, small ears almost hidden, a wide mouth set in whiskers and feet like a dog's, although more splayed with a web of skin between each toe. He observed and noted every detail carefully, and shared the cub's enjoyment of their games, turning on the hosepipe under the apple tree while the animal rolled ecstatically on its back trying to bite the jet of water, which smoothed the bulrush fur until it looked like a small brown seal. Affectionate and faithful, the otter knew no fear of the two men and would run to them; but it remained suspicious of strangers.

When the soldier had to go into hospital because of his war wound, the otter came back to stay at Skirr Cottage. During the day it was kept inside, as its presence still had to be hidden from the locals; but at twilight the young otter accompanied Henry and Billjohn down the valley, hunting the stream for eels and trout. One evening the animal strayed. Henry was alerted by a sudden chattering ahead, and then Billjohn's agitated barking. Running up, he found the frantic otter twisting and rolling in the grip of a gin-trap, one of the vilest of man-made weapons still in use; but he managed to throw his jacket over the struggling creature, and held it still while he opened the iron jaws. From a glimpse of the injured foot, it seemed that three of its toes were missing — then the coat was empty. Henry searched for hours, calling, listening; but he never saw the cub again, although he caught a glint of eyes in the churchyard one stormy night in 1923 and wondered if the otter had returned to the stream 'and been anguished with sudden memory'.

The loss heightened his interest in otters and he continued his study of the animal. In those days he saw many of them killed, as he walked beside the Devonshire rivers with Gypsy's father and brothers as guest of the Cheriton Otter Hunt, which met several times a season. He once took me with him on an otter hunt when I was a boy, and seemed less enthusiastic than the others. No doubt he watched those first pursuits with mixed feelings, wondering always if they would find the particular otter he had loved. At the same time, the writer in him must have rejoiced in the experience he was gaining: he recognized that the otter cub had given him a rare opportunity to study the animal from one point of view; the otter hunts gave him another.

Far from expressing any disapproval of otter hunting, Henry went to the experts for advice. He was told by William Rogers, Master of the Cheriton Otterhounds, that a story of his in the *Tatler* (about a hunt down the River Lyn to Lynmouth) had amused his members because it was so inaccurate. The Master advised him to abandon his proposed book on otters since it was obvious that he had no talent as a sporting writer; nor was there any need for such a book, since the ground had already been covered. Many writers would have flinched from such a humiliating rebuke, but Henry recognized that it came from a man whose knowledge of otters could not be faulted — both as a Master of Otterhounds and as a naturalist who had tried to breed otters in captivity. His wise reaction was to send a conciliatory letter asking if the Master would do him the honour of reading his finished typescript, to make sure there was nothing wrong. The mollified Master sent a detailed reply which determined Henry to 'put nothing into Tarka which was not based on actual country' — for it was *Tarka the Otter* that he was now writing.

He was true to his vow of accuracy. His research was so scrupulous that when he explored the streams of Exmoor and Dartmoor he said he almost used a tape measure, making copious notes afterwards. In writing *Tarka*, Henry believed he was inspired by this particular countryside. He felt, because of his Shapcote ancestry, that he belonged; and it was this sense of belonging, this extra inspiration, that transformed Tarka into a masterpiece. 'The writing you do when you're on the right beam is almost automatic,' he once commented. 'You are a medium for it and you mustn't muck about with that talent.' Writing to a former fellow officer, he was able to state without his usual reservations: 'I'm still

above, left Skirr Cottage, which Henry rented for a few pounds a year on his arrival in Georgeham after the First World War.
above, right Crowberry Cottage, to which he moved after his marriage. Here he wrote *Tarka*. *Daniel Farson*

below Henry outside the Hut, c.1950. If there is ever a Williamson Museum, this is where it should be found. *Daniel Farson*

It was characteristic of Henry's lack of sentimentality towards animals that he took me to this otter hunt when I was a boy. *Daniel Farson*

Portrait of Tarka by Henry's friend, Barry Driscoll, who illustrated
Tarka the Otter for the Nonesuch Press in 1964.

doing *Tarka the Otter*. I *know* it's good . . .' This does not mean that the actual writing was easy, far from it: from 1923 to early 1927, Henry revised the typescript seventeen times, and he was in a state of continuous torment over the revisions.

Tarka had been simmering for several years. It was started after the loss of the otter cub and an original version was drafted in 1923. That was put to one side. Two years later, Richard de la Mare (Henry's best man) accepted the 'otter story' for publication by Selwyn & Blunt, on condition that it was published in a limited edition for sale to otter-hunt membership. Henry disagreed with this condition (though he changed his mind later), and started revising it for Putnam's (London), where Constant Huntington took a person interest.

There was a general lack of enthusiasm for animal stories, which must have been disheartening. 'Sordid', said one editor; 'too sad', said another; and a damning 'people are not interested in the countryside', from a third. The editor of *Pearson's Magazine* warned him not to restrict himself to the 'animal-story market' and, when Henry protested that he could only write as he felt, accused him of being obstinate and having a 'kink'. 'Secretly, I thought all these editors were an illiterate lot of semi-fools,' Henry confided in *The Children of Shallowford* (1939), his detailed and delightful account of this period. So he persevered, against their advice.

The final version of *Tarka* was not written at Skirr Cottage, as is generally believed, but at Crowberry Cottage, where Henry and Loetitia moved five months after their marriage. It was only a few yards up the lane, where it bends on its way to the sea; and though the new home was larger, it was darker and so damp that Henry had to cover the worst parts with concrete. The cottage seems to have lacked the warmth and ramshackle happiness of Skirr.

Their first child, a son, was born on 18 February 1926, three miles away at 'Montevideo', the ridiculous name given to the midwife's house; and, true to family tradition accorded to the eldest son, he was christened Henry William Williamson. Henry's emotions were mixed as he looked at his firstborn: there was a tinge of resentment as he 'saw how completely mother and child were one, and upon me grew a feeling of aloneness, and a desire to fade into the world of my book, which had been broken off more than a year...' But Henry found it difficult to 'fade into the world of my book', for the child fell ill when he was brought home to Crowberry weighing less at nine weeks than he had at birth. To make matters worse, Loetitia too became ill (suffering from cystitis, an inflammation of the bladder). Recalling all this in 1938, Henry had some justification in giving the heading 'The Simple Life Becomes Complicated' to chapter three of *The Children of Shallowford*. The doctor's prescription for the sick baby was callous — 'Shove him in a room and give him a water-bottle and let him cry' — but this was the vogue at the time, it being considered bad for a child to be cuddled. 'The very opposite of the truth', Henry protested, 'and I wouldn't and couldn't — and cradled him and gave him his food and he'd be sick and then he'd go to sleep.' Given this brief respite, Henry would then seize the opportunity to write a few more words of *Tarka*. 'Fact, fact, fact, and I might do a page at night. Then, about three in the morning, when the candle had burnt itself out, I'd go upstairs with my eyes stinging and hand over the child to his mother who lay in bed with fever — and I'd sleep.' But, with Loetitia stuck helplessly upstairs in bed with a soaring temperature, it was Henry who had to wash and nurse the boy — who soon became known as 'Windles' after the times when Henry, trying to ease his wind pain, patted the small of his back saying, 'Windees, baby dear, windees'. At such times when a sudden smile of relief lit the child's face, Henry felt the pang of paternal feelings he had missed at birth: 'He smiled at me; he was my little boy, my poor little boy . . . Then on with the book.'

There were times when the child's crying was unbearable for Henry, as if it reflected some nervous weakness in himself. The doctor recommended cow's milk and warm water, but still the baby cried. Henry grew his beard then, as a protest against what he felt to be his own frailty. Visitors called with advice and succeeded only in distracting him. On top of all this, his uncle gave him interminable lecturing advice, expressing general disapproval of Henry's politics, and even his work: 'People say your novels are rotten and you oughtn't to write any more.' Finally, pursuing Henry into the back garden just as he was going to sling a rotten onion onto the compost heap, he called out, 'Don't waste that, eat it!' And to his astonishment Henry did exactly that, earth, roots, stalk and all, on the spot. Eventually, Loetitia's grandmother volunteered to pay for the services of a trained nurse, but Henry took a stony dislike to her, which was heartily reciprocated. She went around Georgeham complaining that 'the awful man' had stolen ten pounds from her. It turned out that she had never brought the money to the cottage in the first place, but it was an added aggravation. Writing to a friend, Henry moaned at the expense of the family's illnesses: 'It irritates me silently.' One can imagine the fury of that silence.

When filial tears and avuncular advice distracted him beyond endurance, he left his desk shouting that he could not continue like this and something would have to be done. By now he was half way through the revised *Tarka*, but his pleasure in the book had dimmed into a 'prolonged monotony' and he was tempted to abandon it and wander instead along the coast in the open air; but he forced himself to continue, the baby crooked inside his left arm as he took advantage of the quieter hours of the night. 'And *that*,' Henry pounded the

49

table as he described the episode to me fifty years later, 'is why a friend told me that every word of *Tarka* was chipped out of the breast-bone.'

When things were quieter and Henry could break free, he walked the coastline as he had done before his marriage; and, as he confessed later in *The Sun in the Sands*, mused upon his ideal soul-mate: 'While I walked along the shallow foam-nets of the waves, the water and sand scarcely over my toes, I imagined a maiden to be walking beside me, and completing my life wordlessly. Often I imagined that somewhere under the sky was my companion, my sun-maiden, who would share with me all the loveliness of my new world.'

It was a cruel irony that, while he continued to search for his ideal companion, he failed to recognize her in Loetitia — although at that time it is hardly surprising, with her lying in bed with a temperature that sometimes reached 104 degrees, unable to relieve Henry of the burden of caring for Windles. To get her temperature down she was prescribed a diet of spring lettuce with bread and butter, and this Henry carefully prepared for her. Her recovery was gradual, and even as late as July the doctor warned her to 'go slow until September'. Removed from her by illness and tiredness over caring for the boy and writing *Tarka*, Henry returned from his solitary walks, 'Deeply mortified that Loetitia and I seem to live in different worlds; and continually reproaching myself for my deficiencies.' It was gentlemanly to accuse himself, yet there is the curious feeling that he was really blaming someone else.

This familiar pattern of frustration and exaggerated distress must seem unduly self-indulgent to those who did not know him well: but for Henry, self-absorption was the novelist's prerogative. He allowed no experience or emotion to go to waste, and in this case drew on his baby's struggle for survival in his portrait of the young Tarka, hungry in the winter cold because its mother did not have enough milk to feed it: 'The thin little cub, on its couch among the reeds frozen and bent like the legs of dead spiders, greeted Greymuzzle with husky mewing whenever it heard her coming, and would not be comforted by tongue caresses...' Inspired, he imagined incidents that later proved to be true: 'And I found out afterwards that they'd happened there exactly as I wrote them, but a long time ago.' Elliston Wright suggested he must have known about them, but Henry was adamant: 'No, I imagined it, because I could feel all this in my blood.'

In the summer of 1926, life became better at Crowberry Cottage as Loetitia recovered and Windles gained strength. Characteristically, Henry claimed that this was because he *willed* him to do so, transmitting his own life force into the sickly child; but Savory & Moore's baby food helped.

Tarka The Otter, His Joyful Water-life And Death in the Country of the Two Rivers was published in August 1927 in a private edition of 100 copies for subscribers, signed by the author with his owl-sketch, on handmade paper. It shows his uncertainty that Henry should have asked The Hon. Sir John Fortescue to enhance the reputation of the novel by writing an introduction, which he did with the grudging reservation that the author's 'artistic conscience is rather too sensitive'. (It was dedicated to William Henry Rogers, Master of the Cheriton Otterhounds, which seems ironic today in view of the lovable, vulnerable image of the otter which Henry helped to create.) But Henry was so certain of his objectivity, and so determined to sell the book, that he wrote round to the secretaries of numerous otter hunts asking for lists of members to whom he could send his prospectus — which he assured them would itself become a collector's item. He failed to realize that people who hunt otters do not necessarily wish to read about them; nor did they. In the following week, nine copies of the private edition of Tarka were sold, and only four in the week after that. Henry had to face the unpalatable fact that the private edition was a failure: 'Poor old Constant Huntington paid out a lot of money on an expensive production (after 100 rageful letters from me he agreed to do hand-made paper and vellum for £3.3s instead of machine-made and cloth) of 100 signed copies. They didn't sell, except to my relatives, and wife's.... Putnam's did 1000 others [in October], same printing, but other paper and binding, without signature. They sold 50, and got very gloomy...'

The early fortunes of *Tarka* clearly dismayed Henry, and not without justification. There were in fact two editions in October of that year, and there were to be a further four by November 1928 — so some copies must have sold. The book was also most certainly being talked about by the great writers Henry so admired — even if this did not have an immediate effect on sales. But for Henry, the initial failure of the private edition in August seemed conclusive. According to him, Putnam's too were so gloomy that they refused to pay an advance on his next book. And yet he knew they were wrong. At this critical point in any writer's life, his own faith in his talent remained unshaken: he knew that 'the prose was straight, keen and true-to-facts.... It is all here in Devon, if you just happen to see and hear or smell it.'

By chance, at this very point, Henry's roots in Devon were about to grow even deeper; for he was negotiating for the purchase of Ox's Cross, the field on top of the hill above Georgeham, where the Owl Club gathered on summer nights. It is a superb vantage point, looking down over Braunton Burrows towards the estuary where the rivers Taw and Torridge together flow out to sea over Bideford Bar. Henry had long ago fallen in love with the place during that fleeting visit to Georgeham in 1914, as described on the last page of *The Labouring Life* (1932, a companion to *The Village Book*):

> I discovered Windwhistle Cross in the spring before the War, when the leaves were fairer, the valleys and the sea and the hills immense with unknown beauty. Yet the trees are dearer now, with so many pilgrimages to their standing place against the sky. Memories of grass and corn seen from the hilltop; of Dartmoor tors rising blue in the south; of Exmoor smooth and grey, nearer and more intimate, in the east; of the estuary sea-widened under the lesser hills beyond the village; of sunshine and summer wind shared with friends, four-footed, winged, rooted, human: some gone, others to return and renew delights in the ancient earth and sun.

Windwhistle Spinney, at the edge of the field, gained its name from the row of beeches on one side, sliced by the edge of Atlantic gales. A white owl lived there, emerging at sunset to swoop around the field, making it even more magical. Apart from the spinney, the field was open in those days, without the shelter of the tall trees that circle it today, many of which were planted as wind-breaks by Henry himself.

The field is marked prosaically on the map as Oxford Cross, at the cross roads to Braunton and Georgeham, Morthoe and Spreacombe; but Henry dismissed this airily, even though the field was listed as such in deeds 300 years old. With excruciating mimicry of accents, Henry told me what he imagined had happened long ago:

'My theory is that some chap was hedgeing up here and somebody came along and said, "Now my good man, what do you call this place?"

'"Arr! Us call'um Oxcross, zur."' Much tugging at forelocks on Henry's part.

'"Oh, exactly. Oxford Cross."

'"Ay, aye, zur," with the peasant's anxiety to please the gentry.'

This, said Henry, was the reason it had been entered in the deeds as Oxford Cross.

'As it *is* on the signpost today,' I reminded him.

There was a long pause. 'Yes — well, they're bloody fools!'

With no ford on top of the hill, and Oxford hundreds of miles away, Henry's insistence on Ox's Cross is convincing: oxen stopped here on their way to market 'and had a hell of a great meal so they could go to hoof at Barnstaple the next day and not sweat it out'. The field lies half-way between Ilfracombe, where the beasts would have been brought in from Ireland, and the famous cattle market at Barnstaple; and it was fenced or stoned-in for the traditional fattening up before the beasts were sold. As further proof, Henry claimed that the manure left by the cattle after their night's rest accounted for the unusual richness of the soil.

Regardless of the name, Henry knew that he had to own that field: 'If only it were ours, I said a dozen times a day to Loetitia.' Then the dream became a possibility when he heard that it was up for sale. He and Loetitia went up there every afternoon with the baby, planning the house he would build when he was famous — for of that there was never any doubt! Wishful-thinking was followed by panic when he heard that someone else was after it and had offered £100. Acting on impulse, Henry went straight to the owner and offered £125, which was accepted. He wrote out a cheque for £25 as a deposit, which cleaned him out; but at that moment he believed that there was nothing to worry about, since the total royalties from the private edition of *Tarka* would earn him exactly £125. The arithmetic was perfect!

Author's survive on optimism, but even Henry's began to falter when the otter hunters failed to materialize as buyers of books. In desperation, he took the train to London, selling three copies to strangers on the journey, one to the editor of the *Daily Express*, and six to J. G. Wilson of the celebrated bookshop, Bumpus, at the usual trade discount of twenty per cent. Considering that the editor of the *Express* had *bought* his 'review' copy, Henry was relying on the generosity of friends rather than on genuine enthusiasm. By the time the owner of the field asked for the remainder of the purchase money, only twenty-nine copies of the private edition had been sold. As the farmer-owner was also the local butcher he knew about unpaid debts, but Henry talked him into a temporary stay. It was an anxious time: not only the field but his literary reputation hung in the balance. Then, one joyous morning, Loetitia brought him a letter with his cup of tea. It was the moment of triumph that every writer dreams of: he had won the coveted Hawthornden Prize.

'A hundred pounds and fame!' cried Henry.

The field was saved.

When Henry welcomed 'fame' in 1928 the word meant something, unlike today when anyone can become famous doing anything, provided they do it often enough on television. In his day, literary fame was an achievement, earned by work and genuine talent. The distinction gave him class, and if it had not been for his subsequent politics, Henry would have ripened into an old age rich with honours, titles and awards. As it was, he relished the early fun of it hugely. Meeting 'Queenie' in London a few months later, he rushed her into the Victoria and Albert Museum where there was an exhibition of original manuscripts of classic books on nature, telling her that *Tarka* was among them. 'Oh, don't be such an ass, Henry!' she laughed. But there it was.

Always a mixture of confidence and diffidence, Henry had been anticipating the reactions of his 'seniors in the literary world' to 'this new talent among them'. In 1924 he had boasted of an imaginary compliment paid to him by John Galsworthy. This was a fabrication, but it proved surprisingly close to the praise he did receive four years later, when Galsworthy presented him with the Hawthornden. It is perfectly true that Galsworthy also wrote to Edward Garnett in 1926, on publication of *The Old Stag* (a collection of hunting stories), recommending it, and adding: ' . . . he's got one in press on the life of an otter that he thinks is better.' On another occasion, Henry had the bad luck to make a speech quoting 'encouragement' he had received from Arnold Bennett — only to find himself caught out, as Bennett's sister was in the audience. In 1926, the year before *Tarka* was published, he even pretended that Thomas Hardy had read the novel in manuscript form. 'All those lies were uttered by my jittery, off-poise self,' he admitted later. Lies they were in their specific detail, but they were a foretaste of what Henry rightly believed would be the reaction of his 'seniors' to his work in time.

The praise of such men meant everything to Henry. Not only did he fabricate their association with his work before it was published, he went so far as to visit them uninvited. Henry has described a visit he paid to Hardy in 1927, shortly before the publication of *Tarka*. As soon as he knocked at the door of the writer's London house he felt the impulse to turn and run. Before he could do so, the maid appeared and he was ushered in. The grand old man was resting; Mrs Hardy went upstairs to ask if he would see his young admirer. When Hardy descended, Henry found him 'quiet and afar' — which is not surprising, for Henry paced the floor nervously rattling off a volley of names, such as J. C. Squire and Galsworthy, claiming their praise for the forthcoming novel in order to justify his audacity in calling. 'Wasn't otter hunting rather cruel?' Hardy asked gently. Henry admitted he did not like it himself, but had tried not to show it in his book. At the end Henry said that he got up 'and murmured

DEVON AUTHOR'S SUCCESS.

THE NORTH DEVON AUTHOR Mr. Henry Williamson (seen with his wife) has leapt into fame by winning the 1928 Hawthordean prize of £100 with "Tarka the Otter," a story with the Rivers Taw and Torridge as its setting.

AUTHOR OF "TARKA THE OTTER"

Mr. Henry Williamson (left), the winner of the 1928 Hawthornden prize of £100 for his book "Tarka the Otter," is here seen being congratulated by Mr. John Galsworthy. Mr. Williamson, who is 31 and lives in North Devon, followed the otter hounds to get local colour.

Inside the Hut at Ox's Cross on the eve of his 80th birthday, waiting for the honours that never came.   *David Steen*

something about Keats and Coleridge — having lived alone for so long, in detachment of life, I had a different standard of life from the normal — while tears fell from my eyes and I hurried away.'

Afterwards he realized that his 'nervous overspilling' might have embarrassed Mrs Hardy, but she proved sympathetic, even writing to tell him of an abortive visit to the same house by W. H. Hudson, who paced outside for an hour without the courage to venture inside. 'Therefore, Hardy was doubly glad the author of *Tarka* had come to his door.' And though Hardy was near to his death, on 11 January 1928 Mrs Hardy encouraged the use of his 'quote' in the publisher's advertisement for *Tarka*.

Yet another 'senior' he had descended on uninvited was Galsworthy when, in 1924, he arrived at his Sussex home just before a tennis party. Henry resented his reception, which consisted of a drink and an apology: 'If you could let us know beforehand when you're going to be this way, we could always put you up.' Henry rationalized his dismissal as tiredness on Galsworthy's part, believing that 'perhaps even then the tumour which killed him was growing in his brain'.

In the end, *Tarka* brought the acceptance that Henry craved for. Edward Garnett wrote to Arnold Bennett shortly before its publication: 'There is an extraordinarily fine thing to be published on Oct 12th. "Tarka the Otter" by Henry Williamson. It's beautifully written. If you take it up you will see what I mean.' Arnold Bennett did take it up, and reviewed it in the *Evening Standard* — '... the writing of it is marvellous' — while Thomas Hardy hailed it as 'a remarkable book'. Edward Garnett had also sent proofs of *Tarka* to T. E. Lawrence, then in Karachi, who gave the book qualified praise, though he had the pages stitched together 'to lend the irks' (presumably a condescending reference to the ranks). Assuming this was Henry's first novel he wrote back to Garnett: 'He's tried his uttermost to write this one better than his power allowed him,' and was tactless in asking Garnett to forward his letter to the author. Two months later, he was dismayed to learn that Henry had written so much: 'If I'd known he was so practised I wouldn't have dared write him.' He kept his reservations over *Tarka* but not about Henry, for he wrote to Jonathan Cape Ltd in 1928, 'I'm glad you are annexing Williamson. He is a writer by birth and profession, and will do a lot more good work. Don't worry too much over Tarka: he will surpass that later.' Rudyard Kipling, too, had reservations and declined to review *Tarka*, possibly from pique, after the *British Weekly Review* had declared that *Tarka* was 'as fine a piece of observation, record and constructive imagination, as anything in Mr Kipling's "Jungle Books"'.

Writing in 1972 to his friend Father Brocard Sewell at Aylesford Priory, Henry recalled his acquaintance also with Hilaire Belloc and G. K. Chesterton: 'being recognized and accepted, is a serious and delightful and aweful thing in youth. Can this they praise, be *me*?' But the praise he respected most of all was from Arnold Bennett and the 'Order of Merit fellows', as he referred to Thomas Hardy, John Galsworthy and John Masefield. It was Henry's proud boast, which he told me time and time again, that the three assured him there was no need to worry if his books did not survive, because he had written more classics than anyone else in England at that time — 'You deserve the OM as much as we do'. This cannot have been the literal truth, as the three men were unlikely to have spoken in unison or to have made such a comment simultaneously to a young writer on the threshold of his career, unless they sent him a joint testimonial. The claim should be seen as Henry's interpretation of their genuine encouragement, which meant so much to him that his elaboration of it *became* the truth as far as he was concerned.

After the presentation by Galsworthy of the Hawthornden

Prize in June 1928 at the Aeolian Hall, Henry found himself 'hailed by all artistic London', becoming a target for interviews and leading articles. The irony did not escape him: 'It was all very exciting, and I could not understand it. I was famous... At first it was a strange feeling, to be greeted in friendly fashion by the people in the village and roundabout, who before had been inclined to deride and excuse the things I had been saying, for years, about my books.' Until now the first editions had been given willingly with generous inscriptions: 'For in those pre-Hawthornden days I was single-minded and keen, and anyone I met in the pub or who came to the cottage was given a set of my books.'

When T. E. Lawrence came to see him in Georgeham in 1928 he said, 'I suppose you've got a lot of people coming to see "the greatest living writer of English prose"?' And when Henry murmured a modest 'No', Lawrence prophesied that with the first hundred callers he would be shy and somewhat aloof, but after that — if he had any sense — he would say 'Balls!' The deluge duly came and Henry, recognizing the rôle he had played earlier with his own heroes, at first endured his visitors in long-suffering martyrdom. It would have been better had he retaliated with a cry of 'Balls!', for his resentment against callers who asked him to sign copies of his books grew to an obsession and eventually he burst out. Then he regretted his ill-temper afterwards, and suffered remorse from 'feeling discourteous'.

The 'pre-Hawthornden days' were over.

FOUR

Relationships at Shallowford

HENRY CONSOLIDATED HIS SUCCESS quickly with the publication of the fourth and final volume of 'The Flax of Dream'. He cared for *The Pathway* as deeply as for *Tarka*, for in it his own philosophy was reflected through the young Willie Maddison, of whom he wrote in the Foreword: 'William Maddison appears to me as a young brother, whose life has been recreated from scenes we both knew, and sometimes shared.' Many of Henry's admirers find such an affinity with Willie and his romantic yearnings that this is their favourite among his books. It was the only one Henry urged me to read, writing to me at Pembroke College, Cambridge, around 1950: 'I gather you haven't had time to read *The Pathway*, you should if you are going to write that article, for it is to this writer what *Bondage* was to Maugham.'

He had been contemplating the novel since 1919 and suffered the usual labour pains, haunted by the fear that he would die before it was finished — 'I had to force myself to write each word and sentence'. This was to be followed by the usual post-natal depression: 'the completion of my book did not, as I had hoped, free my life of agonized meditation. My idiom of life remained as before — always the struggle.'

This time he could not complain of neglect, for his readers responded enthusiastically: 2000 copies were printed for the first edition and two further impressions were called for within a month of publication. So what was the matter? It is tempting to suggest that little was the matter except that Henry's complexity made it so. Even at this exciting moment of literary triumph, it is plain that Henry suffered from a deep sense of insecurity. It is hard to explain satisfactorily, but those who knew him well confirm his complexity by the very divergence of their views: Walter de la Mare thought he possessed genius; J.C. Trewin remembers him as shy, concealing it 'by a flippancy that would sometimes worry the serious-minded'; Kenneth Young considered him 'a trifle mad'; and 'Queenie' agrees, 'he was as mad as a hatter!' I did not find him mad at all, but as wily as a fox. My father, Negley Farson, accused him of being a masochist, while author-critic Colin Wilson admitted that he found it extraordinarily difficult to write about Henry Williamson because he was 'a very complex bag of tricks'.

It should be remembered that Henry was a show-off, preferring fantasy to reality, which is not a bad thing for a novelist but confusing for anyone who tries to pin him down. Clues abound in his books but they tend to conflict; indeed, it is hard to differentiate between fact and invention in a book like *The Sun in the Sands*. Which truth does one believe in? 'You say things which are not, my dear boy,' says the literary lady, Mrs Dawson-Scott, in that particular 'novel-autobiography'; but, of course, it is Henry himself who repeats such devastating comments against him.

Paradoxical though it may seem, Henry was one of the most truly truthful men I have known, a view shared by the painter Edward Seago: 'But if there are several sides to a person, each one entirely genuine, then why this conjecture of the real self, for are they not all of them real? I am certain that the various Williamsons are all of them very real, for I have never met a man more completely sincere, nor so stead-fast in his search for truth.' Truth was Henry's lifelong objective and hope: 'I would learn to see all things as the sun saw them — without shadows. Detachment — complete and absolute detachment.'

In the preface to the American edition of *The Village Book* (see pp. 29-30) Henry, now aged thirty-five, explained his philosophy. He started by acknowledging the difficulties in writing truly of one's fellow beings — 'all attempts appear as failures' — but this was his aim, nevertheless: 'to write the truth about one small community, Ham village, as the truth had never been written before'. And he ended with this declaration of intent:

> ... as man and writer I would like to be as the sun which divines the true or inner nature of living things. When the rain drifts grey and cold in winter, when the north-east wind dries the lanes and withers the fields and gardens, when the frost racks earth and water in agony, then it is not seemly to seek Truth; but when the sun shines, there is a Being which unlocks and discovers the spirit of man or beast. The sun is entirely truthful; the sun sees no shadows. It is possible, by a sun-like understanding, to discover among the crotchety and cantankerous, among the so-called cruel and vicious, the same person as oneself: the human being which has grown from a child to its present shape, and which in its heart still has the solar innocence of the child. To be like the sun is to see all things plain, and to draw all life to oneself.

Perhaps it was the fervour of this quest that caused Henry's dissatisfaction, which sometimes reached despair; perhaps it was an intrinsic flaw in his character.

'Queenie' told me that 'he was always going to commit suicide, always telling us that he was going to kill himself.' I asked if she knew why. 'I don't know really. No reason I could see. He wanted to drown over Bideford Bar, like

Shelley wasn't it? I'd say, "Oh, do shut up, Henry! Don't be such a damned fool!"' Her ridicule was the right reaction. 'One had to laugh at him, but he took it all in good part. He liked being teased.' But why did Henry talk of suicide in the first place? Was it the need to cast himself constantly in the rôle of injured party? 'Queenie' shook her head uncertainly: 'As I say, I don't know. You see, we regarded him as such a joke. Was it because he was kicked out of home and was so awful to his parents in that ghastly house in Lewisham?'

Whatever had been the immediate cause of Henry's leaving home, he certainly regretted his past disputes with his father and saw them as a tragedy, writing later in his father's defence: 'I did not realize then how much I had worried him with my irregular ways.' He yearned for his father's love and felt lost without it, and this seemed to put him beyond the bounds of an ordinary family existence. In *The Sun in the Sands*, he tells how isolated he was by the normality of 'Queenie's' family life: 'I felt my attitude was due to a defect within myself. The difference was, perhaps, in that they were a happy family and the more natural; while I had been one of an unhappy family and was therefore the more unnatural.' This was alibi talk: his childhood had its acute emotional disappointments for one so sensitive, but it was not as cruelly unhappy as he liked to make out. Significantly, the dedication in his first book, *The Beautiful Years*, reads: 'In deep affection to my Mother and my Father, this story of far away and long ago is given'. In later editions this was changed to the empty and pretentious, 'To THE MOTHER and to THE FATHER'. The original rings more true, with Henry conveying that love which could never be reciprocated as deeply as he wished.

This emotional lack explains his continual, self-defeating search for the 'ideal companion', in the course of which he denied himself the gradual appreciation of such humdrum qualities in other people as simplicity, serenity, perseverance

— which are in fact extraordinary. In rejecting compromise, one lets the real thing escape. I would hesitate to take his 'search' seriously, except that he referred to it so often himself. It meant that every relationship had to be forged by fire, tested, taunted, teased, twisted and threatened. Few relationships could survive. It is proof of Loetitia Williamson's patience and wisdom that their marriage lasted so long and with so much happiness.

When I talked to her a year after Henry's death, I suggested that he was a 'cruel' man, but she would not accept this. And later that day she was able to speak of him with rare tenderness and sympathy, and slight regret: 'He could not accept that the children had to come first. When he finished writing he wanted to walk and for me to go with him, but I had to stay with the children and he couldn't understand that. When you have children they're bound to come first; he needed a companion, but I didn't have the time or energy to go for walks with him.'

As the family grew, they moved from Georgeham to the long, low, thatched house near the stream at Shallowford, returning to Ox's Cross to camp out with the children on special occasions like the King's Jubilee, when they looked out to Hartland and the great bonfires lit in celebration along the coast. The atmosphere conveyed in Henry's own account, *The Children of Shallowford*, is one of warmth, and this is confirmed in an *Essay on Henry Williamson, The Dreamer of Devon*, published in a limited edition of 250 copies by the Ulysses Press in 1932. Herbert Faulkner West describes a visit in March of that year, with Henry collecting him from Taunton station in his Silver Eagle which was capable of 80 mph. In the evening they sat around the fire in comfortable armchairs listening to records of *Tristan and Isolde*:

... the author's secretary ... was knitting by the fire. Gypsy, Williamson's wife ... sat quietly and serenely by the fire, her hands moved rapidly, making a sweater for Windles, the oldest boy. The light from the fire reflected a red glow on their cheeks. There was silence for a while, and after London, an astonishingly satisfying peace. Here at Shallowford Williamson lives, as Thoreau lived at Walden Pond, in his own silences amid quiet and lovely surroundings.

The restful atmosphere is plainly accurate, and a further description of Henry in his slippers beating time with his pencil as he corrects the proofs of *The Labouring Life* to music from *Tristan* is delightful. But the romantic portrait conceals the reality.

Concurrent with his writings were a series of relationships. If these suffered from the drama which seemed inevitable with Henry, at least they provided distraction. Towards the end of his life particularly, girlfriends became secretaries, and secretaries girlfriends, and the secretaries left and so did the girls. Curiously enough, far from preferring women he could easily dominate, Henry admired women with spirit and intelligence, provided they were prepared to surrender their will to his.

Loetitia maintains that when he was a younger man it was the women who ran after her husband: 'Henry had so many girl-friends at that time. Some of them were very hard to get rid of. There was one lady — we practically had to carry her away.' She smiled at the recollection of a predatory millionairess who pursued Henry through the southern states when he visited America.

Did she mind him going off on his own? 'No, I had plenty to do without him. Children! But I was able to join him later and we lived in New York for a short time, on our own, which was marvellous, one of the happiest times of our marriage. We rented an apartment in Greenwich Village while Henry lectured on Hamlet.' There, for two months,

65

Loetitia was able to fulfil the rôle of companion without the distraction of other responsibilities, and then they sailed home together.

Her loyalty was absolute throughout, and Henry knew it. 'Loetitia is the heroine . . . ', he wrote to his publisher during the political hostility against him in the second world war; and he told his daughter Margaret to remember that, 'whatever qualities you children may have, you got them from your mother'. Henry was lucky in the particular patience of his wife who remained so steadfast and understanding. She had need of her serenity.

In that description of his visit to Henry in 1932, Herbert West mentions one particular secretary. Since she prefers to remain anonymous, I can only say that this was another relationship that survived against the odds — as did Henry's with Loetitia alongside it — for nearly two decades. One day, perhaps, the full story may be told.

Though Henry found adult relationships difficult, he enjoyed a rare affinity with children. He was proud of his own, and the photographs in *Shallowford* of their radiant young faces prove how happy they could be. Yet there are moments in the book when Henry lacerates himself as he describes how cruelly he could play upon their emotions, as he did with Margaret when they examined a dormant hedgehog rolled up in leaves for the winter's hibernation. Hedgehogs, Henry whispered to her, ate snakes by nipping them by the tail and then curling up so that the snake would beat itself to death on the spines.

> 'The hedgehog is probably rather hungry, Margy.'
> 'Yes, it probably is rather hungry, Dad, ban't it?'
> 'Shall us give the snake to it for its dinner, Margy?'
> She nodded. 'Then th' aidge-'og won't be no more hungry, will it, Dad?'

'But what about the poor snake, Margy? What about its children.' I put false pathos into my words.

'That poor snake will cry if it don't see its children no more, won't it, Dad?'

'Well, certainly it won't like being eaten.'

'No, it won't, will it, Dad? Us mustn't let the nasty old aidge-'og eat the poor snake, must us?'

'But the snake might eat the mice, Margy. Aren't the mice pretty ... ?' [And so on, tantalizing the child, until the awful demand:]

'Then what shall we kill, Margaret?'

Afterwards with his scrupulous honesty, he admits: 'How easy it was to prejudice the children's minds. How easy, too, to upset their natural balance of feelings, and make dominant, for example, the sense of pity.'

His teasing sounds cruel, but when I reminded Margaret of the episode it had made so little impression that I had to describe it again. 'Simply a case of wanting to see how people would react,' she explained. 'He could be very tender to young people and animals, but he wasn't always kind to my four brothers. We were never asked to do something, we were told.'

'Did you ever rebel?'

'I think with Henry that he inspired you to get on with things.'

'Did you have fun, as children?'

'Oh yes! He was blessed with humour. He could turn the smallest thing into something amusing. He was a jolly difficult man by any standards, but he had tremendous compassion, the ability to forgive and forget and see the other person's point of view. He had great integrity, but he took it out on people around him. He needed sustenance from other people, and, as an artist will, he rejected those he needed most.'

Remembering the strictness of his own father, Henry veered in the other direction, demanding too much of Windles while giving too little guidance. When the daughter of the Master of the local otter hunt was married, Windles was allowed to run up and down the aisle during the service, gurgling and noisy, much to the annoyance of the wedding guests. 'But Henry thought it was a joke,' says 'Queenie', who was there.

I am told that, on the night that Windles was born, Henry had expressed the hope that he might raise his son as one of the leaders of a new generation, destined for peace rather than war. Romantic ideals are hell to live with and worse to live up to, and it is not surprising that the boy was intimidated. 'Now my son is in his seventh year,' wrote Henry later, 'and what have I achieved? Nothing.' With his usual detachment, he recorded, 'My little boy did not want me'; for he would ask his son to come for a walk and there was always the quick reply, 'No thanks.'

One night, with an obvious effort, Loetitia told him the truth: 'Windles is afraid of you.'

'Of *me*?'

'He thinks you don't like him.'

'But he doesn't seem to like me,' replied Henry, casting himself as the injured party.

'He thinks you like John better,' she added, smiling and flushed with nervousness. 'John is very companionable, isn't he, dear?' Henry stared at the fire in the nursery where they were having supper. 'Don't be hurt,' she continued, 'but you make Windles afraid, I think. Sometimes those things you say to him, he says afterwards — "Are there *really* green eyes in the wood?" — to me. He is very nervous, you know, and also has a dread of making a fool of himself before you. And don't mind my saying this, but he is really *terrified* of "green eyes". After all, he is only six and has a vivid imagination.'

Windles may have been six, but Henry, who was always an injustice collector, felt himself aggrieved. Telling his son about 'a dear little man' who lived in the Deer Park on slices of Christmas pudding, he had to twist the knife sadistically by adding, 'He has such tiny little hands, much smaller than baby Margaret's. I hope no one shoots him, it will be such a shame.' Noticing his son's alarm and his wife's anxiety, Henry thought, 'she is afraid of me... of my ceaseless criticism'; but when he reassured them he felt bitter:

> [that] such easy, careless words of mine could apparent-
> ly make both mother and son happy. It was a kind of
> dishonesty; like the gracious insincerity of good man-
> ners which could make people feel fine, when an
> apparent interest was taken in them and their doings.
> Yet good manners, graciousness, was only as oil to a
> laden axle which otherwise might overheat and break.
> Friction was loss of energy, of life. The use and employ-
> ment of graciousness was one of the fundamentals of the
> art of living. I knew this, but seldom used the knowledge.
> With good-mannered people I was good mannered, and
> with gauche or careless people I was awful: a poor
> example for my son.

Narcissus detesting his reflection. 'Henry did not find him-self easy to live with,' Margaret told me after his death.

Already Henry had tried to transfer his traumas to the fictional Maddisons. Originally he intended a happy ending for Willie in *The Pathway*: 'Immortality is now, he is going to make all happy as he can — to use his genius for making others see that what he sees is Truth, and seeing, so may they come to happiness. For most people are like children looking for the mother they have lost.' But as the tetralogy drew to a close, he funked it. The Great War has come to an end and Willie has fallen in love with Mary Loetitia Ogilvie, ex-periencing the piercing innocence of young love; for once

69

there is no regret. The setting is Braunton Burrows, with the estuary of the two rivers beyond:

The rain was blown away up the estuary, and swift sunlight brought brightness and colour to the grass and stones before the hut. The faded heads of the sea-thrift trembled on their stalks rising from the saltings. He asked her to tell him if she loved him, and she would not reply: he asked her again, and she said that she did not know.

'Yes, you must know,' he pleaded, and she said he knew already. 'Well, do you like me?' he asked, and she nodded.

'When did you first begin to like me, then?' She whispered that it was after he had talked with the Vicar on Easter Sunday night, when she wanted to take care of him. 'You seemed to be so all alone, and a poor boy altogether.'

'Not before then, Mary?'

* * *

His long arms held her closer, and he leaned down his head, and touched the sun-burned neck with his cheek, as though seeking shelter. He murmured to her in a voice rapturous and sad, and with a rough movement unfastened her blouse, so that the first soft swelling of the breasts showed white beneath the sunburn. 'Oh, my Mary,' he said kissing her, while she clasped his head and looked with wonder past the faded flowers of the spring. He asked her if she had ever loved anyone else, and she shook her head.

* * *

My virgin, Mary, he thought, while his eyes filled with tears and he went away from her again. How sweet a thing it is to be pure! And with desolation in his heart he fell to thinking of Eveline Fairfax, and of the things he had said in love to her and now might be saying to Mary. Never again could he be as Mary, natural and pure, as God meant a maid to be. He strayed down to the shore, and, looking at the sky, felt no remorse for having known love before; only regret. All the acts of men, that priesthood called sin, rose before him; but no human action could seem sordid under the blue space around the world. I regret nothing, he said to himself.

This was written after Henry's marriage, when he was beginning to recognize his own frustration. 'You are in harmony with life;' Willie tells Mary. 'I'm a reactionary, in harmony with an imaginary life. I shall make you miserable, and anything that makes you miserable is blasphemous.'

'You don't make me miserable, silly,' Mary replies; but Willie, like Henry, knows better.

'I have a daemon, Mary — as the old people used to say: and when I work, I dissolve the daemon out of myself, and am free to be happy.'

In 1920 he predicted a happy ending to 'The Flax of Dream', because he considered it 'truer for the modern world whose makers will be the young men tried in the hell of war, given a wisdom beyond the material wisdom of old men. He *refuses* to die, to be drowned, to be crucified.' But by 1927 Henry knew he had to kill off Willie Maddison before his youthful illusions were tarnished by the truth; the drowning was neither accident nor suicide, but a literary murder. In *The Sun in the Sands*, he describes how he planned it while walking along the sands from Crow Point to Bideford Bar: 'The sea was narrow in the estuary, with long lines of white where rollers broke on the sandbanks of the bar. "That is where Maddison dies," I said despite myself. "He is drowned in that far estuary."'

Nearly fifty years later, as we walked across those same

sands for a picnic beneath the site of the old lighthouse, Henry pointed to the whiteness of the Bar and told me of his overwhelming emotion when he came to write that scene: 'I was just in tears, I finished about eleven o'clock at night, I wandered about outside, almost muttering "Willie's dead". I didn't want my imagination to lose control.'

'Were they tears of regret?'

'No, I had the feeling I had done something I could be proud of, because there is no brutality or any unkindness in the writing ... '

So, at the end of *The Pathway*, due to a misunderstanding with Mary's mother who does not trust him, Willie Maddison is stranded on a ridge in the estuary as the tide rises and cuts him off. There are no passing fishing boats to save him, for this is the start of September and the salmon-netting season is over. He burns the pages of his literary masterpiece, *The Star-born*, but no one sees the flare and Maddison is drowned.

It is not surprising that Henry was genuinely moved by his death, for he was killing his younger self. When Barbara Rogers, an admirer who lives in Appledore, met him for the first time when he was an old man, she told him that she wept when she read the chapter of Willie's death. Henry replied, 'Oh yes, that was my other self. He had to die.' For in this way, Henry's 'psychical' self was to be spared the harsh entry into the adult world where hopes and promises are unfulfilled, and life becomes muddier, and marriages fail. He knew that the sea cleanses absolutely: 'How many times one has thought of dissolution and peace in the tide surging north past the Morte ... ,' he wrote to me in 1950. Henry was too brave a man to take his own life, but in killing off Willie he was expunging his own problems, which is the author's prerogative and freedom.

John Middleton Murry, talking of Williamson in *Katherine Mansfield and Other Literary Studies* (1959), claimed that it is impossible to separate *The Pathway* from Henry's own background:

> Here, it seems, is the reason why Mary Ogilvie's engagement to Willie Maddison is broken off in the novel. The marriage could not be realized in fact. The reality denied the dream. Here, too, from the other side, is the reason why Willie Maddison had to die, in spite of the author's previous determination that he was to live. In the flesh he could not cope with the problems of day-to-day living with his wife.

Murry examines Henry's malaise further:

> The dreamer cannot in fact come down to earth. What inward conviction can sustain him in his indictment of those who cause the unhappiness of children and so cause the misery of war, when he, in bitter fact, is himself perpetuating that unhappiness by his estrangement and incessant irritation with his wife? What does it avail to find in himself a growing sympathy for his once hated father, whose fatal withdrawal and irritability he sees being reproduced in himself, when the sympathy is purchased at the price of a growing impatience with his mother whom he had loved? The very foundations of the novel which he dreams of writing, he knows, are shifting sand.

Colin Wilson suggests in his *Eagle and Earwig* (1967) that:

> Since Williamson was writing *The Pathway* after his marriage to Loetitia there was no solution, except to confess that Willie would have made a mistake in marrying Mary. This may be the reason that their separation is crudely contrived, followed by Willie's death. But this cannot be the whole reason; Williamson's defeat complex was reappearing, the romanticism about death (there is a strong element of this in Jefferies's

The Story of My Heart) that had been so obvious in the
animal sagas and that was now making its way into the
human world.

Valerie Belsey (*Devonshire Association Report 110*, 1978)
writes that Mary is competing against no mere human rivals
for Maddison's love, but with the ghost of the Great War
and the predatory cycle of natural things: 'It is not clear
whether suicide has been committed or not, but what is clear
is that the young author was always fighting to be at one
with nature, a state which could perhaps only be achieved by
his losing his life through some natural disaster.'

It could be true that Willie's death also appealed to
Henry's sense of drama, as Steerforth's did to Dickens.
There was an element of play-acting in his own suicide
threats, and 'Queenie' did not believe them for a moment
when Henry made them to her.

Henry allowed his characters to remember Willie with
gratifying sorrow. '"I see it all!"' Mary cries out. '"He was
too good to live among us, and so he was taken away."'
'"The legend begins,"' murmurs Willie's cousin Phillip to
the priest. '"If we had understood him better, he would not
have needed to go away at all."' Mary hears him and
laments, '"Yes, that is the truth! I failed him!"'

Before we hear the echo — 'You'll be sorry when I'm
dead!' — Henry checks himself. '"Nobody has failed anybody,"' says another of his characters. '"Nothing you or
anybody else could have said or done would have made any
difference. He would never have changed."'

A liar in search of truth, a pacifist in love with war —
with such a complex mind as Henry's it is as difficult to 'pin
him down' as it was for Richard Maddison to capture the
Camberwell Beauty he pursued at the beginning of *The Dark
Lantern*. Or was it the promise, the innocence, of childhood
and adolescence that he tried to hold on to?

Henry once surprised me when, in 1950, he expressed admiration for Orson Welles's film *Citizen Kane* (I never saw him as a cinema-goer). He compared the film to a Sherlock Holmes story: 'Mystery all the way, and the Rosebud dénouement is masterly and strictly the true story. Psychology be blowed; it is a story; and a true story. Ask Beaverbrook.' 'Rosebud' (Kane's final word as he dies at Xanadu) is revealed at the end of the film as the rose transfer on his childhood sleigh, which is thrown into the furnace of unimportant possessions after his death. Did Henry have his 'Rosebud' as well? If so, I suspect it belonged to his childhood, too; or to that later bewildering period of adolescence where everything has a brightness which is never quite recovered; or to the war, that sudden growing up which was too sudden in his case. Far from bringing him to maturity, the war arrested his natural development: Henry was left suspended between the innocence of childhood and the unnatural innocence of war, which was like a continuation of his schooldays with the fine comradeship of men. Throughout his life Henry demanded a return to such purity, yearning for a heavenly landscape where the sun would shine all the time as in those long hot summers of remembered childhood. 'It is true, however, that between those years, between the ages of seventeen and twenty-two, I had learned nothing to fit me for what was called a normal life.'

'Julian Warbeck' (quoted in *The Sun in the Sands*) also dared to suggest that Henry was still an adolescent in 'that uneasy period between puberty and adulthood'. Henry asked sardonically if one can only become an adult after committing adultery, but he accepted the truth of it: 'I had long perceived this inability to assert myself, to say what I thought was right and fair, to be the cause of much of my past unhappiness; yet the inability or impotence remained. I blamed my schooling for this; together with the excessive love and protection given me by mother as a boy, and the constant fear of my father when at home.'

If Henry had his 'Rosebud' it might have been, like Kane's, something he had lost or never fully known — a photograph of a girl, exchanged across barbed wire during the Christmas truce; or the symbol of the barn owl, painted on the side of his Norton motor-bike which took him back to Devon in search of the peace he had known briefly before the outbreak of war, and always hoped to recover.

FIVE

'The vermin pole'

ACCORDING TO HENRY, he once introduced J. B. Priestley at a New York party as 'the great English humorous writer' — prompting Priestley to introduce Henry as 'the great English *un*-humorous writer'. Whether or not this is true I cannot be certain, because years later Priestley has declined to comment; but if it was not, at least Henry had the wit to invent the story against himself.

When people claim that Henry had no sense of humour, they usually mean that he did not share *their* sense of humour; for he had a strong brand of his own. When he relaxed, which was more often than I (or Henry) have suggested, he could be as giddy as a schoolboy, using words like 'soppy', 'bilge' and 'rot', which featured incongruously in his every-day conversation (Edward, Prince of Wales, was known as 'the Pragger-Wagger — such a dear boy!') Henry described himself as a mischievous boy, and the mischief never left him.

Shortly after he arrived in Georgeham, he and some friends indulged in a prank, covering the sign outside the village hall with newspaper. It sounds a silly thing to do, though hardly serious, but the villagers took umbrage over the desecration of their George and Dragon, and Henry was forced to own up in a letter of apology to the secretary of the Institute:

Sir, With reference to our recent conversation about the apology for the pasting of the Institute sign last Whitsun by myself accompanied by two friends as witnesses, when two sheets of the local newspaper were affixed with gloy to the corners of the aforesaid sign, I beg to confirm with willingness that on Whit Monday I with my fellow culprits went to the Rector as Chairman of the Institute Committee and humbly confessed and apologized for our act of vandalism and that our apology was most graciously accepted by the Rector. I have the honour to be, sir, your obedient servant, H. W. Williamson.

This was characteristic of his dry wit, but it is probable that the less humorous villagers accepted his 'apology' literally.

Many people found his humour uncomfortable, including one magazine editor who complained that a reference to a stag 'rolling in its soiling pit' was 'not quite nice' for his readership. Henry explained patiently that a stag rolls on its back in a sort of peat-bath to destroy the scent when it is hunted, and that 'soiling' came from the Anglo-Norman word meaning 'to wash off'.

'I see you don't understand what I've been saying,' sighed the editor.

'Well, if you think it's a tiny bit nasty, shall I put the stag in a pair of bathing drawers?' Henry suggested helpfully. Instead of the expected burst of laughter, the editor glared at him huffily:

'That's the end of it, if you can't be sensible.'

Henry's verdict was straight to the point: 'The man was just a silly ass'.

The intensity of Henry's writing may give a grave impression. Nonetheless, even in later years he was an envigorating man to meet, with a sense of fun and a blazing smile which made him a welcome guest at parties. Strangers were often astonished by such vivacity in an old man. When other spirits flagged, he felt compelled to perform, playing the 'giddy goat' or leap-frogging over bollards down the street. When sitting by himself in a pub he would attract attention by imitating the call of the cuckoo, which tended to startle people who had no idea who he was. 'Bloody cuckoo's right,' I heard one holiday-maker mutter uncomfortably. But children loved his childishness, until he became too intense.

Henry had mixed feelings when the joke was against himself, though he could be forgiving. His close friend, S. P. B. Mais, who appears in various guises in Henry's novels (though he is also referred to by his own name, 'Petre'), lampooned Henry in one of his own (*Orange Street*, 1926). The novel begins as a successful publicist, Nigel Baring, flees from London to the West Country and the home of the poet, Brian Stucley, who greets him brandishing his latest work: '"I want you to listen to this. I think it's great."' Before Baring can murmur a 'How d'you do?', Stucley tells him: '"I don't want you to say anything, it's damned good and I know it."' As he starts to read, Stucley explains that this is the first chapter of his new novel: '"I've now fashioned and re-fashioned it ten times. It is very long. It takes an hour to read."' It took longer 'owing to the fact that he periodically stopped to kick his dog away from his feet'.

'Lydia', with black hair and brown eyes and much in love with Stucley, is based on Loetitia as plainly as Stucley is on Henry, with his characteristic outbursts of self-torment: '"What about me? Have you no pity on my loneliness? What have I left but my work?"'

An affectionate but irreverent portrait, and at first Henry was wounded: 'I'd been hurt to think he could be so friendly in life, and so mean in fiction. I know now old Petre had never seen any true connexion between the real me and the fiction me. He had merely been making up a story.'

Although Henry could rationalize in this way to his own satisfaction, and forgave magnanimously, disgruntlement was apt to linger. Priestley's comment in New York, for example, rankled; but this may have been due also to his earlier and deadlier comment that Willie Maddison was 'half-baked, with all the trappings of a prophet without the prophecy'. There was enough truth in this to hurt. As if to his own detriment, but really to his advantage, Henry further quoted Priestley at that New York party: 'Isn't it queer, but there's a clique in London, quite a small one but it definitely exists, of people who think you are a first-class writer. I can't understand it.' When Priestley continued by quoting the opinion of J. C. Squire that *The Pathway* was 'a really big novel' — adding, 'Yes, Jack's got a queer streak in him' — Henry protested faintly that Squire might have liked the book 'because he liked me'. 'Damn it all, *I* like you!' Priestley exclaimed; but he confirmed that 'it's a fact you have no sense of humour'. Henry allowed himself the last word, explaining Priestley's apparently boorish behaviour:

> Then he sat down or rather flopped down on a sofa, uninterested in the party. It was Priestley's first forty-eight hours in New York and he must have been tired out — the lion who refused to be a lion, and was just himself, rich but honest Jack Priestley. One can't help liking the fellow; and one can't help believing that a first-class writer would never accuse a second-class writer of having no sense of humour. I suppose the first-class writer wouldn't dare, realizing the parochialism of such a judgement.

With such a bitter comment he came close to proving Priestley's point.

When Henry tried to be funny in his writing he often

80

resorted to whimsy. In his heart he knew this failing, dismissing *Scribbling Lark* (1949, a children's book) in a letter to me in 1950 as 'my cigarette-card storyette'. By contrast, his serious short stories have a savage power seldom equalled in this century; and these are the ones that matter.

Many of them end in death. In 'Redeye' (*The Peregrine's Saga*), for example, the hunted hound of that name collapses in the Nightcrow Inn (based on The Rock Inn, Georgeham, with recognizable local characters), 'run stiff — heart burst and broken — muscles set'. In 'A Crown of Life' (*Tales of Moorland and Estuary*, 1953), Henry tells the story of a faithful mongrel dog whose drunken farmer-owner commits suicide after ostracism by the villagers. Finally, on Christmas morning, the starving, frozen dog enters the church:

> ... those remaining in the pews began to notice a small chiming and clinking in the air about them, and as they looked up in wonderment, the movement of other heads drew sight to the figure of the old grey sheepdog walking up the aisle. With consternation they watched it moving slowly towards the light beginning to shine in the stained glass of the tall eastern windows above the altar. They watched it pause before the chancel step, as it stood slightly swaying, as though summoning its last strength to raise one foot, and a second foot, and again one more foot, and then the last foot, and limp to the row of kneeling people beyond which the rector moved ... [the verger tiptoes up but the rector shakes his head imperceptibly]... The dog's paw was raised to the rail as it sat there, with dim eyes, waiting; and at every laboured breath the icicles on its coat made their small chimmering noises.

'A Crown of Life' (first published in the *Adelphi*, with a dedication to Benjamin Britten) made such an impression on me that I asked Henry if I could include it in my anthology *In*

Praise of Dogs (1976). He agreed generously, signing my manuscript (for reasons I still do not fully understand): 'There was my belief—ended but still alive. Henry Williamson. Georgeham.' Later, I discovered that this was one of his favourite stories, although he gave me no sign at the time.

The finest of his short stories concern animals. Apart from his moments of calculated whimsy, Henry's attitude towards animals was sympathetic but seldom sentimental. I remember my mother saying that, when she heard the hens screaming and saw the cat flash through the window while the dog slid under the table, she knew that Henry was coming down the drive; which makes me smile whenever I see him described as 'the great animal lover'. He knew animals, he understood animals, but he did not love them as people love their pets. This lack of sentiment was the strength of his appeal to children, for whom he was the antidote to *Winnie The Pooh*.

When Henry took me on that otter hunt along the banks of the River Taw in my childhood, I do not think he relished it as much as the others; but even then his attitude was unemotional, which surprised me. At the end of his life he was more reluctant to declare his support publicly, but he was always in favour of hunting in principle. As he saw it, this was only realistic. In a broadcast in 1936, he justified stag hunting on the grounds that stags damaged the crops of farms lying under the moor. Farmers were given approximately £1,500 from hunt funds not to attack the deer themselves: 'Otherwise, of course, the presence of the deer would be a burden on the farmers, and they would soon be shot, trapped or poisoned.' As proof that hunting was a form of protection, he cited a period seventy years earlier when the red deer were threatened with extinction because the hunt was supported so feebly that the farmers were killing the animals by their own, more indiscriminate methods. (With Henry's endearing, turn-about 'objectivity', he was then compelled to add that deer do not feed exclusively on crops but also on heather tips, whortleberry shoots, ivy, ash-sprays, acorns and new bramble.)

It is an emotive subject. The very idea of any animal being chased through the countryside is sickening to many people; argument in favour of it, however logical, does not impress them, especially now that animals have to survive the threat of pollution and the spread of 'development' as well as pursuit by ladies in bowler hats. It is hard not to be prejudiced by the image of an animal as splendid as the stag hunted into the sea where it drowns, or driven into the corner of a building where the trembling animal is shot. The hunted seem always so beautiful compared to the hunter. In his BBC script for 'The Red Deer of Exmoor', which underwent several revisions, Henry tried to strip such images of their brutality:

Will you be patient and listen to the reason why I do not believe that the stag, or any hunted animal, suffers the mental pain called 'fear' while it is being hunted?

Men in battle do not feel fear . . . Before the action starts, yes: a most awful paralyzing cold fear: but when it is happening, one enters another world wherein ordinary feelings are lifted from one. One is, as it were, in a fourth dimension, a kind of clear-headed delirium, which is often at first exhilarating, because reality is not so terrible as one had imagined, and because one is still alive . . . Although at the time one is not conscious of loss of energy, afterwards the heaviness of one's body and limbs is apparent . . . . One sleeps like a dead man. Later, one begins to feel the satanic blasts of high explosive, and the horror of disruption, and the loss of friends. And so while the stag is running, and when at last he is at bay in water, surrounded by a nightmare unreality of figures and noises, I do not think he feels fear.

If I had the choice of being say, a bullock in a pasture or a wild deer on the moor, I would choose to be a deer, so that when my turn came I would have a chance in the open instead of no choice in the confined horror of an abattoir.

Henry's identification with the stag is impressive, and a far halloo from the complacency of fox-hunting ladies and gentlemen who claim that the fox *enjoys* being hunted. Their joy in riding across the English countryside on a glorious day is acceptable, so long as they do not insist that it is all for the animal's good.

Inevitably, Henry's views were controversial. After his broadcast, the President of The League for the Prohibition of Cruel Sports complained to the BBC for allowing him 'to justify the sport' which was 'inhuman and barbarous . . . and a disgrace to a civilized nation'. This produced the evasive reply that Mr Henry Williamson was 'one of our most distinguished living writers on natural history'.

The murder of a red deer on Exmoor can indeed seem tragic; but is it worse than a rat's lingering agony from warfarin, or the hideous explosion of a rabbit infected by myxomatosis? The manner of death concerned Henry as much as the death itself. When a 'shaggy fellow' offered him ten shillings in a pub near Shallowford to trap the rabbits which were swarming into his field, Henry thought of them playing there, and possibly courting, and refused. Even the wilful uprooting of a wild flower would anger him unless it was being transplanted. For Henry, it was reasonable to kill an animal for food, and part of nature for one animal to kill another; hunting was justified when it helped preserve the species, wrong when it placed that species in danger; a clean kill was good, a messy one lacked skill and was unforgivable:

'What ploughman or rabbit-trapper or whipper-in to hounds or wildfowler was ever a sadist, or blood-luster?'

He could sympathize with worms while exploiting them, 'I have impaled them on hooks; and have flung them, poor innocents, into the river for trout and salmon; yet always with a feeling of the wrongfulness of it, as they writhed in desperation in the swirls of the current.' He felt for the aged salmon stranded in a river pool where he had to run in winter: 'Poor old fellow, he was lonely and shut-in by this small moorland stream: condemned to hide all the summer days under some muddy elder roots — unless someone stuck a dung-fork through his back first.'

Although he rejoiced in the survival of the fittest, Henry had compassion for the victim too — as when, on one occasion, he observed a baby bird mesmerised by a snake. But afterwards he reflected: 'As for the grass snake, it had to feed somehow, I suppose. Mice and young birds were its chief food. And one robin less would mean, perhaps, a few more happy worms.'

Like the dedicated naturalist, Sir Peter Scott, who once told me he was going to kill one of his geese at the Wildfowl Trust for his Christmas dinner as a form of culling, Henry had no mock scruples in devouring meat and fish; but the irony did not escape him. When one of the speakers at a Foyle's Literary Luncheon praised him for *watching* the fish as well as catching them, the audience applauded as if a great truth had been propounded. Henry remarked dryly that it would have been more becoming if they had not just stuffed themselves with salmon mayonnaise.

Henry suffered with the animal when the odds were against the innocent. In *Tales of a Devon Village*, he bemoans the bloodlust of a badger dig, which contaminated everyone taking part, including himself as he is 'blooded':

I submitted; after all I was a guest. I was given a pad

covered with short black hairs, with five black digging claws, three of them broken. I murmured thanks, and tried not to look unpleasant, as I wondered if the boar had broken them as he dug for the safety of his mate and himself. His labour availed nothing, for the pick and spade and harrying terriers working along a tunnel are more speedy than ten claws scratching on hard stone and earth. Now he was a lump without a head and paws, and his blood was on my brow and cheek. I felt I had been false to myself, and yet another thought told me such feelings flourished only in nervous weakness. Why worry? And yet, only ten claws.

As so often with Henry, there was the converse side as well. He is alleged to have seized a kitten and smashed its brains out on the kitchen floor of the Norfolk farm, when he caught it destroying the fish dinner laid out in honour of a titled guest. A vile incident, if true, even though it was performed in the rage of the moment; yet, in a horrifying way, consistent, for the animal was eating the food which had been prepared in a time of rationing for a valued friend. Henry simply acted like the animal itself.

He had witnessed the cruelty of nature when he was a boy, allowed to search for birds' nests in Holme Park Woods in Kent. Arriving at the gamekeeper's cottage, he leant his bicycle against the hedge, climbed two stiles, and headed into the woods to the vermin pole where the keeper hung the corpses of hawks, weasels, stoats, rats and cats as a warning to other predators after young pheasants or the eggs. It was a gruesome ritual but it fascinated Henry, who was twelve or thirteen at the time: 'All the animals seemed to be grinning horribly in death. Some looked as though they had died with teeth clenched in rage.... My sympathy was with the victim of the gallows tree.'

Anyone who has seen an animal soon after death will

recognize that unsettling, mocking grin; but, far from haunting Henry, the spirit of the slain animals affected him in a way that was strangely enjoyable: 'a secret solitary feeling which I hardly dared expose even to myself in my thoughts'. He watched with sickly fascination as a weasel circled a rat, sharing the victim's 'helpless desire, sharp-sweet, deadly cloying, to give itself to the hunter'.

When Henry poked his stick into a gin-trap to render it harmless, he knew where his allegiance lay; it was harder to differentiate between the animals themselves. Charging at a stoat once, to save a bird hanging from its mouth, he was bitten through the nail on the forefinger of his right hand, which left a scar that was never erased 'in spite of having pressed a rifle trigger thousands of times with that fore-finger, and having held a pen which has written many millions of words'. And his effort was fruitless, for the bird was dead, leaving sixteen babies in the nest which died from slow starvation. Characteristically, Henry then removed the carefully woven home of webs and feathers and took it back to the 'museum' he shared with his friend 'Bony'.

A week later he was given an opportunity of seeing the stoat's viewpoint, when he returned to Holme Park Woods to find a shot female stoat stretched on the pole while her mate struggled in the gin-trap beneath. Two young stoats, barely weaned, were jumping up to reach their mother; the keeper struck them down, then beat the dog-stoat to death while it screeched defiance and tried to seize and bite his stick. The boy Henry was dismayed, but knew this was the rule of nature: 'It had been a killer all its life, and now its turn had come to be killed.... I felt very sorry for the stoat; indeed my tongue seemed to be drawn down my throat, so that I could not breathe properly. But afterwards, when looking at him and his mate and their little family strung up on the gallows, there was a tranquil sadness in thinking they had all died together.'

Such experiences excited rather than discouraged his interest in nature. Once, forgetting his 'unhappy childhood', Henry told me, 'As a boy in Kent I was always wandering about on my bicycle, it was marvellous. I was as happy as anything.' On expeditions with his friend 'Bony', their haversacks stuffed with bread and butter, apples and cake, they recorded their discoveries in their 'Nature Diaries', in a clumsy code that was easily broken. Rival naturalists in the same class, they tried to surpass each other and it seems likely that their schoolwork suffered accordingly. Quoting a terse end-of-term report — 'His standard of honour should be raised' — Henry's reaction was philosophical: 'I did the next best thing to looking out of the window, which was to imagine what the country outside was like.'

When I asked Henry to contribute to *Panorama*, the magazine I started at Cambridge University in 1949, he was kind enough to send me an article called 'My Friends the Crows' (*Panorama*, Spring 1950): he found loveliness even in these ungainly birds that lived in the trees near Ox's Cross, unlike the farmer who hated 'the bliddy craws, they'm worse than thievin' bliddy rats or magpies'. After releasing a crow caught in the farmer's gin-trap, Henry contemplates the balance of nature as it flies into the sky: 'It is one thing to have your eggs and poults taken by flamin' bliddy craws; another to watch them benevolently.'

He watched them all benevolently, the snake, the stoat, the 'bliddy craws', the worm, but the finest passages in his books were often inspired by the noblest of their kind — the red deer on Exmoor, or the salmon vaulting from the water on his journey up the river to the place where he was born. Even Henry's lesser work is enhanced, as in *On Foot in Devon* (1933), when he wrote in praise of a falcon glimpsed in a gale at Morte Point:

And in the midst of the colossal wind which blew out my eyelids whenever I opened my eyes, I saw a peregrine sweeping down out of the sky like a fragment of falling steel. It hit one of the gulls, which seemed to break into two pieces amidst a burst of feathers, and the falcon was gone a mile along the line of the cliff in about twenty seconds, glorifying in the playfulness of its element.

A passage like this redeems a hundred pages of whimsy.

Henry achieved an extraordinary grace and freshness in his writing with two themes in particular, animals and children. For he understood both. The delicate evocation of the joys and pangs of boyhood in *Dandelion Days* and *Donkey Boy*, for example, is matched in his simplest animal stories such as 'The Story of a Norfolk Owl' (contributed to *Country Company*, compiled by Richard Harman, 1949) — a delightful account of an owl called Hooly, befriended by the Williamson family. It is here, rather than in his messianic writings, that we find Henry Williamson at his best.

SIX

Traitor or patriot?

HENRY WAS ONE OF THE most fiercely patriotic men I have known. He loved his country passionately. But his patriotism was frequently misunderstood — and not without reason. With his right-wing views, he went against the literary movement of his time: how different it might have been had he fought in Spain, joined the Communist Party, spied for the Soviets...

If proof is needed of the double standards of patriotism, you have it in the attitude of the Fellows of the British Academy who voted overwhelmingly in July 1980 against the expulsion of Anthony Blunt, refusing to pass an amendment deploring his conduct. Defending Blunt against the criticism expressed by Max Hastings in the *Spectator* (23 August 1980), Hilary Rubinstein, Blunt's literary agent and the brother of his solicitor, replied in the same magazine: 'He would clearly like Professor Blunt to be treated as an out-and-out pariah.' This is precisely how Henry was treated during and after the Second World War, when he was guilty only of sincere belief.

Of course he was politically naïve — naïve about fascism, naïve about Hitler. Henry always did show a striking naïvety — a quality (or weakness) which endeared him to some but which many find baffling in a grown-up man. It

was his failure to anticipate the fury his political views
would arouse, as much as those views themselves, that made
his naïvety so damaging.

The trouble started with the rash statement in the foreword to 'The Flax of Dream' (1936, first composite edition)
— 'I salute the great man across the Rhine, whose life
symbol is the happy child' — a declaration which cost him
the loyalty of countless readers. To Henry, Nazism was a
logical outcome of the Great War: he saw Hitler as the 'man
of strength' that Germany needed at that time. Identifying
Hitler with the 'young German soldier' who had shared in
the traumatic experience of that war, Henry saw the idealistic vision of the Nazis without seeing the dangers. And
because he held this belief consistently to the day of his
death, many people never forgave him.

Harry Williamson, Henry's son by his second marriage,
has described an incident from his childhood when Henry
came to visit him at Millfield School on a parents' day. Henry
struck up a conversation with the father of one of Harry's
schoolfriends, each unaware of the other's identity. The
father was Lew Grade (now Lord Grade), who seized an
opportunity a few minutes later to ask an aide who that
interesting man was. When told that it was Henry Williamson,
he turned on his heels and left. At least he did so in
silence, unlike the man in the Lobster Pot at Instow who, in
1974, interrupted one of Henry's readings with a cry of
'Bloody Fascist!' and walked out, to the embarrassment of
two hundred people — while Henry continued as if nothing
had happened.

Henry's mistake lay not in his passionate opposition to a
second world war (he did not survive the muck and bullets of
the first only to acquiesce in another, which he believed
would change his country into a second-class power and lose
Britain most of her empire) but in his naïvety in falling for
Nazi glamour; like most boys he could not resist the boom of

91

the big parade. He was not alone in Britain in failing to recognize the threat of Hitler's vaulting ambition, for pro-German sympathy was common in this country up to 1935. Even after the occupation of the Rhineland in March 1936, the British were far from disenchanted: 'The consequence surprisingly was not alarm about Germany or hostility to it, but a display of pro-German sympathies or even enthusiasm,' wrote A. J. P. Taylor in his review of *Fellow Travellers of the Right* by Richard Griffiths (*Observer*, 31 August 1980). 'Germany had become respectable. Anti-semitism was played down; Hitler made a friendly compromise with Austria; Berlin was lost to the Olympic Games.'

When Henry joined his lifelong friend, Sir John Heygate, in Berlin in 1934, he was impressed by a nation apparently vibrant under a new leadership. A different Germany from the place he had visited in the 1920s, when he witnessed a state close to civil war with thousands of Communist and National Socialist casualties: 'It was terrible, machine guns in the streets and pubs being bombed, seven millions out of work, coming from the Treaty of Versailles in July 1919 when chunks of Germany were cut off and given to other countries. It was then that Foch pointed to Danzig and said that's where the next war will break out in twenty years' time. He was wrong, it was twenty years and two months. All that was unjust and wrong.'

Highly susceptible, Henry was easily deceived by Hitler's transformation of Germany. Like many decent people in Britain at the time, he could not believe that such a régime was inherently evil. Ironically, though he would have been appalled by the National Front mentality today, he was dazzled by Hitler's show of strength, perceiving it as a glorious gain for the ordinary German with whom he had identified since his experience in the Christmas truce of 1914. Though he must have heard rumours of the bully-boy tactics, he preferred to accept the apparent nobility of the promises made at the Nuremberg rallies. Back in England, working on *Goodbye West Country* (1937), and observing a hive of bees about to swarm, he compared it to one of the rallies:

> I was witnessing a natural phenomenon resembling one I had observed recently on the Continent, when millions of men and women had cheered their leader and national inspirer. Then I had been carried away by the mass emotion, even as a strange bee, wandering into the orbits of the mass of bees here, would be stimulated and excited. The feeling I had while among the masses of people listening to Adolf Hitler at Nuremberg was one of their happiness and goodness.

It must have seemed to him that the promise of the Christmas truce was being fulfilled at last, and he built on this idea audaciously, suggesting in his foreword to *The Pathway* a parallel between his theme and the concept of the new Germany: 'The ideology of the NSDAP is not war-mentality, but ex-frontline soldiers' mentality. We older ones wouldn't care, I guess we've seen through life, peeled the onion to the core, and found — endurance.' He thought of the boys — 'all the merry little chaps in the towns and villages' — and searched for an opening sentence to the foreword with which to arrest the reader. He succeeded: 'On Christmas Day 1914, the author of this history had a conversation with a young soldier of the 133rd Saxon Regiment in no-man's-land, in front of the Bois de Ploegsteert. Although he did not realize it fully at the time, that experience altered his entire conception of the world.' There are other references which imply, without actually stating it, that the young German soldier was Hitler himself. Henry returns to the idea of a personal truce with the German Führer in the penultimate 'Chronicle', *Lucifer Before Sunrise* (1967), with an extract from one of Willie Maddison's German notebooks:

The inflation has ruined all classes in Germany. Jews arrive daily from the ghettoes of Poland, with a few roubles and become property owners of houses, streets of houses, small businesses and firms, almost overnight. The *morale* of a nation depressed by defeat, is temporarily destroyed. A phrase used by Sir Eric Geddes, who at the outbreak of war was a railway manager in England and ended a Cabinet minister, is often repeated in my hearing, 'Germany is a lemon to be squeezed until the pips squeak.'

The pips are more than squeaking. They are shrieking. They shriek through one man's voice. He has the truest eyes I have ever seen in a man's face, he is an ex-corporal of the Linz Regiment which opposed my regiment under Messines Hill on Christmas Day 1914. We made a truce then, which must never be broken.

In fact, as reported correctly in the earlier *Children of Shallowford*, Hitler enlisted in the 1st Company of the 16th Bavarian Reserve Infantry Regiment, known as the *List* Regiment (named after its commander rather than after Linz, the town).

Henry returns to the truce in his notorious foreword to 'The Flax of Dream', which is significantly dated Christmas Day 1935:

During that truce the seed-idea of *The Flax of Dream* was loosed upon the frozen ground of the battlefield. During the years that followed it lay dormant; to quicken, suddenly, three months after the Armistice, on reading an old copy of Richard Jefferies's [The] *Story of My Heart* . . .

The fulfilment or materialization of that idea has been the mainspring of life ever since; for many years in a solitariness of desperation; but now with hope, because the vision of a new world, dreamed by many young soldiers in the trenches and shell-craters of the World War, is being made real in one European nation at least.

I salute the great man across the Rhine, whose life symbol is the happy child.

Henry was astonished when people took offence. Quoting a reaction from *The Bookseller* — 'The spectacle of one of our more sentimental writers enjoying a sort of vicarious toughness by becoming (at a safe distance) the evangelist of the rubber truncheon is among the more interesting manifestations of current literature . . .' — he comments plaintively: 'I wonder who wrote it, and how old he is. I don't think anyone over 30 would write like that, not a man, anyway.' Among the many letters he received was one from a reader, 'amazed and hurt because the foreword seems to be a complete reversal of what I've imagined you to be, and to stand for, since I first read and re-read *The Pathway*.'

Henry felt his special affinity with Hitler because they had been through the same war, and he would have agreed with Hitler's comment at Hamburg in 1934 that it was 'the greatest of all experiences'. However, such phrases of Henry's as 'moral beauty' do tend to stick in the gullet. By contrast, the journey to see 'mein Führer' with Sir John Heygate in 1934 sounds fun. Everyone was friendly as they bowled down the autobahn at 82 mph in an open MG with a Union Jack fluttering above the radiator cap. The splendid car belonged to Heygate who was seizing a break from the UFA film studios in Berlin, where he supervised the English versions of German films. The two men indulged in overtaking other fast cars, racing a Mercedes-Benz for forty miles. 'I'd never seen so many smiling motorists,' wrote Henry, 'truly a party spirit.'

Stopping at an inn, they heard first-hand stories of the Leader on his journeys south to Bavaria. (Once Hitler invited everyone there to have a drink, and, as Hitler was known to be teetotal, one man after another ordered *fachinger* tonic water sycophantically, until one old man demanded beer. 'Ha!' said Hitler. 'At last I meet an honest man.') Henry met only one man who did not admire Hitler: a technician at the UFA studios, whom he dismissed as 'a wizened little chap who insisted on telling me, with offensive gestures of the pre-war gutter, the difference between English and German girls'. Otherwise Henry was determined to see the best in everyone and everything.

They arrived in Nuremberg to a horizon glowing with fireworks and dilated as though from gunfire. With their invitation cards as guests of the Leader, they were waved through by SS men controlling the million extra people who were pouring into the town for the rally. Flags and banners stretched from roof to roof, and at dawn they woke to the steady beating of drums from faraway bands: 'Many drums, many bands. The bom-bom-bom grew more insistent. It was Sunday morning. The sky was red in the east, the sun almost risen. Switching on the light, I read that Hitler was to speak in the Luitpoldarena; we must be in our places before 8am.'

I can sympathize with his excitement for I was in Germany around that time and have a clear image of a crowded, noisy street dramatically festooned with crimson and black swastikas as I leant excitedly from a hotel window in the Vier Jahreszeiten in Munich before a similar rally. But I was only seven years old and, as well as the excitement, I remember a sense of dismay, probably instilled by my parents, for my father had reported the rise of Hitler for the *Chicago Daily News* and distrusted what he saw. His affection for Germany, where I spent much of my childhood, waned as the speeches grew more strident. He was unimpressed by 'those grotesque parades, in the lovely old city of Munich, of the bulging Brown Shirts with their fat behinds'. I, on the other hand, wrote to my grandmother: 'Munich church was very nice, figures came out and knights fought. Munich is a nice town, and the proseicuns [processions] were very nice. Hitler's speech was nice.'

'Nice' is hardly the word Henry would have chosen for the man who wanted peace for a thousand years and the creation in the West of the greatest civilization the world had ever seen. This is Henry's eye-witness portrait, from *Goodbye West Country*:

I wandered about, went to the headquarters, saw Hitler quite close, talking to several people. He was very quick in his head movements. He spoke rapidly. I got the idea his natural pace is much swifter than the ordinary, his eyes falcon-like, remarkably full of life. A man of spiritual grace; he calls himself a medium; which means the small inner voice has been developed until it possesses the physical brain. Saw, too, Von Papen, Von Krupp, Von Blumberg — a fine chap — and other faces. Amused myself by wondering what I should say, if by chance of Time's wheel, the minor country writer was brought up before Hitler. I'd have nothing to say; knowing that those things which were fancied to be common or parallel experiences, should not be obtruded. I'm happiest hidden in a crowd, anyway.

The critic, Eric Hiscock, wrote to me about Henry: 'He was an odd-ball, as you must know. Always, like Byron, saying "I want a hero". He found him in T. E. Lawrence, then Hitler and Mosley. The 1914-18 war scarred his soul: as I know myself, Flanders was no place to be at seventeen.'

Henry's hero-worship of the legendary Lawrence of Arabia is understandable. Both men were unable to escape their childhood: Henry with his difficult father, denying him the love he yearned for; Lawrence brought up by his disciplinarian mother, dreading the revelation of his illegitimacy. Trying to hide their faces from the materialistic world, Henry drew closer to nature, while Lawrence assumed the anonymity of 'Aircraftsman Shaw'. Henry found parallels between Lawrence and Hitler (who was also a vegetarian): 'Neither drinking nor smoking, giving the dividends from his one book to German ex-servicemen's funds, owning nothing except a small retreat in the mountains — the equivalent of Lawrence's own cottage on Egdon Hill.' If Henry was thinking of Berchtesgarten as the 'small retreat', he was stretching the comparison considerably. In a letter to *Time & Tide* in May 1936, he referred to Hitler as 'a very wise and steadfast and truth-perceiving father of his people: a man like T. E. Lawrence, without personal ambitions, a vegetarian, non-smoker, non-drinker, without even a bank balance...', and described him during the purge of Roehm as 'actually in tears as he waited in his room', comparing him, and the occasion, to Lawrence 'when he had to shoot an Arab murderer with his own hands'. Once again, Henry was twisting comparisons to prove his point.

Now Henry conceived a bold plan to save Europe from war, using Lawrence as a figurehead; for, although Lawrence had opted out of public life, he still remained a living legend. In his study of pro-German sympathizers, in *Fellow Travellers of the Right* (1980), Richard Griffiths suggests that Henry imposed his own fantasies on Lawrence; which seems a fair judgement of the whole venture, for it smacks of the *Boys' Own Paper* and John Buchan — heroic, foolhardy and slightly vain.

Convinced that Hitler was the only true pacifist in Europe, 'releasing and reaffirming the aspirations of the ordinary man in Germany, and so gradually converting a nation in the image of himself,' Henry decided to seize his opportunity: '... it was time something was done about the pacification of Europe through friendship and fearless common-sense. The resurgent Europe must not be allowed to wither.' Consequently he saw it as his mission to start a 'whirlwind campaign' to bring the two prophets together in the cause of peace: 'The new age must begin: England was ready for peace. Lawrence was the natural leader of that age in England. I dreamed of an Anglo-German friendship, the beginning of the pacification of Europe. Hitler and Lawrence must meet. I wrote this to him.'

According to Henry, Lawrence was receptive; he was prepared to accept that the press had misrepresented Hitler as much as himself:

> He read the speeches of Hitler, and was confirmed in his divination. A man who had served in the ranks of the infantry, been wounded, and blinded by mustard gas, a man who loved Beethoven and lived only for the resurrection of his country's happiness — a nation's honour — a man who was the ideal of youth, was one who not only knew the truth, but could speak it and convey it to the minds of others. He was a corner-stone for the new, realistic pacification of Europe.

How was Lawrence to impress this on the British people? The answer lay with the old soldiers; only they could cope and understand. Henry proposed that 'a mass meeting of ex-servicemen be held in the Albert Hall in London, a meeting that would get the greatest publicity because he [Lawrence] was calling it, and a speech broadcast, that because of its truth and balance, would show complete understanding of and sympathy with the French and German and English family man'. And he wrote Lawrence accordingly.

On 13 May 1935, Lawrence replied by telegram — 'Lunch Tuesday Wet Fine Cottage One Mile North Bovington Camp' — and crashed his motorbike as he drove back to Clouds Hill from the Post Office, dying from his injuries five days later.

'I believe,' wrote Henry later, 'that had he lived, Lawrence would have confirmed the inner hopes of every ex-serviceman in England: that the spirit of Christmas Day 1914, already hovering in the air, would have swiftly materialized and given ... a vision of a new conception of life.' Asked to contribute to a book on Lawrence the following year, Henry compared him to Hitler and received a query from Lawrence's younger brother asking him if he really meant this, failing to understand that from Henry this was the highest praise.

There are two baffling postscripts to the whole intrigue. Robert Skidelsky, in his book on Sir Oswald Mosley (*Oswald Mosley*, 1975), quotes Henry's intention to fly to Germany to see Hitler in place of Lawrence: '"If I could see him as a common soldier who had fraternized, on that faraway Christmas Day of 1914, with the men of the Linz [List] battalion under Messines Hill, might I not be able to give him the amity he so desired from England, a country he admired?..."' Then there was the rumour that Lawrence's crash was not an accident but a premeditated murder by Zionists to prevent the proposed meeting between the British hero, Lawrence of Arabia, and 'the great man across the Rhine'. A sinister black limousine was reported racing from the scene after the crash, and this rumour became exaggerated with time.

Writing in the *Daily Express* (29 June 1977), Douglas Orgill referred to the possibility of Lawrence as Dictator of Britain, 'as someone ineffably suggested to him in 1935'. Henry was partly to blame for such distortion, and it is possible that the idea of a Zionist plot appealed to him. He remained enigmatic and mysterious, neither confirming nor denying the rumour about Lawrence's death, although on one occasion he told Rex Aylmer in Mugford's public house in Barnstaple that he believed the rumour true; but, when I asked him categorically in my television interview in 1975, he was scrupulous in his denial: 'No, I don't think so. His bike went because his tyres skidded.'

And that is probably the truth of the plan to save Europe from war, a truth bizarre enough to leave one wondering what might have happened had Lawrence lived.

In view of their mutual admiration for Nazi Germany, Henry's support for Sir Oswald Mosley was a natural consequence after the death of Lawrence, although they had little in common otherwise. They were introduced in the late 1930s by Dorothy, Lady Downe, a member of the British Union.

In many ways, Mosley was everything that Henry wished to be, moving easily in a world which Henry envied. Where Henry was naïve, Mosley was sophisticated, a baronet and connected by marriage with two of the most extraordinary families in England: his first wife, Lady Cynthia Curzon, was the daughter of Lord Curzon, Viceroy of India and British Foreign Secretary, and extremely rich; his second wife was the Hon. Diana Guiness, one of the talented Mitford girls, and the most beautiful. It was intended as a personal compliment to her sister, Unity, that Hitler attended their wedding in Berlin in 1936, rather than as a political endorsement of Mosley as the potential leader of Britain.

Mosley was self-confident, an aristocrat among dictators, provoking Herbert Morrison, the Labour statesman, to complain that Mosley spoke to him like 'a landlord addressing his peasantry'. Henry did not have the arrogance which prompted Mosley to snarl at a heckler, 'I fought in France for Great Britain so that rats like you might live.' Mosley had been in the trenches for only six months; Henry, who had seen more, would never have dared be so presumptuous.

Politically, Mosley was one of the most intriguing chameleons of the century, standing for Parliament first as a Conservative, next as a Socialist, then as an Independent, and, finally, outside Parliament, becoming the leader of the

British Union of Fascists. Old newsreels confirm how closely he aped the Nazi rallies, with the solitary figure of the
leader marching through a phalanx of his followers, their
hands raised in salute. While Mosley had the glory of centre-
stage, Henry watched from the wings; and though he had
little political cunning, he had absolute integrity. In some
ways he was more idealistic than Mosley himself, who rather
took Henry for granted, in spite of his good fortune in adding
such a distinguished writer, naturalist and ex-soldier to his
cause.

Referring to Henry's plan to fly to Hitler in place of
Lawrence, Diana Mosley admitted, 'My husband had no
such romantic feelings.' Certainly Mosley was no romantic,
and I had first-hand experience of this as the first person to
interview him for television after the war, when a press
boycott kept him hidden from the public. This led to several
meetings with Mosley, who surprised me at once with his
sense of humour. Wit from a dictator is disconcerting,
especially when directed against himself. Referring to the
massive posters decorating the East End of London, which
showed Mosley striding forward under the headline, 'HE IS
COMING', he smiled disarmingly as he admitted that he
found the comparison to Christ a bit embarrassing. After
lunch at the Hyde Park Hotel he made a remark on the steps
which has puzzled me ever since, or rather his motive for
making it.

'We've been in Venice, and we were having luncheon one
day when I noticed another English couple in the restaurant
talking about myself and Diana. A friend of ours was
lunching there too, and told us what they said after we left:
"Mosley doesn't look all that bad," said the man. "I don't
think he'd have sent us to the gas-chamber." "No," said his
wife, "but *she* would have!" Thank, you, Mr Farson.'
Mosley gave me a mad smile, 'I've enjoyed our lunch,' and
stepped back into the hotel.

above Henry at a Fascist meeting in 1939.
BBC Hulton Picture Library

below Henry and Christine, with the landlord of the Rock Inn, Georgeham, which features as the Upper House in many of his stories. *Daniel Farson*

above 'Henry at the barricades': a demonstration outside Downing Street in the late 1960's against the Vietnam War.   *Oswald Jones*

below Henry reading aloud in the 1970's, at the Lobster Pot, Instow, where he was once interrupted by a cry of 'Fascist!'   *Tony Freeman*

Another time we lunched in the comfortable domesticity of Cheyne Walk, which was equally strange as both Lady Mosley and her sister, the Duchess of Devonshire, treated 'Tom' with patient tolerance whenever he tried to interrupt their torrent of gossip with a major pronouncement of his own.

The final television film was historic (I fear it may have been destroyed, although Granada TV kept the interview with Mosley which Malcolm Muggeridge made later). My interview gave him the first opportunity to speak his mind and he seized it; he was startlingly frank about his political views, Hitler and Unity Mitford, and confirmed that he was still restless for power.

'Do you believe power corrupts?' I asked.

'Only small men,' glacial smile, 'never *great* men.'

'Thank you, Sir Oswald.'

Mosley's story fascinated me. I thought that the way he was absorbed by the British without either persecution or martyrdom was proof of our native good-humour and common-sense. Unaware of my views, Mosley agreed that I should write his biography and be free to say anything I liked provided that he was given the last word in a final chapter written by himself. As he was dreaded for the libel actions which he brought (and invariably won) when accused of 'treachery', this seemed an admirable solution and a good selling-point for the book as well. At a cocktail party I told someone about it and, when asked where I thought Mosley had gone wrong, was rash enough to say that his weakness was vanity. This was reported in the Londoner's Diary of the *Evening Standard* the following day, and Mosley subsequently cancelled our arrangement.

However distasteful Henry's views may be, *he* could never be accused of holding them for the sake of expedience. Once he declared his loyalty, he remained constant — even after the Second World War, when Mosley retired to the comfort of the Temple de la Gloire outside Paris, awaiting the call which never came, while Henry had to contend with local gossip directed against him in North Devon.

When I asked him in 1975 if he had suffered for his allegiance to Mosley, he replied emphatically, 'Not at all. I gloried in it...'; and defended him as 'a great friend and colleague who tried to stop the war with Hitler because he thought it would mean the end of Europe. *He was no traitor!*' He added wistfully, 'I haven't seen him very often.' Explaining the beliefs which drew him towards Mosley in the first place, he said: 'I know Fascism is a dirty word, but what we wanted was to get on with the welfare state and of course the Communists, who were very idealistic people in their own way, would come to his meetings and smash them up, and there was so much fighting the police had to move in. But it wasn't Mosley who caused it. He was a brilliant person,' Henry assured me, 'the only thing was that he started at the wrong time.' By this Henry meant that they were *before* their time in fighting for the welfare state and putting Britain first. Henry often told me of 'three little girls, very thin and skimpy, playing with a skipping-rope, and they kept on falling, and it was dinner-time so I asked why they weren't at home.' Henry imitated the girl's high, piping reply: 'Oh, sir, it's not our turn to eat today.'

Such memories of the Thirties moved him greatly, and he said that Mosley told him it would be criminal not to write about the poverty and the piling mass of unemployed ex-servicemen. One phrase of Mosley's made a particular impression on him: 'Wherever you find talent and quality, whether in a castle or a cottage, that's where we want it. But remember that a gentleman can live in a cottage and a cad in a castle!' It would have been wittier the other way round, and just as true, but humour had no part in this. Henry was left with the conviction that 'all this business of privilege is no good unless you earn your spurs in each generation.'

SEVEN

A farm in Norfolk

FULFILLING MOSLEY'S CONCEPT of 'a new resurgent Britain', Henry embarked on the next phase of his life with the purchase of a farm in Norfolk. Here he would grow food and make his contribution to society in defiance of the general decline of British agriculture at that time, when many farms stood idle and neglected and changed hands for derisory sums. *The Story of a Norfolk Farm*, published by Faber in 1941, described the venture and became one of Henry's best-selling books. With the problems involved in running a farm, it is astonishing that he found time to write it at all.

With no previous experience of farming, it was not only a bold project for him but a rash one and, like many an idealist, Henry lived his dream at his family's expense. The strain was mental as well as physical; there was constant financial worry quite apart from the threat of a second world war. Henry was fortunate in having Loetitia to share the experience, appease the people he offended and cope with everyday life. She told me how they found the farm after Henry had crossed England to check on properties advertised in farming magazines: 'He chose one that was completely run down and derelict. Thistles as tall as yourself, the river polluted, no proper road. But he liked this particular farm, even though it took a bit of time to buy it because the owner wanted to sell the Old Hall with the six cottages as well.'

Henry finally bought them all, with 250 acres, in 1937 for £2500. The sum is almost meaningless today, an apparent miraculous bargain; but it was substantial then and left them with little to spend on the crucial repairs. Henry took it on as a challenge, and Loetitia admitted that it was at the cost of eight years' unremitting slog to his whole family.

'But he wanted to feel that he was safeguarding us by having his own land where he could grow his own food.'

On one level it was wholly advantageous, for it provided him with new material for his work: 'He was writing all the time, partly for his weekly column in the *Daily Express*. He worked eighteen hours a day.' (Her daughter, Margaret, added: '*She* worked twenty.')

'Was it necessary to work so hard?' I asked Loetitia.

'Yes, it was. We had only three men and nothing mechanical until the first Ferguson tractor. Horses were slow compared to today. Very killing. Very hard work. We had cows, poultry, turkeys and sheep to look after.' (At a meeting of the Henry Williamson Society at Stiffkey in 1981, someone asked Loetitia what she remembered most of those farming days: 'Having to look after all those damned turkeys!')

With the declaration of war came the red tape of officialdom. Holding the views he did, Henry was automatically suspect. This is understandable when you look at the map and see that the village of Stiffkey (pronounced Stewkey) lies a few miles from the marshes of Blakeney Point on the North Sea, a vulnerable part of the coastline if the Germans invaded, as then seemed likely.

Henry did not make it easy for the authorities, nor himself, when they came to the farm. He described their confrontations in his contribution to *The Pleasure Ground* (ed. Malcolm Elwin, 1947). In the chapter entitled 'The Winter of 1941', Henry's tactlessness and tiredness, as well as a petulance with the military, is revealed. A sense of injustice cries out from every page, as well as an utter contempt for the temporary officers he had to deal with, whom he compared unfavourably to those he had known in the First War. Sometimes he used a favourite trick of feigning a sympathy which was transparently false. Referring to a claims officer, who had a supercilious expression and highly polished boots, Henry comments: 'I learned also that his job before the war had been the selling of little houses on a Housing Estate on the hire purchase system, with weekly payments extending over a quarter of a century or so. I expect he was a good salesman.' After this damning snobbery, he is equally unconvincing when he blames himself: 'It was no doubt a weakness in me that did not allow me to stand up to him with his own manner and attitude, or to see the comic side of the affair; I remember that his remark about the pigs being ground into the mud hurt me deeply, perhaps because in my youth I had seen so many dead men, and wounded men not yet dead, lying in mud during and after battles, and also my isolation in a district where I was unpopular...'

At least that unpopularity was real. Believing that a vindictive black marketeer had turned an advance party against him, Henry was as difficult as only he could be when they started making arrangements for a temporary army camp, insisting on full security procedure: 'How do I know you are not German parachute troops in British uniform? May I see your identity card, please? I am entitled to ask, you know, as the owner of this land.'

The startled, florid major resorts to his stand-by sentence: 'We've never had a complaint yet'; and Henry tries to explain, 'half-apologetically', that he regards the farm as a unit in the home-front, to be maintained in full efficiency for the nation: 'Can't you possibly go to your proper camping site which was allocated to you?'

'We've never had a complaint so far,' the major repeated.

No doubt the major was a tiresome man and the claims officer sounds mean-minded, bargaining for every penny of compensation for the fouled woods, the broken fences, the missing animals, and for the roads, which had at last been completed and were now churned up by the military vehicles:

> The ruined roads, costing so much in ceaseless work in the past, were a symbol of the vanity of hope and constructive endeavour. Was it for this — to be arrested and imprisoned without charge or trial, as a suspected traitor — that one had gone through the Somme and Passchendaele? For this, that one had striven to clarify the mind, to see, and then to tell in words the truth? Life without honour was a mere existence; it was more honourable to be dead.

Presumably, a hundred arguments ended with the outraged cry of officialdom, 'Don't you realize there's a war on?', but it becomes clear that Henry wished to cast himself here too in the heroic rôle of martyr. Why paint the Mosley lightning-flash on his house and car otherwise? 'In the mood of frustration that bound my life at this period,' he recalled later, 'it seemed more and more true that honour existed only among the dead and those about to die, and in those in prison without trial.'

'In prison without trial', 'arrested and imprisoned without charge or trial' — references like these, with Henry's confirmation over the years, have led to the general acceptance that he was interned under the regulation known as 18B. But the moment I started to research this I was confronted by confusion. Henry always told me that he was interned for fourteen days; my father, always sceptical where Henry was concerned, reduced this to four. Loetitia remembered that he had been questioned by the police, but she was doubtful that he had ever been sent to prison. It has not been easy to find out the truth, for there was never any specific 'charge' when Regulation 18B was invoked, which is partly why it was so criticized: it was a means for holding people under suspicion and was used to great effect with Sir Oswald and Lady Mosley, who were detained for three years. With his well-aired views it is hardly surprising that Henry was suspect too, but this was largely due to the personal malice of the black marketeer who made accusations of such gravity against Henry that the police were compelled to investigate.

An example of how far-fetched these rumours could be concerns the field at Ox's Cross in Devon, which Henry is supposed to have whitewashed with lime in order to direct the German bombers to the nearby air base of Chivenor. A clumsier means of spying could hardly be imagined, but this is still believed by Devonians today, and what makes their conviction so depressing is their absolute sincerity, even when I point out that Henry was in Norfolk at the time, which is where the rumour originated. Loetitia says it was started by the black marketeer, who talked 'about Henry cutting a field in a certain way to point it in some direction or other, but the village people did not believe there was anything to this'. Even so, there are people in Norfolk today who will tell you that Henry tried to signal to off-shore U-boats on his evening walks beside the sea, or by placing glass tiles in his roof.

Detesting gossip, Henry rose above it — 'Usually a public story about anyone is true only in its strict opposite...' Nevertheless, in my television interview with Henry in 1975, I wondered what had been his reaction to the gossip against him from the men of Norfolk (who boasted of shooting through the farm windows at the naked light-bulbs when Henry deliberately defied the black-out — or so they said) and to the rumours of the Devon field sign-posted with lime for German bombers. He replied with weary impatience: 'I don't care about people like that, they make me ill, but there are always poops all over the place, you know that, but if they go on like that with sulky eyes and brooding...then there's something wrong. That's a rubbishy thing, painting a twenty-acre field with lime....' the words faded away bitterly. However, it seems that there were times when Henry's lack of tact did give genuine offence: for example, his complaint after a Beaufighter crashed a few hundred yards from Langham, killing both the crew, that the rescue services had ruined a fine crop of sugar beet. 'I remember the smell of burning parachute,' Richard Williamson said in 1981, adding that his father's grumblings had been 'much misunderstood'.

Antagonism increased and rumours spread, until there came the knock at the door which might even have been welcomed by Henry in these peculiar circumstances. Basically it was a routine message from the Chief Constable, asking Henry to see him. Loetitia remembers it as 'a formality, in order to silence the gossip from this individual'. Trying to recall the episode after thirty-five years, she added: 'I am certain Henry was never interned'.

I received further evidence from two contrasting sources. The Chief Constable of the Norfolk Constabulary sent me this straightforward report in 1980:

It does appear reasonably certain that Mr Williamson was detained for one night in Police cells and there is little doubt that this would have been at the then local Sergeant's station at Wells. Local opinion is that Mr Williamson was engaged in espionage and even that certain of Hitler's female friends had visited him at Stiffkey. A few days before his arrest, he apparently burnt a number of documents in his garden and is said to have remarked, 'they wouldn't find enough to keep me long'. He was a regular contributor to the local press on farming matters and made several radio broadcasts. It is said that he was strongly sympathetic to Sir Oswald Mosley and his party and it is understood that the house in Church Street, Stiffkey, where he lived, still displays a Fascist emblem on the front.

My other source is Ronald Creasy, who was in the area at the time of the 'arrest' and sympathized with Henry's political views, as he indicates at the start of his letter, dated 29 August 1980, in which he referred to the 'inspired and outstanding capability of Sir Oswald Mosley which with his followers would have saved the British Empire from being sold to America in a fratricidal war schemed for ulterior purpose and which left us in ignominy, bankruptcy and shame'. After this declaration, Mr Creasy suggests that Henry's 'internment' might have been a case of wishful thinking:

Henry Williamson, in his intelligence, would have appreciated the honour conveyed both currently and in future history to those who were incarcerated in condemned prison cells and the Concentration Camps of Britain under the lawless section of 18B. H. W. possibly felt he *should* have shared the honour and from such feeling told you that he was interned under 18B. He did come under such restrictions at his home under house arrest while the peculiar quirks of the Home Office, under secret direction, decided on their intention in satisfaction of mob propaganda. He was not sent to the infamous Liverpool Prison or to Brixton. Doubtless he was 'interned' in his own home for 14 days under the eye-wash of 18B. On this point you can put the record straight once and for all.

Mr Creasy rightly took me to task for referring in my letter to a 'charge' under 18B:

Those who were the scape-goat victims were held without charge or trial. They were forced, under armed guard, to attend an inquisition in secret which was less exposing of themselves than a mock trial. The Chief Constable of Norfolk was asked by the Home Office for a report on the political activities of Henry Williamson on which it could decide the extent for propaganda under the 18B falsity of coverage. Not to investigate a charge as stated in your letter. Following his house arrest for 14 days under 18B, as with numerous supporters, he was put under an Alien Order for an unspecified time restricting him to a five-mile radius.

With this information, I reached the conclusion that the Chief Constable had investigated the rumours in order to give Henry the opportunity to clear his name; that no charge was made against him; that he was not interned, but held overnight at the local police station and possibly restricted in his movements afterwards; that in fact Henry had been denied his martyrdom, for this differs from his protest that he was 'arrested and imprisoned without charge or trial'. Then I had the luck to receive a detailed account of the 'arrest' from a friend of Henry's (who prefers to remain anonymous) who was staying at Stiffkey at the time and witnessed the events, which took place shortly after the fall of France when invasion seemed imminent.

All the local signposts had been sawn off, to confuse the invaders, but Henry knew the way as he drove her along the coast one night to dine with an old friend, who was a retired army officer. Unfortunately, there was another guest, a designer for the old Russian ballet, who took such a dislike to Henry that she refused to sit in the same room with him, though she kept on opening the door with a shout of 'Filthy spy!' It cannot have been a pleasant evening, and it was lucky that the roads were deserted when they drove back, for on the following morning Henry discovered that the lady had painted swastikas all over the Alvis. The police (in plain clothes) arrived in the afternoon, as they were taking tea. The 'arrest' was made with no comment from Henry, who went quietly within a few minutes. Two of the men stayed behind. Their search was lengthy but they found little more than a few photographs of the Nuremberg rally, which they took away: they failed to look under the fitted carpet where, unknown to his anxious companion, Henry had hidden a quantity of Mosley's magazine, *Action*.

Her vivid recollection clarifies the problem of Henry's 'internment'. It seems that he was kept in the police cell for less than a week and released, after investigation by the Chief Constable, as a 'harmless eccentric'. Plainly, the police behaved impeccably. In Germany at that time, he would have been sent to one of the concentration camps referred to by Mr Creasy; in Russia he would have been killed or cast into oblivion. The British have a genius for *assimilating* people who hold unusual views — a solution that can be more deadly than martyrdom. To be called a harmless eccentric was a bitter acquittal.

At the same time, the true wretchedness of his situation should not be under-rated. 'Nearly every day in Norfolk was a little death,' Henry wrote afterwards; he and his family lived in daily dread, the contents of their dustbins sifted by neighbours for evidence against them, or so Henry claimed.

At Ox's Cross a friend and neighbour, R. W. Thompson, broke into the loft over Henry's studio and destroyed a small swastika flag in case the police searched it. Henry's reaction was typical — 'I thought this windy cheek' — and one can see his point. It must have seemed to him that the England he had fought for and loved had turned against him. During a visit of Henry's to the Savage Club in London, an elderly member shook a fist in his face, mentioned Dunkirk and said that Henry should be in prison. This was the common reaction.

Henry was lucky to have Stiffkey to return to — with the welcome always provided by Loetitia, a fire burning in the open hearth, and his children to greet him. Loetitia gave the solace he needed, calming the prejudice against him; for she was popular in the village, where she played the organ in church, ran the library and was President of the Women's Institute. Her daughter, Margaret, told me that it was Loetitia's tact that united a community hitherto divided by wealthy, autocratic newcomers; and for this she received a vote of thanks from the Parish Council. Because of her there was no local prejudice against the children, who in any case were hardly seen as they worked so hard on the farm.

Henry never failed to acknowledge his debt to his wife: 'Loetitia, always kind and ready to smile, annulled much of the negation of the world, wherein Britain seemed to be dying.'

As for his sympathy for the German people, can we altogether condemn him? The answer is unequivocal for many, including the writer and dramatist, Frederic Raphael, who disagrees with everything Henry stood for but is fascinated by him nevertheless. I recognized Henry in Raphael's scathing portrait of an elderly fascist in his controversial novel, *The Glittering Prizes* (1976), powerfully played (and with disturbing accuracy) by Eric Porter in the BBC television dramatization. The only critic to comment on the resemblance was Philip Purser of the *Sunday Telegraph*, so I wrote to Raphael for confirmation, anxious to learn his opinion of Henry which would help me to see him from another point of view.

Raphael was kind enough, and sufficiently interested in Henry Williamson to reply in detail, explaining what he thought of Henry when he first created the part in 1959 in a play which was never produced. For *The Glittering Prizes* apparently, the character of Stephen Taylor was also partly based on Frank Lloyd Wright:

> whose organic architecture at one time seemed to be a kind of three-dimensional image of the Good Right. I elected to invent a Williamson/Mosley/Wright compound largely because I wanted to be free of the obligation to be 'accurate'. I didn't want to get into Mosley's pretentious nonsense but to find an awkward target, for myself and my 'hero', a man who held appalling ideas but was not himself appalling or untalented.

Unlike many of Henry's critics, Raphael tried to separate the man from his politics:

> I wanted to set myself a hard nut to crack, though I suppose I always meant to be sure that crack it would. I certainly never met HW, nor would I have wanted to, except for coldly curious reasons. I am not among those who find it necessary or amusing to find justifications for Fascism, or rather murder, though I notice it has become fashionable lately. It would be satisfying to agree wholeheartedly with Sartre that it is impossible to write a 'good' right-wing work of literature (you're familiar no doubt, with the arguments in *What is Literature?*), but the thornier truth is that much of what critics regard as the essence of modern literature is indeed of the 'Right' — Pound, Eliot, Windy Lewis, etc. The high opinion held of W's nature books (and the idea that 'nature' is now a kind of God, whose worship automatically cleanses the celebrant) may have something to do with the determination of certain 'liberals' to find redeeming features in W as a man and as a 'thinker'. (The same is, to a degree, true of the even more rapt veneration accorded to D. H. Lawrence, of which all of us have been, I daresay, guilty — if guilt is

the right term — in our time, or Leavis's.) It seems to
me there is a measure of excess in the admiration given
to W's nature books, because I remember finding them
pretty dull when I read them as a child, but I am willing
to believe in their merits.

As for the 'Chronicles': 'I did indeed try to get into them,
but found them more tedious than wicked. There is a tone of
noble whine, of Stoic grousing in W which seems to subvert
the notion of the true character of Britain about which he is
so gruffly strident.'
Returning to Henry's politics, he asks:

Can one ever take seriously the finesse, the literary
consciousness, of anyone who went on believing that
Hitler had been 'misunderstood', etc.? Damn right, he
had, but by those who gave him credit for 'ideas' and
could believe that murderous paranoia was a recipe for
salvation. The only charm which W has for me is that
he and his vicious friends, even allowing that he was
brighter than most of them, are defeated relics of a
complacent brutality which, whatever else happened,
did not actually prevail, at least not in the form they
might have welcomed. The sympathy which W is
accorded is that which can be given, and sometimes
should be given, to losers. Had he been empowered to
be the muscled apologist of the doctrines his poor mind
found agreeable, we (or at least I) would have been
dead before we could take a well-balanced view. There
would have been no well-balanced views.

The redeeming qualities about which you ask me are,
I suppose, those of the self-sufficient man, who believes
in simplicity and in the rural life, though even here we
can recall the cheeky view of Paul Johnson that the
industrial revolution, however beastly and smoky, was
seen and experienced as a *liberation* by many of those

stout yeomen and their thinner rural proletarian cousins whose lot W elected to regard as nobly old English. If we are honest, there is something clammily seductive about visits to torture chambers and viewings of atrocious films, but that does not, I hope, mean that one finds something good in torture or atrocities. I think the Maddison sequence (of which I have read perhaps two or three, dutifully) does *something* to advance Sartre's argument; W was not a bad writer, but his intellectual prejudices prevented him from being a good one. As for the 'virtues' of the Right, there is a certain charm in the idea of the institutionalization of 'values', in a society somehow transcending the cash nexus, though I am sure that any attempt to incarnate such a spirited notion must lead to corruption, rant and oppression. Thus such a notion can better invigorate poetry than prose. W had a prosaic mind and a poetic appetite. Such men can easily become the Ramsay MacDonalds of literature.

In a postscript, Raphael adds the wry comment: 'How we all crave strong men, though we know they are an illusion! Now we've proceeded to strong women, of course. Better? Hum?'

Frederick Raphael's strong feelings are understandable. But I cannot agree that Henry was *favoured because* of his right-wing views. Surely he *suffered because* he was out of step with his times? (Loetitia says 'he was terrified of Russia; he was very farseeing'.) In any case, his experiences in the First War had placed him irrevocably apart. Writing to a former officer in 1926, he asked if he was going to a Regimental Dinner: 'I feel always a little bewildered and sad at such functions. Living in the Salient most of the time, in the immensity of the past.... Brilliant — always at night, at Night. Only soldiers understand the feeling.' In *The Sun in the Sands*, twenty years later, he refers to the Great War 'still

117

continuing in the minds of many young-old soldiers: they were solitaries.' Henry remained a solitary.

As part of the television interview in 1975 I sat with Henry in North Devon, beside the breakwaters below the site of the old lighthouse on the Torridge estuary, and he spoke dramatically of Hitler.

'Of course he was a great man, but so many great men turn out to be fiends and devils because they go too far. He wanted to avoid war with us, but went the way to get it. He was a very brave soldier and he loved England.'

Anxious to put the record straight, I asked if he had met Hitler.

'Yes, of course,' he whispered.

'How did he strike you?' I asked unwisely, for this gave Henry the chance to indulge in some shadow-boxing.

'He didn't strike me. I laid him flat first!'

At least this broke the tension, but after the laughter the hushed reverence returned with a remark about saintliness which forced me to ask if he were comparing Hitler with Jesus.

'I am in a way, of course I am, because Hitler was human and Jesus was human, he wasn't just floating about in coloured pyjamas or something like that! Hitler told me there must never be war with England; if so everything would come to an end. There were tears in his eyes. He was a very emotional man.'

There were tears in Henry's eyes too, as he told me this: although I had asked my question about the meeting with Hitler in all innocence, I suspect that the fantasy had taken over. Unless Henry had made further visits to Germany which he did not write about, his account in *Goodbye West Country*, where he watches Hitler but decides against talking to him, is the one that rings true. This was confirmed by Sir Oswald Mosley, who wrote to me from Paris in 1980. 'I had a great regard for Henry and found him truthful and reliable.

118

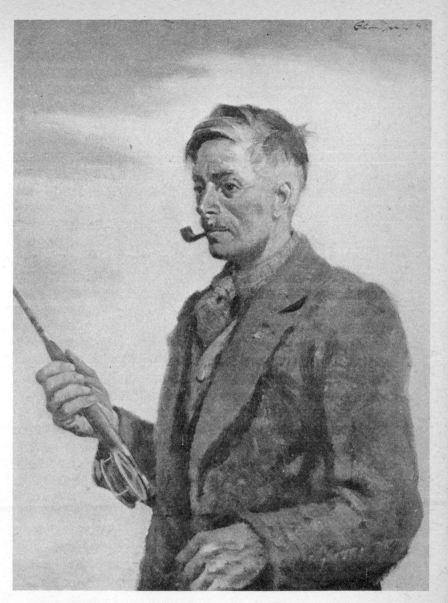

Edward Seago's portrait of his Norfolk neighbour, c. 1940: 'He will
not be captured easily on paper ... his biographer will find that he is
writing the life of more than one man.' *Seago Estate*

Henry posing quite happily for once, *c.*1950. The sack on the hedge is from the farm at Stiffkey in Norfolk. *Daniel Farson*

He may have developed some fantasies before the end. We never heard of him being at Nuremberg, or with Hitler whom I last saw in 1936.' Loetitia Williamson also told me that she doubted if her husband ever met Hitler.

It makes little difference now. Henry was eighty years old then, and entitled to his fantasies. It was, however, my responsibility to check on them, as too on his other claim that he had lunched at Buckingham Palace — which was rather a swing of the pendulum, but stated with such conviction that his family believed him. If true, it makes the denial of public honour all the more baffling. The Palace has no recollection of the occasion, although the Queen's equerry has said that this does not prove that he had never been there.

If there was any deception on Henry's part, it was the gentlest kind, a wistful dream. Perhaps there was a slight *folie de grandeur*, as Middleton Murry has suggested (see pp. 72-73): he was 'always tempted to see himself in the rôle of the rejected prophet'. Middleton Murry also examined Henry's personal identification with Hitler:

> It is scarcely surprising that in this turmoil and mental confusion, Mr Williamson should have succumbed to the seductions of Adolf Hitler. He persuaded himself that Hitler was putting into practice the dreams of Willie Maddison; he even persuaded himself, without any evidence, that Hitler was among the German soldiers who fraternized with the English at Christmas 1914; he persuaded himself, too, that he had an immediate and intuitive understanding of Hitler.

Referring to the notorious declaration to 'the great man across the Rhine', Murry continued:

> The real cause of this aberration must, I think, be sought in Mr Williamson's frustrations as an artist. His identification of himself with Hitler — for it amounted to little else — was a kind of vicarious self-expression,

119

and a radically false one. What Mr Williamson ought to have been doing in these years of frustration and self-repetition was to create Willie Maddison anew, setting himself resolutely to the heavy task of facing all the reality which had been evaded in 'The Flax of Dream'. Nor could he altogether deceive himself. Every now and then, in the autobiographical books which were themselves the outcome of his evasion, he let fall an indication that he was fully aware of his creative duty.

Middleton Murry reaches the unpleasant conclusion that Henry saw Hitler as 'the man who is free to realize Willie Maddison's prophetic intuitions — chiefly because he did not have a Mary Loetitia Ogilvie to frustrate him'.

In *The Children of Shallowford*, Henry admitted this frustration openly: 'I wanted to go away for two years and write a long novel, in three books, with the London cousin of my ex-soldier as chief character. And here I was surrounded by the noise and movement of an alien world. For my own world of the past was the one in which my being longed to re-enter.' The 'alien world' he referred to consisted of his wife and family, with the obligations involved. This frustration festered in Stiffkey, contributing to the final breakdown of his marriage.

The daily existence with Henry became unbearable, even for Loetitia Williamson. It was not his politics that mattered, she told me; and indeed I suspect there was no specific reason for the break up. For Loetitia it must have been the strain of Henry's dissatisfaction — not the shout in anger, but the whisper of his constant crucifixion. I asked Mrs Williamson if she thought Henry had been a happy man, and she shook her head; 'No, I wouldn't say that, he was always wanting more. He lived in the future, never happy with the present.'

'Why did you divorce him?'

'I realized there was not much point in going on. We just found it difficult to live together.'

'Was he a cruel man?'

'Not cruel — *impatient*!'

Speaking of him with the warmest, gentlest affection after his death, she referred to the crucial interruption of his adolescence by the Great War: 'That's what coloured his life; he was a sensitive boy.'

Henry had won his battle with the farm, raising it to 'A' classification against the odds, including a disastrous first year when he lost £800 in his struggle to make the farm a paying proposition. But he did so at a punitive cost to his family and, ultimately, at the cost to himself *of* that family. Loetitia Williamson divorced Henry at the end of the war; Windles, come of age and able to confront his father on equal terms at last, blackened his eye and emigrated to Canada.

In his conclusion to *The Story of a Norfolk Farm*, Henry referred to his exhilaration during a brief, snatched holiday at Ox's Cross:

> I came as near to bliss as any man can come in this world. I had earned my holiday; I had worked for this field: I had worked for my farm . . . and I thought of all I had seen during the day, being part of the same earth of England, and in me there was no division of spirit, no homesickness, and I would return after my holiday, and start afresh, and harm no other man in the world by that work — growing food for my own sort, English people.

This idyllic picture is so removed from the reality of the ruined roads and house arrest that it might have been a rare attempt at diplomatic public relations. There is no deceiver like a self-deceiver.

Edward Seago placed Henry in a more convincing perspective in his book, *Peace in War* (1943):

Today there is Williamson the farmer. Several years ago he left his beloved Devon to farm in Norfolk. I think he left his heart behind. The farm of his ideal has not materialized. Perhaps it will do yet. I hope so, or perhaps the dream will become an emcumbrance no longer bearable. Just now in the second great war of his life, he is a tired man, toiling with his hands on the land; still steadfast to his principles, seeking 'orderliness' and 'regimentation', believing that only through clarity, and universal comprehension of all points of view (through knowing oneself), can un-understanding and that mass un-understanding called modern war be avoided; and finding that he is a voice crying in the wilderness. Tormented always by the thought that he, himself, may be the discord, yet knowing that it is not within his power to strike a different note.

Seago doubted if Henry was a happy man: 'I wish that he could find peace of mind, but I'm afraid that if he did the spark which burns fiercely inside him might die.'

The dream was over and Henry returned alone to his beloved Hut at Ox's Cross to work on the novel he believed it was his 'duty and destiny' to write, which grew from one book into the fifteen volumes comprising 'A Chronicle of Ancient Sunlight'.

PART TWO

Fulfilment and Retribution

A little of the glamour I have tried to put in this book: when you think of me, forget that I am lank and ugly and unprepossessing, and remember only the strange shouts of the birds, the trees, the stars, and that lovely spirit in men's hearts!

always your friend,

Henry Williamson

EIGHT

'Tarka the rotter'

MY FIRST IMPRESSIONS of Henry were formed when he returned to Devon. I had recently become, at the age of seventeen, a Parliamentary and Lobby Correspondent in the House of Commons, working for the Central Press Agency and spending my holidays with my parents at Sedgebanks, the bungalow at Vention which they rented until they bought the Grey House, two houses away, in 1945. (Sedgebanks was later bought by the writer, Malcolm Elwin, who was instrumental in persuading Macdonald to publish 'A Chronicle of Ancient Sunlight' and became Henry's literary executor until they fell out.) At that time I had dual nationality. I enlisted in the American Air Corps in 1945 when I was eighteen, later transferring to the army newspaper, the *Stars & Stripes*, in post-war Germany. After my demobilization I chose British nationality, but the generosity of the G.I. Bill of Rights enabled me to spend two contented undergraduate years at Pembroke College, Cambridge, where I started my own magazine, *Panorama*, in 1949. Whenever I could I returned to Devon. Henry became a regular visitor to the Grey House, while we were equally welcome at the Hut (where he worked) and the caravan (where he slept) at Ox's Cross, which was only a few miles away.

My father, the American writer Negley Farson, had

known Henry for years as a fellow member of the Savage Club in London, which Henry called The Barbarians in his novels. They were not so much opposites as complements, with their enthusiasm for words and nature; but Henry was introspective whereas my father was described by *Time* as 'the great extrovert', one of the last of the legendary breed of foreign correspondents. My father had a shattering zest for life which soured with drink, while Henry remained detached, an observer of life rather than a participant. They were old sparring partners.

I cannot remember the exact date but I was still in my teens and woefully naïve and susceptible to influence, when I met Henry for the first time. I have the impression of a lean, vibrant, almost quivering man, with dark hair flecked with grey, and blazing mesmeric eyes. He had an exceptional presence. His determination to achieve an immediate and intimate rapport with any young person made me uneasy to begin with, for adults did not usually behave like that. I felt conspiratorial and slightly treacherous when he advised me to be patient with my father — who must resent the threat from 'the young bulls' — for I did not understand what he was talking about. He asked me to forgive my father when he was drunk because 'he has so much to contend with in life'; but I had lived with my father's drinking for as long as I could remember and felt this should be a personal problem, kept within the family. When he spoke like that in my father's defence I felt uncomfortable, for it seemed that Henry was trying to condemn him at the same time.

Most upsetting of all, as we raced along the country lanes in his beautiful open Alvis on summer evenings, was Henry's outspoken admiration for Hitler as 'a great and good man'. This left me speechless as I fought back tears of impotent rage. My innate schoolboy patriotism had been influenced by my father's dedication of *Bomber's Moon* (1941) to 'The last Nazi', and I was genuinely shocked by Henry's justification of Hitler which seemed evil at that time. It was difficult to relax in the presence of such intensity, but I was flattered that he should take a boy into his confidence, and gradually accepted Henry as Henry, which was, of course, the only way.

At the time, the secretary-companion was still very much in evidence. She had her own way of handling Henry. I remember her as slightly harassed, but kind and patient: she needed these qualities. On one occasion I remember, in June 1948, my mother and I called on them and left when she told us that he was busy writing. She was protecting him from interruption, but Henry wrote to my mother that evening a letter which seemed intent on castigating her rather than mollifying us: 'I heard voices and when [she] didn't come and tell me, imagined that friends of hers had called in and for some reason she didn't want me to see them. What must you be thinking of me?... I expected her at any moment to come and tell me who it was....' The letter protested at length in this vein and it was obvious that he had worked himself into a state of exasperation. Considering that he detested intruders, and other 'men from Porlock', this was unfair to his companion who knew that few things are more deadly to a writer than a pointless visit from 'droppers-in' with little to say of importance and a tendency to linger. One such 'lamprey', as Henry described him, had been a persistent nuisance over the years, descending on my parents after visits to Henry, to slander him, then returning to the Hut to spread further gossip about them. The 'lamprey' even went to Ireland where he confronted Henry's friend, Sir John Heygate, airing petty grievances for five hours with the conclusion that 'Henry was a very awkward fellow'. When the 'long, thin, dull lamprey' had the temerity to come back to Ox's Cross, Henry let fly: 'Ever since 1935,' he wrote to a friend, 'I'd been false-face to him, and now my real face was a hiss and chatter of teeth and would he LAY OFF.'

Yet, far from appreciating his secretary's invidious rôle as

127

buffer, Henry exaggerated his apology to my mother out of all proportion, unable to leave it alone:

> It's only strange faces suddenly appearing at the door, and myself unpresentable, that I try to avoid — the sudden shock as it were. Heavens, I am regretful at missing you, and hope you won't think any more of it; I'm not 'shy-made' at all, and of course there's no cause at all; but alas, almost everything seems to go wrong nowadays, everything is upside down, a colossal sense of irony and negation seems to be brooding over this life, the exact opposite or negative of everything that is asked or required being the outcome.

Henry was indulging in his pastime of transferring his frustrations on to someone else; exacting his revenge when his work was not going well.

It is worth noting that, at exactly this time, Henry was acting as editor of the quarterly magazine, *Adelphi*, which he had agreed to take on in 1947. It was a rash assignment when he was overworked already, and a little obtuse of him considering the unpopularity of his politics, which were less easily overlooked in his new role. The *Adelphi* had been run by its founder, John Middleton Murry, since 1923, and it was only reluctantly that he had handed over the editorship to Henry. Henry regretted his decision and wrote to me in 1949 that he was 'giving up *Adelphi*, it is an energy-waster, it leads nowhere, it costs money I haven't got to lose, and it interferes with my own WORK, which I must do now, or perish. It's now or never, and so it must be now!'

It is also worth noting that Henry was at this time already involved, and somewhat stormily, with the girl who was to become his second wife — Christine. The strains on his household must have been considerable, and it is no surprise that his long-suffering secretary-companion of two decades had left for good by the end of 1948.

She was not the only one to find Henry difficult. At one time or another almost all of us suffered from his intolerance and frustration, and some of us certainly provoked him. In my own relationship with Henry in those early days, my queasy blend of gaucherie and dogmatism must have exasperated him, as some of his letters confirm. I was once presumptuous enough to ask him to sign one of his books for me, when he came to the Grey House for dinner. I can only plead that I was young and thought that authors *liked* to be asked; but I upset him, and Henry explained his refusal in a letter dated 30 December 1950:

Dear Dan,

You accused me of being rude to you in your father's house the other evening, over the matter of not signing or inscribing a copy of a book you asked me to. I wonder if you would accept an explanation of the avoidance of so doing? This author has many similar requests; and has had a considerable number in the past. One collector known to him, by letter though not personally, has about 50 books which he has bought over the years, all this author's books, all signed and inscribed: in one case, eleven copies of one book. There are other collectors who possess similar collections.

In those days I used to sign almost every copy presented to me, as well as give away hundreds of copies to friends, acquaintances, etc. Then, later, I used to issue signed limited editions of each book; and to keep faith with the subscribers (usually two guineas) I stopped diluting the number with casual inscriptions of ordinary 'trade' editions. It seemed only fair; it also gave me a good reason for doing what I had come greatly to dislike when requested to do; but which, freely, gives me great pleasure to do — inscribe a book, when it is truly given, truly a gift. I like to reserve the

129

right, as it were, to give; and having given away many hundreds of books to people who didn't care for them/ want them, almost, in the past, I now like to retrieve my character, and my right to give, to myself.

It is amusing to learn the names of people who, often sooner rather than later, offer the inscribed books for sale. Generally speaking, and I hope without egotism, those people who were not my sort, and — in the period before you were born, I kept in my small way, open house, and was usually full up with visitors, the more the merrier, so to speak — were usually the ones to cash in on the books right away, and this actually went with stories about the author's defects, etc. etc., all no doubt quite true; and so it was, in a way, quite right that they should dispose of their copies for a few guineas or so (those were the days when a copy of *Tarka*, of the vellum original edition published in Georgeham, sold for £100 and more) and allow them to come into the hands of people who did, in a way, care for them. But when once I had a list of such books from a collector in Liverpool, I decided then and there to give my books only to those who would care for them for themselves; and to distinguish such people required a certain amount of time.

This may sound pompous and conceited; but in my small way and scope, in my own little life and sphere, it is how I feel. When one is asked to write in books, it is always a little frustrating: it isn't a spontaneous thing: writers know this feeling, and perhaps, in the trade as it were, seldom ask one another to do it. It is in a way like love; it has to be the genuine thing, or it is no good at all, and should be avoided. Or it is like having a trout stream; the knowledgeable do not ask to be invited; they would not have the hands for throwing a fly exactly so, if they did. What does one do when a man turns up, complete with rod, etc., and says, 'You don't mind if I have a day on your water, do you?' One used to say, 'Yes, but may I send you a line first, next time, so that I can be sure of the water being free for you?' But some of them, in the old Shallowford days, did not understand that way of talking. They thought perhaps the owner was rude. No doubt he appeared so; but he had so many requests like that, and each caller was unique to himself, and did not know that he was but one of many. Of course they were unknowledgeable; as we are all, until we learn.

This had been typewritten, now he added by hand:

So please, Dan, try to see the question of the avoidance of signing of books by direct request — some write a letter first, thus showing some awareness of reality — as something other than rudeness on the part of him from whom a fair number of such demands are made, & quite often! I have always hoped that one day we might become real friends, so that I will be able to give of my own free will. That's about the only freedom left to one who has many responsibilities — whatever superficial adjudging might indicate!

H.W.

Even I, with all the arrogance of youth, was mollified by such a sympathetic letter. I assume that I replied with some understanding, for he wrote to me again from the 'Hut Field':

Glad you saw my point about signing books. My worst moment was in 1947 at Bradford, where I was chosen (?) president of the Lit. Society. I liked the secretary, a Mr Macdonald (? memory dull), much. But some of the others were alarming. Thus I arrived for a speech at 7.30, at 6 as asked. To meet the Committee. About 45-60

131

men and wives. Shake hands all round. Then an old
gent avec cape and palsied hand descends on me with a
BIG ATTACHE CASE of books, bends over me, shaking
and sibiltailing [*sic*], poor fellow, and says I have waited
for you for years and now I have got you and with that a
faulty catch of said bag or case 24″ x 15″ x 8″ flys off and a
shower of mouldy books of mine, Collins imprint 1921–
23, descends into my lap. Quite TWENTY. I am compos-
ing my speech, and a pint of cold beer is in my feeble
hand. I have already motored up there in a faulty
motorcar oiling plugs all the way and titubating [*sic*]. I
murmure [*sic*] feebly about etc. etc. and might I sign one
and I do so while he grumbles and says I am rather rude.
Later I see that one copy in a list for £6/6/-. RARE first,
autographed. I always wanted to keep my chastity for
those I liked, and could freely give; having nothing else
of value, for me that is, to give; all else stripped away
by my own goolishness [*sic*] in the past then To Dick and
Harry & Co. were my friends; and carriers away of
little bits of portraits of a genius but. Now it isn't genius
anymore, and the but is a shrug. To me it is a great deal,
to be left free in that respect. I am sorry if this is silly;
but all things are relative: a gash is as painful to one as
an amputation to another.

This was a generous explanation, and typical of the man that
he should spend several pages giving his reasons for refusing
to sign a book. Other people besides myself were bewildered
by Henry's attitude when they proffered his books, and felt
offended as if he had rejected a hand outstretched in friendship. Even so, Henry's disinclination is understandable. It is a
damned nuisance when a stranger trespasses on a writer's
time, and the indiscriminate signing of books under this form
of blackmail diminishes the pleasure for the people to whom
one *is* giving spontaneously, and reduces their value. My

father, who was asked to sign his books less often, did so with relish. I remember also an afternoon in a small mid-western town in the States, when I watched Somerset Maugham sign dozens of books with infinite patience because he was staying in my godfather's house and he knew it would help his tattered reputation locally — even raising a wintry smile when a woman plunked an entire *Collected Works* on the table, explaining that her husband had been furious over such a waste of money when she bought them but might forgive her if they rose in value. Recognizing a shrewd commercial instinct, Maugham signed each volume graciously. Henry on the other hand suffered greatly from this kind of pressure, and was constantly betrayed by his friends, who cajoled him to sign his books in order to sell them at a profit. There is no excuse, I now realize; for this is never the author's intention, and though the recipient may need the money the gift should remain sacred and personal.

When Henry signed a book of his own accord, he did so with care. Presenting my father with a copy of *The Old Stag*, he found the right words and inscribed them warmly:

To dear Negley Farson, whose smile is like the sea and the sands of Woolacombe Bay,* with every good wish from H. W. June 1944

* A phrase that would be totally misunderstood in the Café Royal but not in the lumber woods, or on the lakes, or the beaches of Normandy in summer 1944.

Unwittingly, I gave Henry further distress when I took photographs of him. I had no idea how much he disliked this until I received the following letter:

Dear old Dann'll
   Don't sell too many of the copyrights of your photographs until I've seen 'em, will you? This looks like

conceit; but it isn't really. It's the knowledge that at times I feel and look like death; and then in the right company, can flood with life and so change the aspect of the machinery. Photography to be good must consider the subject, not as a camera-eye (otherwise photographic grilling) but as the personality within the machine. The camera is the servant of the machine; the portrait painter strives to illuminate his subject, to get its *spirit*. That isn't done by flattering; or by caricaturing, as [Augustus] John did some of his pompous subjects, in his attempt to get to the real man under the façade of business, etc. There is a façade; then there is the pretension of the man; then under that is the natural creature; and under that, his spirit. It is your job to bring out that spirit. And it ain't done by innumerable chuck-and-chance-it snaps. That's not the right way to go about it. If you had tried to co-operate with me, and talked alone, apart from others (remember I am always, under my affection for Negley, half-scared of him. I was scared when once or twice in the Savage Club he 'picked' on me, no doubt telling the truth admirably from one point of view, but without any form — which I think is important — he said aloud, again and again, 'Henry's all balled-up about sex', and then proceeded to mention the name of a woman, etc. etc. I didn't really mind; I knew it was the current superficial-silly opinion of half-a-dozen semi-sensitives there; but it BORED me, and I did my best not to react, or to hurt *his* feelings, 'if you understand my meaning, Dan'l'.) ... Anyway, I couldn't in honesty really object, since I had been in the past and probably in present also, so damnably blatant and stupid about myself, egocentric, arrogant, etc. etc. — all of which I deplored since the machine did know better ... There is some of this feeling in your photographs, only one of which, in my opoinion, so far as I can judge, is near positive. The others are negative: the machine stopped.

His letter may well have been more revealing than my photographs, with the candid comments on my father and Henry's self-indictment. As usual, Henry followed up his rebuke with a further explanation:

> To be frank, I was somewhat abashed when I was aware that you were going to snap me in your house that night. Do you mind me being frank? I rather disliked myself for it; but I couldn't help feeling that as I was a guest, I ought not to object; also I didn't want to hurt your feelings knowing how sensitive you were. I wanted to say, 'Wait till the SUN-shines: then let us get a sun-shadow series, I know my photogenic angles, also the dud ones.' I wanted to say, 'MY sort of author is best-served by no photographs; it is a special kind of illusion; and easily disturbed.' (I have known it 27 years; you must permit me to know in this, what ill-serves my little reputation, what serves it. I usually am the worst server of it, for I do silly things on impulse, and also say silly things, 'running myself down', as someone put it).
>
> Well, that's my confession! One other thing I'd say to you, as a friend or younger brother; Keep most of your reactions to yourself. That is what I ought to do too, but seldom do. I have been in someone else's house or club and criticized fellow-members or guests; and then got the reaction for my gaucherie. The man who says little about others is usually happy; he falls into no boomerang-traps or alleys.
>
> Well, enough of that sort of bilge!
> The field is plowed....

Perhaps he referred to his gaucherie because he recognized it in me. Altogether it was wise advice, even if it was hopeless to tell me to keep my reactions to myself. When Henry protested 'I wanted to say...', he should have done so, directly and humorously, and it is just possible that I might have listened. At the end of another follow-up letter, he added the postscript: 'So you have sold my ugly face to Faber. Will he stick pins in it? I HATE MY FACE. IT IS RUINOUS AND CHARRED WITH SIN.' Why did Henry hate his portrait so vehemently? Simply because it was a poor photograph? Or did it reveal an animal cunning that shocked Narcissus? Whatever the reason, the aversion to photography was constant; and when Dennis Knight showed him the portrait he had taken in his Barnstaple studio, Henry was so enraged that Knight thought he was going to strike him. Today I understand that taking someone's portrait can be interpreted as a sort of theft. That fine writer, Jean Rhys, was reluctant to be photographed when I visited her home near Exeter, and I respected her wishes — to my lasting regret. I am glad now that I persevered with Henry: my photographs in this book must speak for themselves.

In my defence, I was eager because I had just become a professional photographer. The date is pin-pointed in a letter Henry wrote to John Hanson on 5 July 1951: 'Then there is a local lad who takes photographs, all my faces are dead weary in his camera; now he has joined *Picture Post* and wants a series. I could do them much better myself; and with some blood in the face.'

A satirical feature of mine in *Panorama*, in which I photographed an actor in the style of various magazines and newspapers — including one on a bomb-site in the dreary socialist fashion of *Picture Post* — brought a summons from *Picture Post*'s managing director. I was unaware that a few hours earlier he had announced the dismissal of the editor, Ted Castle, brandishing a copy of *Panorama* as proof to his staff of where their policy had failed. I was being interviewed as a potential editor; but when I was asked how much I was

Henry at work in his Hut at Ox's Cross — one of the photographs I inflicted on him c.1950. He enjoyed the attention but mistrusted the results, and stiffened accordingly. *Daniel Farson*

Negley Farson in front of the Grey House, Putsborough Sands. *Daniel Farson*

earning I made the disastrous mistake of telling the truth. Having just started as an apprentice copywriter in an advertising agency, my nominal salary was roughly £4 a week, and I could feel his interest evaporate when I told him. 'Oh well,' he sighed with disappointment, 'I expect we can do better than that'; which was how I joined *Picture Post* as a staff photographer. This proved far more interesting than a desk job, for I worked with such distinguished writers as Robert Kee, with whom I went to Majorca to photograph Robert Graves, and the late Kenneth Allsop who became a close friend.

This formed another link with Henry, for Ken had known him since the age of twelve, when he picked up *The Lone Swallows* in a public library and experienced 'a confusion of excitement, wonder, disbelief and, almost fear. For the first time I had encountered someone who, it seemed, felt as I inarticulately and gropingly did about birds and the country-side.' Ken persuaded his parents to take him on holiday in Devon and he wrote to Henry, who arranged for Windles to show him the countryside on his bicycle; but it was Henry that Ken wanted to meet. When Ken was twenty-one he gave Betty Allsop 'The Flax of Dream', and she suspects he would have called off their marriage if she had not liked it. They spent their honeymoon in North Devon, making love in Spreacombe Woods unaware of the cold March day; and it was after this that they called on Henry in the Hut: 'Of course he read to us from the book he was then writing,' Betty Allsop remembers. 'He seemed very lonely and talked a lot about Gypsy, who had left him not long before. For ever after he was part of our lives — a large part.'

When Ken and I discovered that we were taking our holidays in Devon at the same time in July 1953, I introduced him and Betty to my parents, over dinner at the Grey House. My father took an instant liking to Ken, who recorded his own impressions in his *Notes*:

Negley is a big lumbering red-faced man with faded very short bitten-about hair, walks with a limp (flying accident, wound still open). We liked him very much. Talks in rather thick blurred American. We sat on stone wall of terrace in lovely warm evening sun looking across to Baggy Point on West, Morte Point to East, with waves from Atlantic breaking along Woolacombe beach, drinking sherry. Eve, not the tall, elegant woman I expected: dumpy and fat but charming and laughs a lot . . . Subject of Williamson came up: Eve hates him, said he is 'cruel and treacherous'. Negley actually keeps a black-list and HW is on it. Negley said 'Tarka and Salar and the Old Stag are wonderful — Tarka makes me weep'. But he thought nothing of the novels. We had a good dinner, talked a lot . . . .

Reading this recently felt like eavesdropping, with the same unexpected shock. Memory dulls the edges. Was my mother really so dumpy? I suppose so. But if she 'hated' Henry this was due to her defensive loyalty to my father. And I cannot remember any 'black-list'. However, it was perfectly true that resentment between Henry and my father had been brewing for some time. This was not due to rivalry (for their work was so different), but to Henry's tendency to take the centre of the stage when he visited the Grey House to read aloud from his latest work. He did so brilliantly, but he gave us no choice. He paced his words with the skill of an actor; his voice was clear and emphatic — but he loved the sound of it. Williamson reading Williamson could be a solemn business.

Sometimes the sentences were whispered with such intensity that the words faded away at the end as if overwhelmed by emotion. Interruptions were not tolerated, though there was a grudging respite allowed for coffee or clearing of throats. My father, who relished the give as well as the take of conversation, chafed with restlessness and sometimes registered his protest by clumping noisily to bed while Henry read on.

When he finished there was the awkward silence while we wondered what to say, like suppressing the impulse to applaud after a memorial address. On one occasion, my gallant, elderly grandmother broke the tension, swearing slightly in her anxiety to rise to the occasion: 'Henry, that chapter has damn-*all* in it!' she exclaimed emphatically. It sounds apocryphal, but she was known for her eccentricity in taking slang literally (in this case it means the opposite) and I heard her say it. So did my father, who regarded her with new admiration! Henry, on the other hand, recognized the compliment she intended.

As my father also enjoyed reading his own latest work aloud, usually for the benefit of my mother's advice over breakfast, I can see there was a genuine resentment, but to be fair to Henry he was eager for advice as well. He proved this in a letter to my mother after a reading from the manuscript of *The Phasian Bird* (1948) the night before: 'Thank you for everything last night ... You will understand, I know, that the broody state was due to a suspended artistic problem. And it was most helpful to hear your views and see your reactions.' Henry then proceeded to list the various points carefully, so this was not mere politeness.

1. It makes me see that I must link up more parts, bring the bird in the foreground .... Negley walked out at the point where I began to steal descriptions from the Norfolk farm ....

2. I must keep the sympathy for all concerned as the spine of the book. I felt this from you, Eve.

3. Dan showed that the two themes can be combined,

provided they *are* combined & don't come, like the strands of a bad rope, loose and fuzzy.

Henry was touchingly appreciative, though he always managed a dig at my 'poor' father:

> I am most grateful to you for your patience & have nothing but admiration for your tenacity and stoicism. I hope the coffee restored poor Neg. He is a valuable sounding-board; and he *is* right. Alas, in this work, at least, & for the last time I hope, I must try & combine fire & water. So long as the result is steam up, Neg will forgive me, Dan will approve, & Eve will be able to read without having to close the petals.

The friction between Henry and my father was that of old colleagues. Henry brooded on grievance, while my father relished his barbs against his closest friends after their visits to the Grey House: 'Victor [Gollancz] has written another letter to the *Times*; his heart bleeds so much he must be anaemic'; while he condemned Kingsley Martin for his 'wet woollen-underwear socialism'. My mother remarked that guests were rather like fish, they went off after a few days. But they made such remarks with glee rather than malice, and my father's enthusiasm was so infectious that he filled the Grey House with laughter when such guests did come to stay. He was the most compelling raconteur I have heard, partly because he enjoyed his stories so much; but this was a pleasure denied him when Henry came to dinner.

After one such dinner party, Henry made a sudden excuse and left, possibly sensing my father's dread of the inevitable 'reading' afterwards. Understandably, when the conversation started up again it centred on Henry, who was always an interesting subject. We were not particularly indiscreet, but everyone felt an acute sense of guilt when we went outside to look at the sunset and found the initials 'H.W.' carefully composed in twigs left near the dining-room window. It was typical of Henry to eavesdrop — and let us know it. My father stared at the initials with wonder and disbelief: 'Tarka the Rotter!' he exclaimed, 'the elfin son of a bitch!'

The feud simmered merrily with grudging admiration on both sides. If anything, our visits to each other became even more frequent until the arrival of the Allsops, which brought, in all innocence, a new element of jealousy. One morning, Ken and Betty drove to Ox's Cross where they found Henry morose and aggrieved. He emerged half-naked from his Hut saying, 'Went down to the pub for two nights looking for you but you didn't turn up'. Ken's *Notes* describe how they left their children with Christine (Henry's second wife) and 'Poodie', (the nickname given to Harry) — 'who has blond hair cut like a medieval page-boy's, long as a girl's. Our children still don't believe he's a boy' — and drove Henry into Barnstaple. As it turned out, this was taking a lamb to the slaughter, for it was market day, which meant that the pubs stayed open all Friday afternoon.

Ken's *Notes* continue:

H a bit more cheerful. Then we went into the Three Tuns and had beer, he's brought along a lunch tin with Vitawheat biscuits, excellent Irish cheese, tomatoes, while he talked to two women opposite. Offered them biscuit and cheese and told them they ought to eat brown bread, white bread being poison and would kill them, old woman said she was 82 and had been eating it all her life. Then he said they must listen to radio on Tuesday at 10 o'clock when he was broadcasting.

Then Negley Farson lurched into view: on one of his 3 monthly breakouts: he was very drunk, sat down, leered at Betty, mouthing 'sweetie' and making significant signs. He began to attack Henry in most outrageous way. Went something like this: 'I met these two people last night and thought they were nice people. What are you doing with a fellow like this? I don't like him and he doesn't like me. You're just trying to make a legend about yourself.... Now all this stuff about your Devon forbears — you said your mother came from Ireland, now you're of old Devon stock. You're bogus, Henry, you're bogus...'

All this in a pretty incoherent stream, very drunken and blurred, and HW sat there shrivelling under it, his face stiff, eyes big, until after making one or two vain attempts to ward it off, first to joke about, he leaped out and said, 'I'm going, I'm not going to stand any more of this.'

Outside he was raging. Swearing about that man — explained he had written to Negley saying that the Genealogical Society had found that his mother descended from an old Devon family now extinct, and that he believed that the reason he could write about Devon and the Devon people so well was because of this — like a swallow returning to its English birth-place: in blood.

Ken Allsop went off to have a haircut and Betty was left with Henry, who walked her towards the banks of the River Taw describing previous incidents. She takes up the story:

Apparently Negley used to attack him in the same way in the Savage Club telling him he was bogus and all balled up about sex. Ken's haircut must have taken a remarkably long time because H and I spent about two hours sitting on the wall or walking about, Henry deciding to throw himself in the river and deciding *not* to throw himself in, and I repeating over and over again that I wouldn't allow it because I loved him, Christine loved him, Ken loved him and we all loved him.

Finally, Henry decided he would like someone else to fall in the river so he could dive to the rescue and dash his head against the rocks and drown. Betty Allsop pointed out that as the tide was out he would only land in the mud. At this he decided to return to the Three Tuns to tell my father that he would have him in court for slander; but when he got there he found that my father had been collected by taxi, denying Henry even that satisfaction.

It was surprising how many of his victims forgave my father, but Henry was not one of them. I cannot blame him, for the tirade could be merciless in its repetition, the dreadful home-truths inflicted hour after hour, and as my father was a big man it was difficult to escape, especially when compressed in one of the cubicles of the Three Tuns. It must have been particularly mortifying for Henry to be humiliated in front of friends he respected. My father had a fatal knack of finding the Achilles Heel and probing it. One story he related with relish concerned a remark that Henry had been rash enough to confide in him after Henry had eloped with the wife of a fellow Savage Club member, who had told him: 'Henry, there is no one I would rather she ran off with than you.' 'Yes,' said my father cruelly, 'and you know what he added after you'd gone? "Because my poor, foolish wife will go through such hell with Henry that she'll come running back in a couple of weeks pleading for forgiveness." And she did!'

It would have been understandable if Henry had kept away from the Grey House after that, but he returned as if for further punishment. It was not a happy time for him, as I shall explain, and once he confided to my mother that he thought he was going mad: 'I find myself shouting in the Hut and banging my head on the wall'.

In 1955, *A Fox Under My Cloak* was published (the sixth volume of the 'Chronicle', which has since become a collector's item. At the time, a few critics hailed the novel —

which described the year of the Somme — as one of the most powerful studies of war ever written. Kenneth Allsop wrote: 'There is an analogy here between subject and author, for Williamson, committed for a decade to building this bridge of narrative .... is like the war itself, overlooked and underestimated, a misfit genius whose sense of authenticity and scale of composition tower in the literary background.'

Henry presented my father with a copy and, on a subsequent visit, basked for a moment in his unexpected praise, finding my father in a most expansive mood having just returned from the pub in Croyde. Then my father went to his bedroom, drank most of a bottle of whisky he had brought home with him, and descended to demolish the smiling Henry with a cascade of 'truths', including his dislike for the character of Phillip Maddison and his suspicion that Henry had gleaned his war material from old copies of the *Illustrated London News*.

By now Henry was out of favour with Macdonald and my father was apprehensive that he was going to ask him to encourage his friend Victor Gollancz to publish him instead. My father had already placed *Tarka* with his own publisher in Sweden; although the fusion of Williamson and Gollancz sounds improbable, Victor had a real affection for my father, as well as being his British publisher, and would have listened to his recommendation.

Henry's confidence had been further shaken by an unpleasant letter from his American publisher, which he brought to show to my father, scrawled over with his vituperative comments. The letter informed him that they proposed to melt down the plates for *Salar the Salmon* (1935) unless he wanted them himself at the cost of $200. Knowing the difficulties which had engulfed Malcolm Elwin, who had persuaded Macdonald to publish the 'Chronicle', my father was not anxious to become involved. As his instinct was usually generous, he may have resented being placed in such an awkward position.

In retrospect their jousting seems childish, for I suspect there was an element of dramatics in it which we did not notice at the time. Certainly my father was desperate for the conversation otherwise denied him in Devon, which has been described as 'an intellectual graveyard': any friction was preferable to boredom. In regarding the feud as serious, onlookers inadvertently helped to make it so.

NINE

Henry takes his revenge

On Saturday 14 July 1956, I drove down to Devon with Colin Wilson (who had just published *The Outsider*) and Ken Allsop in his red, open sports car, reaching the Grey House in time for dinner.

It is good to realize what pleasure our visit gave to my father. Far from resenting the 'young bulls' of Henry's imagination, my father seized on the latest news enthusiastically, even though it was second-hand. My smallest achievement was grist to his mill, and I could hardly have brought him more stimulating companions.

The weather was perfect, as it usually was — thirty years ago. Williamson weather, with the sun so hot that the sand scorched our feet; and the next day was a perfect laze of swimming, reading, eating and conversation. Ken was so mobile that it was easy to forget that one of his legs had been amputated after injury during the war. He was a courageous man and taxed himself far with his determination not to let other people feel conscious of his disability. Nonetheless he was conscious of it himself and refused to join us in the sea until my father offered to support him while he took off his artificial limb and hopped into the water. With his own leg wound, a raw, gangrenous hole dating from his plane crash in Egypt when he flew for the Royal Canadian Flying Corps in the First War, my father was the right person to persuade him; Ken told me several years later that this had been a turning point in his life in helping him to lose his self-consciousness. At this stage it could not have been a happier visit; Ken described the day as 'perfect, ending with a dinner of wonderful peach-fed ham sent over from America'. Then Henry cast his shadow.

Ken's *Notes* reveal that he had been worrying about Henry. He told my mother that he felt he should call on him, especially as Malcolm Elwin had looked in at the Grey House earlier: Henry would be bound to hear of his visit and would be deeply hurt if Ken failed to see him. Of course my mother agreed. Ken drove to Ox's Cross on Monday afternoon, where he found Henry typing in the Hut with the door open. Ken's *Notes* continue:

When he saw me he came out and said (typically): 'I was thinking of you this morning.' He's grown a moustache (quite white). Looked well and brown, green shirt buttoned up to neck. He seemed in good spirits. Henry said about the Amis school of new writers: 'I wouldn't want to sell a million books, I'd feel there was something wrong, but I would like a bit more appreciation.'

That evening Dan and I drove to Georgeham and met Henry in the pub and had some drinks. He has his Tales and Life of a Devon Village exhibited in there at 3s 6d each — the pub is now tarted up like a coffee bar with fancy wallpaper. 'Subtopia', HW said.

Earlier, Henry had described a walk he had taken along Baggy Point with his twenty-year-old son, Richard. Peregrine falcons were nesting on Baggy that year and they had seen three pigeons coming across the sea when the tiercel swooped and took one — 'Just like Farson swooped on me and mutilated me with his talons...' Ken replied: 'Never

147

thought of you as a pigeon, Henry.' Somehow, judging by Ken's *Notes*, the fun had gone out of the visit. He concluded: 'Next morning Negley was obviously in a bad mood. Dan's theory was that it was because we had seen Henry — and he seemed to think Negley was about to go off on another binge. We drove back to London in six hours with the hood down.' I am sure my father did go off on his 'binge' but I doubt if this had much to do with Henry. For this was the pattern by then, a rage of frustration at seeing friends leave for London and Fleet Street and the mental excitement he longed for — a natural reaction.

It was through his connection with the Grey House that Colin Wilson met Henry for the first time. He has since become one of the most controversial critics of Williamson's work, though not always popular with Henry's admirers. Henry himself was unamused by Colin's essay on him in *Eagle and Earwig*, writing to a friend that 'Mr Colin Wilson once wrote that Henry Williamson had no sense of style at all: surely this is a robin pecking at its image in a looking glass.' In 1980 Colin upset members of the Henry Williamson Society by his astringent comments in their journal on Henry and his work, describing a night when Henry stayed with him in Cornwall and asked for Wagner's *Tristan* prelude. As the music swelled, Colin's brother made some remark:

Instantly, Henry turned on him and snarled 'Shut up!' Fortunately, the music was so loud that my brother was oblivious. It was just as well; he also has a temper, and might easily have knocked Henry down. But that was typical. He was in somebody else's house, drinking his wine and about to eat his food; you might have expected him to make an effort not to be offensive. But he simply had no control of his emotions.

Personally, I liked this side of Henry's nature; irascibility was such an integral part of it.

Colin has described how his acquaintance with Henry
began:

I met Henry Williamson under rather amusing circumstances in 1957. I was staying with the writer Negley
Farson, who lived a couple of miles away from Henry,
on the coast of North Devon. I'd heard all about Henry
from Negley's son Dan, and from Kenneth Allsop,
whose novel *Adventure Lit Their Star*, had been deeply
influenced by Williamson's nature writing. I had read
Tarka the Otter in my teens and been enormously impressed; I was not critical enough to feel it was overwrit-
ten, and saw it only as a magnificently objective portrait
of the wild moorland country and its inhabitants. So I
was surprised to hear that Henry was not much liked in
the Georgeham area of North Devon, and that most of
his friends were sooner or later alienated by his neurotic
egotism. Negley and his wife Eve had quarrelled with
Henry long ago; so if Dan wanted to see 'the hermit at
Ox's Cross', he had to keep his intentions secret. And,
one afternoon, Dan and I and my girlfriend Joy set out,
ostensibly for a stroll along the beach — in fact to visit
Henry. Like everyone else, I was struck by his good
looks and his military bearing; he looked and sounded
like a retired Colonel. Joy, predictably, thought he was
stunningly attractive, Henry's wife, a pretty girl who
had been a teacher of gymnastics, gave us tea, and
Henry produced his latest manuscript and read us a
dozen pages or so. I expected it to be about animals —
or possibly about the First World War (he had just
written *The Golden Virgin*). In fact it was a defence of
his attitude to 'fascism', specifically to Sir Oswald
Mosley's Union Movement. I had met Mosley, and
found him brilliant and enormously likeable; so this was
a matter on which we immediately established a bond

149

of sympathy. Henry read on for what seemed like hours, with the consequence that it was dusk when we left. Dan asked me what I thought of him, and I said I'd found him impressive, but perhaps rather too talkative. Dan smiled ironically.

'He intended to be.'

'Intended?'

'That's typical Henry. He knows we're not supposed to see him, so he wants us to be late for dinner, just to stir things up . . .'

The subterfuge to which visitors resorted regarding Henry and my father seems futile now; what a precious waste of time and conversation. It would be nice to think that the two men would have burst into laughter at such silliness had they come face to face on the beach; but instead the tension grew, as Colin Wilson indicated in a letter he sent to Ken Allsop the following year after a further weekend at the Grey House:

Called on Henry on Saturday afternoon, and found him out. Left a note. Didn't tell Negley or Eve. On Saturday evening, the phone rings for me. A heavily disguised voice says, 'This is the man you called on this afternoon . . . can you come over at ten tonight? Don't tell Negley.' So I went over, feeling placed in a horribly false position by this time, and talked to Henry til midnight, then drove a journalist friend of mine back to Bideford (my excuse for going out at 10 in the evening!). All weekend I tried to confess to Negley that I'd seen Henry, but couldn't.

When I broached the subject of Henry at last, said I'd met him in London, and that I'd quite like to see him, Negley said: 'Do go and see him for God's sake! I wouldn't want you to feel I objected!'

Again, I tried to come clean, but couldn't make

it!!!! So I still feel guilty, and hope Negley and Eve never find out, since I can quite straightforwardly go and see Henry next time I go over there!

Incidentally, Henry spent quite a lot of time psycho-analysing Negley, and bitching him vigorously; I tried to defend him, and steer the conversation away, but it made me feel more than ever that Henry rather enjoys placing people in awkward situations!

Judging by this letter, it seems that my father had fewer inhibitions about his guests meeting Henry than they did. But it was too late for the reconciliation which should have taken place. My father died on 13 December 1960, and Henry wrote to my mother the following day. Character-istically, his condolences were tempered:

My Dear Eve,

Do accept the sympathy of Christine and myself in your sudden shock at the loss of your comrade, husband and friend, Negley. I know what good pals you were, to yourselves and to so many others all over the world, including our little family. Negley was a wonder in many ways but particularly in that his nervous system was chronically drained by a wound that would have killed most men, first driving them insane. For one occasion when he was upset — the true personality temporarily in shadow — there were hundreds when the drain on his vitality was equally heavy, but his sunny spirit shone through clearly; he could enjoy life, when, as I said, most of us would have been chronically irritable and morose. This was, in my observation, felt by everyone who knew him, in all walks of life. They divined and therefore truly knew 'Negley'. I have to go to London in an hour's time, on a long-set arrangement, and shall not be back until Saturday (train) & will alas miss the opportunity to be near you when the earth,

151

which loans our lives and nourishes them & in due course receives them back, gives him his 'rest after strive'. So will you please accept my apology for absence at the time. I have asked Christine (who hopes to be able to leave her school then) to pay my respects to Negley, and to you and Dan, with her own. She joins me in this little letter & we both send our love to you three dear people.

My mother died a year later, and it is no exaggeration to say that she longed for her own death after my father's. Her last year was one of appalling grief. I was left the Grey House and on 1 April 1964 resigned from my successful job in television and left my London home at Limehouse to live in Devon and find out if I could write. I am still finding out, but in the course of doing so I have had to sell the Grey House, which was a high price to pay.

When I moved to North Devon, I was unaware that the feud between my father and Henry had swollen to such proportions. Preoccupied as I was with my television work, my visits home had become less frequent, and it did not occur to me that any resentment might have lingered on Henry's part after my father's death. When Henry and I met we had the occasional fall-out, but I regarded that as a natural hazard in our friendship.

Five years later, in 1969, I received a phone call from Eve Elwin asking me anxiously if I had read Henry's new book, *The Gale of the World*. When I said no, Eve explained that she and Malcolm were distressed because it was 'so cruel about Eve and Negley'. She implored me not to read it. I bought a copy that afternoon.

The Gale of the World is the last volume in the 'Chronicle' and the most bizarre of Henry's books. Many of his readers found it shocking, but I was less concerned with the writing than the portrait of my father, wondering if I should recognize him as I read on apprehensively. The moment the character of Osgood Nilsson appeared, there was no doubt of that. Henry had taken his revenge.

Though Osgood Nilsson was boorish, which my father was not, the comparison with the loud-mouthed American journalist was unavoidable. Nilsson had written a best-seller, *Sinner's Way* — my father's best-selling autobiography in 1936 was entitled, *The Way of a Transgressor*. Nilsson boasted of his grandfather, 'a general of Confederate forces . . . evidence of which he exhibited by bringing from a breast pocket an old photograph of a man with whiskers and drooping moustache wearing a sort of frenchified uniform jacket with kepi, sword, scabbard, and shapeless trousers' — I have just such a photograph of my great-grandfather in the room with me now; General Negley was a fearless and remarkable character, but I admit the *opera bouffe* appearance was there.

The comparison with my mother is equally inescapable, for Mrs Osgood Nilsson was given 'Irish lineage' with a father who wrote 'ghoulish *extravaganzas*'. My mother's uncle was Bram Stoker, who was born in Dublin and wrote *Dracula*. The disguise could hardly have been more perfunctory. But the portrayal was petty. I should not have minded if it had been witty (and there was plenty of scope for that) or truly savage, but it was blunted by bitterness. Details were right, like Osgood Nilsson startling his visitors by rolling up his trousers to reveal the hole in his leg, the legacy of his plane crash; but the whole was pathetically wrong.

The portrayal of my mother as a tiresome gossip was unfair. 'Osgood gets so depressed at times,' she tells Philip Maddison, 'it's his leg you know, he won't have it off. He'd have been so much happier without it, but I suppose vanity makes him cling to it.' In fact she had supported my father against a regiment of surgeons who wished to amputate, and rightly so, for he went on to climb the Caucasus, sail his boat 'across Europe' and travel the continent of Africa from one coast to another. As a veteran himself, it was obtuse of Henry to mistake a natural instinct for survival as vanity. My father enjoyed a colossal conceit, but he did not suffer from vanity.

Colin Wilson sprang to my father's defence in *books & bookmen*:

> There is an acid portrait of Negley Farson as the American writer, Osgood Nilsson, of whom he writes primly: 'Self-knowledge, in relation to the defects of others, was denied him; so he remained a second-rate or superficial writer.' Williamson could be describing himself. If Williamson had simply portrayed Farson's alcoholism and capacity for virulent abuse, he would have been perfectly fair; but he shows Nilsson involved in acts of calculated meanness; and whatever Farson's faults, he was never mean. Unfortunately, Williamson was; and it is because this can be sensed in the later volumes that 'A Chronicle of Ancient Sunlight' ends on a level that is so far below its beginning.

I decided that my father's memory was avenged and forgot all about it, so much so that when I met Henry some time afterwards at Barnstaple station we walked back across the bridge together and stopped for a drink at Mugford's in the square. It was market day, which meant it was open all afternoon: Henry should have been warned. At first we drank gently with no curfew hanging over us. Suddenly I remembered *The Gale of the World* and felt a flush of filial loyalty. Trying hard to think of something to annoy him, I remembered a remark made to me by Oswald Mosley and repeated it: 'We like Henry so much, but he will take it all so seriously.' The effect on Henry was appalling. My father's son, I had struck the Achilles heel with unerring aim, and Henry rose trembling from his chair and left the pub.

If I had known the effect my words were going to have I hope I would have kept them to myself. A letter arrived next day, sent from Ilfracombe and dated 9pm, 22 December 1969.

Dear Dan,
   I am most sorry that you felt you had to speak (almost in public) as you did in Mugford's tonight. And I can only repeat, *with truth*, that I have never had to 'get my own back' on your father Negley. I understood him. And how alcohol disturbed his judgement, and released at times, a sense of his own social superiority: as when he produced in public General Negley's photograph in order to say to one or another of his pub-stooges 'you never had a general in *your* family, you're a no-good man.' This was repeated in many local pubs to various people near him.

This was truer of Henry's 'Osgood Nilsson' than of my father, who had no sense of social superiority, never used the phrase 'no-good man' as far as I can remember, and whose photograph of the general was handsomely framed, as it is now. Henry continued: 'I had nothing to get back. I liked Negley but loathed his remarks when drunk. So did everyone. Your mother used to apologize for them. It wasn't necessary — we understood Negley. We knew how his leg sapped his vitality, year after year.' This impression of my father as a tortured, neurotic remnant is far from the truth, but perhaps Henry wanted to believe in the decline he depicted in *The Gale of the World*. His letter to me continued on a note of bitterness which seeps through the pages:

But when he tried to *humiliate* those whom he considered his social inferiors — as he often did when poisoned by alcohol, it was 'a bit much'. It was tedious. He did it to me sometimes but it was water off a duck's

155

back. 'I knew my place.' And I remained overtly and inwardly *friendly*. To repeat, I understood him and his torments: and their expression.

After several more paragraphs, Henry suggested that the character of Osgood Nilsson was not so nasty after all:

> If you read without bias, you will see that Osgood was a 'goodie' at the end. He saved many lives. Good for Goodie Nilsson!! Gradually, bit by bit, idea by idea, the book built itself up. Re central theme you appear to have missed. I understand why. I am sympathetic to ALL my characters. But I found it hard to be so to the rapist Lt-Col. Peregrine Bucentaur.
>
> Your remarks — or quotes — of what OM [Oswald Mosley] said to you are very sad to me. I was never really a fascist. I cared for England, I fought for England in 1914-18. I saw another war coming. And so joined BU [the British Union] as late as *1937* in Norfolk; begged to do so by Lady D [his Norfolk neighbour, Dorothy, Lady Downe] a Blackshirt patriot. And having joined, I was always loyal to OM — though it led to much hardship and suffering. I'd do the same for Negley, or you, if you were in trouble.

It is true that Henry was wholly consistent in his views, when others wavered. His loyalty to his friends was absolute when they were attacked; I heard, time and time again, how he sprang to my defence when I was criticized in turn in North Devon. Henry concluded:

> This is all I can say. I am grieved that you are hurt: but I think you need not be, Nilsson is *not* a bad character. He's a hurt man; and, as it turns out, a good man. So is Phillip. And all the others. But not Bucentaur. He was mean. I am not mean. I am sorry — to repeat — you have been distressed. I will not trouble you again with

my presence, Dan. In any case, I am weakening fast, and have just lost the will to live. It's time to go. Bless you, Dan

Henry

PS   I shall be away tomorrow, else I'd come & see you, hoping to ease your unhappiness with my *sincere* belief that I had 'nothing to get back' to poor old Negley.

A generous letter, though I could not help smiling at the dramatic conclusion that he would never see me again, followed by the postscript with his intention to visit me the following day.

Instead I received a letter a week later, 29 December 1969: 'My dear Dan, I got back from Dartmoor — edge of — yesterday, dead beat, streaming eyes — not 'flu, it's been getting worse for weeks, and (I suspect) is psychological.' Henry quoted the cousin he was staying with — 'a great big ex-boxer RAF Grp-Captain' — as praising Osgood Nilsson as 'one of the best characters' in the book; but his words have a familiar, Williamson ring. He then proceeded to give an outline of *The Gale of the World*, with the attempt to rescue Hess, and the 'terrific storm' near Lynton at the end ('gliders frozen — struck by lightning — pilots burned — fall in sea') which resolves itself in clarity with Phillip able to start his Chronicle at last. Then came a revealing admission concerning Henry's relationship with Mosley:

I believe what you said re OM. He spoke to *me* like that, once, at Nicky's wedding reception at the Savoy (1947 or 1948). I begged him NOT to form another party — 'European Union'. I wanted him to write his Memoirs instead. He was NEWS! but bad news. He let loose a sarcastic glance at me and said 'Your place in our Movement, Henry, is to stand by the Savage Club window as we go past down below, & to say "I

157

shouldn't be surprised if there wasn't something in it."'
Well, I didn't mind that. I'd asked for it. But 20 years
later, Diana said 'You did advise Kit to write his
Memoirs and keep quiet — I remember.' She was then
white-haired and had to be sustained by pills, poor
darling.

After further comments on Mosley, Henry ended his letter
with characteristic sweetness which put my original pro-
vocation to shame, though by now I was absorbed by the
correspondence it had produced:

Thank you for your letter, dear Dan. I'm very low — &
have been for months — all 'elan' gone — & the death-
wish strong & constant. I was so happy, too, when I saw
you in the summer. Your letter so cheering. I worried
that you were so unhappy. You needn't be. I was very
fond of your Papa & Mama, & remain so.
     Love from Henry

A kind, considerate letter, but inevitably there was a postscript, for Henry could seldom leave a page alone. In this
case he returned full circle: 'PS. Since writing melancholy
"screed", I have washed, etc., & eaten honey & bread & feel
better. And perhaps you are right in *feeling* a little of "own
back" in the portrait.' Even then he could not leave it there
but had to make further comparisons between Osgood and
my father, finishing with this surprising revelation: 'I was
always most patient with NF when poisoned with alcohol:
& this led him to write me a single letter — "Have you ever
thought you are a masochist?"' As if to make fun of this,
Henry signed his postscript: 'Yours ever "B. A. Boon" (shall
we say) Ha! Ha!'
     In the psychological sense, I believe my father was
correct.

Fortunately, this clash with Henry was brief and in a curious way our friendship grew stronger for it. The same book caused a rift with Kenneth Allsop, however, which was rather more serious. Henry was Ken's ideal, a writer in the great tradition of Hudson, Thoreau, Jefferies, whom Ken admired. Ken was himself a fine writer, awarded the John Llewellyn Rhys Memorial Price for his novel, *Adventure Lit Their Star*; but he turned his talent instead towards journalism, a field in which he felt more confident of shining. His nature articles for the *Daily Mail* and *The Sunday Times* proved how fine he could be. Finally, he became one of the few television personalities whom the viewers respected — but by this time he had become the victim of his success. A perfectionist to the last, Ken confided in me that he was unhappy if he made less than £1000 a month, which was a great deal of money ten years ago, and a considerable burden. By now he owned a beautiful home in Dorset, a former mill house which he loved; but the upkeep was expensive and the terrace, which he insisted on paving with York stone, had to be paid for. Which meant that it had to be worked for. Ken told Colin Wilson how much he envied Henry those early years in Devon, when he spent his days walking over the moors and his nights writing by lamplight. As Wilson records: 'Allsop had become a successful journalist; he said that it would be impossible for him to go back to the days when he had no money, and write more of the books he really wanted to write. He had become too accustomed to driving a sports car and having a bottle of whisky in the cupboard.'

There had already been an earlier falling out two years before *The Gale of the World* was published, when Ken had included Henry in a BBC series, *Personal Choice*. Henry was seventy-two and arrived at the studio expecting a tribute. It is a difficult business, interviewing friends, and neither Henry nor Ken could avoid certain direct questions:

159

Henry, you're a contradictory and complicated man, and your dedication to the ideal of a new man in tune with himself and nature and with his own family has, in fact, resulted in a fairly disrupted personal life. Your marriages haven't worked out, and now you live alone, and you seldom see your children, I think. Do you ever feel that the cost of your sense of mission has been too great upon yourself and upon the people close to you?

By this time Christine had left Henry so it was a devastating question, and one for which he was not prepared. At last he managed a reply:

No, I think the mistake I made was taking on other people's troubles, instead of getting on with my work. But I must say we're a fairly harmonious family now, I see all my children — even my grandchildren call me Henry, which I think is a great privilege. Because I want to feel equal with them. And my wife, Gypsy, who's Mary of *The Pathway*, thinks I've done very well ... she's brilliant ... she's lovely....

A sharp question producing a moving reply, but Henry was dismayed. Even so, he attempted a *rapprochement* two years later, dedicating *The Gale of the World* to Ken. He was rebuffed. Betty Allsop says that 'Ken found it distasteful and disliked it intensely and, although he wrote and thanked Henry for sending it to him, he was unable to bring himself to write further about it.' I remember Ken asking my advice at the time, and my cynical suggestion that he use a euphemism — 'I hope this has the success it merits' or 'Good's not the word for it!' — but Ken had too much integrity for that.

'It was a tragedy for HW,' Betty Allsop recalls, 'because Henry thought this final book would bring him the recognition he had so earned and deserved.'

above Henry in Ireland, 1961, with Amanda Allsop, daughter of Ken and Betty, two of Henry's closest friends. *Betty Allsop*

right Henry and Ken on Woolacombe Sands with Harry and Fabian, 1953. *Betty Allsop*

right Henry with Titus, Ox's Cross, 1964. After Henry had kicked Barry Driscoll's dog, Driscoll threatened to punch him if he ever did it again — and a new relationship dawned. *Barry Driscoll*

above Henry at his happiest, at work on Ox's Cross, c.1950. *Daniel Farson*

Aggravated by Ken's silence, Henry's resentment over the television interview began to fester. In 1973 he sent me a rambling letter with some comments on our own previous television interview for my series, *Something to Say*:

> I well remember the happy times we had, you the Master reporter, on TV some years ago.... I am reminded of this because, while on a half-hour interview with ZX, a well-known BBC TV type — I was not shown questions beforehand — it was suddenly sprung upon me, 'How can you equate your idealism with the fact that you have had two broken marriages?' I had to think quickly, and reply, 'Broken marriages? You should see us all together at Ox's Cross!' Much later, daughter Margaret met the interviewer in a train and he asked why Henry seldom saw him nowadays. She told him. His reply was, 'Well, I am responsible for telling the truth to my public so I must have nothing to hide.'

At the time, I failed to realize that Henry was referring to his old friend Kenneth Allsop.

By luck, they met only a few weeks later at a party. 'To the great joy of both they were reconciled,' says Betty Allsop. 'There is no doubt that both had been very unhappy by the separation.' Amanda Allsop, Ken and Betty's daughter, also met Henry at a party, shortly after the reunion:

> Henry was talking to Gypsy when I arrived. Very drunk (10 pm) and loud. I didn't recognize him at first, much older, more bent. He didn't recognize me. I went up to him and introduced myself. He hugged me and made me sit down (against my will) wandered off to look for wine and got diverted. Eventually he came back. He talks very loudly. I ask him how he is, and he says 'I've been living alone for ten years: I've had to cook for myself, shop for myself...' he changes the

subject constantly and suddenly. Goes on to tell me about a beautiful young girl with whom he parted on bad terms about a year ago. Then he got a Christmas card saying — will you by any chance be in Exeter Cathedral Close at 2 pm on such and such a day. So he went and she was there and everything was wonderful.

Talks about father — saw him at Bill Thomson's exhibition — 'I just went up to him and put my arms round him and hugged him.' Then alternates between deep affection and hurt accusation. Rather muddled story of how dad had suggested he was incapable of maintaining a relationship — 'After two broken marriages...'

Kenneth Allsop died a few weeks after his reconciliation with Henry. He was found at the Old Mill with the telephone off the hook and the front door locked from the inside, propped up in bed in his pyjamas with a clip-board in one hand and a pen in the other, as if he had been working to the very end. The coroner gave an open verdict, saying there was no evidence to show 'how or why Mr Allsop took a drug overdose'.

Ironically, Ken was writing better than ever. By chance his last article in *The Sunday Times* concerned the proud peregrine falcons which meant so much to Henry and himself: 'We poison them, we shoot them, we steal their eggs and young. It is so wrong. We are the predators and killers, not those peregrines. For they and the few of their kind which survive live exalted lives, true to their nature, and we degrade and damage their world which is so beautiful and complex and balanced.'

Henry understood Ken's yearnings better than most people. After Betty had told him 'about the hell of being married to a temperamental writer,' Henry wrote to her on New Year's Eve 1963/4:

It was simply lovely with you and your sweet children at Gurneys last night. What a perfect place it is — the joint work of Ken and yourself. The creation of such a home and family is a very fine achievement: and at the same time, I realize how the strain of Fleet Street & the frustrations of a very sensitive writer like Kenneth, whose gift is for nature & particularly for wild birds, can at times almost overwhelm him.

I speak as one who was for a period overwhelmed and overwhelming. Hold to the truth of a writer's life & depletion steadily and bear with it & never let it overwhelm you. It is not reasonable, logical or true: a mere by-product. The product is the family, the home & the basically good and kind people in it. Never forget this & do not be diverted by cries of pain. with love. Henry.

Betty suspected that this letter described what Henry himself needed and perhaps had once enjoyed: 'I was very moved that he wrote it to me — and it even helped!' She was less moved by Henry's letter of condolence after Ken's death, which returned to the vexed question of the television interview all over again, complaining that Ken's question had been wrong and unfair — 'And this was supposed to be a letter of sympathy on my bereavement!'

But it was Henry who read the address at Kenneth Allsop's funeral (even if it was largely about himself, informing the congregation that he was feeling far from well). And a few years later it was Ken's daughter, Amanda, who read from Shelley's 'Adonais' at the Thanksgiving Service for the life of Henry Williamson.

TEN

The sun without shadows

WHEN I FIRST KNEW HENRY in Devon he read so much of his work aloud that I glimpsed his books in sections instead of reading them for myself. The first Williamson novel that I read from start to finish was *The Scribbling Lark*, which was an unfortunate introduction for it was a minor whimsical exercise. Of course Henry had his faults as a writer: he tended to overlard a sentence, often spoiling the effect by adding to it; he used archaic, almost biblical words to create an impression of deep feeling; and he indulged in overblown passages which I find hard to take, though others admire them — such as the whispered lines in *The Starborn* (1933), which he regarded as his 'gospel': 'In the eastern sky the Morning Star, Eosphoros the Lightbringer, glowed with its white fires. Joyfully the song of water arose in the valley. The poet looked at the maiden, and he knew that his search was ended; for on that brow was sunrise.' It is easy sport picking at passages like this. Finally, a writer must be judged by work that will pass the test of time, and Henry provided this in abundance.

His letters, alone, if compiled by his son Richard, will provide compelling reading for the future. Because Henry was self-absorbed, every detail around him mattered and he described it vividly. He wrote to me that 'a gash is painful to one as an amputation to another', and with Henry it was always a gaping wound though it probably healed itself by the time he stuck down the envelope.

He wrote so much that I have merely skimmed the surface here: his fine study of war in *The Patriot's Progress;* the tetralogy of 'The Flax of Dream', as tender as their titles suggest — *The Beautiful Years, Dandelion Days,* and *A Dream of Fair Women,* though many readers feel a particular affinity with the final, sadder volume, *The Pathway*; a number of short stories that should live as long as people read; and, of course, the animal books, such as *Tarka,* for which he is remembered. But it is the fifteen volumes of 'A Chronicle of Ancient Sunlight' which confirm that Henry Williamson was a great writer: if he had need to redeem himself, which I doubt, he did so here.

Before I read them, I assumed that 'The Flax of Dream' was Henry's masterpiece, a lyrical evocation of England between the wars. I read the four volumes on holiday several years ago, under an Aegean sky which enhanced the gentleness of the English countryside he was describing with such joy. By chance I was in Greece again, more recently, when I read the first volumes of the 'Chronicle', and the distance helped me to see Henry's canvas in perspective. It is immense.

Because of this range, the 'Chronicle' has been compared to Tolstoy, Proust and Dickens. But the image that occurs to me is that of a Breughel painting, which shows us a landscape alive in detail in which every person, going about their business or their play, is granted an equal importance.

Henry portrayed a middle-class England at the turn of the century, when everyone believed that life would get better; a dream that Henry shared himself until his disillusionment in the First War. At first I found his pace leisurely, until I became immersed in the struggles and fortunes of the Maddison family in the suburbs of London, which was swelling before their eyes, advancing into the countryside like a great inky stain. At first I was uncertain if I was expected to feel sympathy for the character of Richard Maddison, and particularly his son Phillip, until I realized this was never Henry's intention and remembered his letter to me, 'I am sympathetic to all my characters'.

This is Henry's strength, that he treats them all with equal compassion, the hypocrites and humbugs as well as the decent men and women with all their wistful hopes and vanities and fears. Henry makes no judgement. At last I understood what he meant by the declaration, 'I would learn to see all things as the sun saw them, without shadows' — which had always irritated me, since light and shade are the essence of life. Henry's extraordinary achievement in the early volumes lies in standing aside, casting no shadows himself, so that the reader can see with absolute clarity and judge the characters and their landscape for himself. Few conclusions will be the same, just as people view a great painting differently.

The 'Chronicle' is unique in my view, so the claim by Roger Mortimore that it is 'the one English novel to rival Tolstoy' strikes me as irrelevant, and the comparison to Dickens as misleading. Dickens dealt in bold brush-strokes and glorious exaggeration, with villains who were insufferably bad and heroines only slightly less insufferably good. Dickens cast his shadow effectively on every page: we know exactly how he felt and intended us to feel. There is no Dickensian morality in the 'Chronicle': Henry tried to convey the truth without prejudice and did so without resort to cut and thrust or the calculated feint. These volumes could not have been written by anyone else. No wonder he was eager to write them after leaving the Norfolk farm, for this is what he had been waiting to achieve since 'The Flax of Dream'.

Henry had set himself a task which would have daunted

most writers: the pursuit of one family from birth to death in a series of fifteen volumes. Imagine the excitement if Dickens had developed the same characters over several books, but I doubt if he would have had the patience, or the time for such meticulous concentration. Henry's research was formidable, but it never shows through. A fine portrait of the tedium of suburban life in the early 1900s was achieved without being tedious.

Mistakenly, I started with the marvellous second volume, *Donkey Boy*. It is better, of course, to begin at the beginning with *The Dark Lantern,* which explains so much about the father and reveals him in another light: for the 'Chronicle' is a saga about fathers and sons and their inability to communicate with each other. To begin with I found it hard to reconcile Richard as the severe, intolerant father, with Phillip as the misunderstood, sensitive child, for it seemed that the son was just as difficult as the father. I missed the point: far from indicting his own father through the character of Richard, Henry is making amends by revealing him also as a man of principle, too virtuous for his own or his family's happiness. Local youths jeer at 'Christ on tin wheels' as he rides past primly on his bicycle, but once he escapes into the countryside Richard is released and we see him on his own, exuberant.

Richard marries Hetty secretly after her hypocritical father, Tom Turney, has rejected his prospective son-in-law with such open contempt that Richard can never forgive. When Turney learns of his daughter's clandestine marriage, he knocks her unconscious. Afterwards she leaves home to live with Richard openly as husband and wife at last, but the banking firm he works for has also discovered the marriage and dismisses him under the rule that no member of staff can marry if they earn less than £150 a year.

From then on, it is a life of forced gentility, with decorum, decency and discipline as the principles to follow. It was audacious of Henry to choose such a background: a father who is dull and almost Pooterish in his respectability; a son who is difficult, a liar, and in many ways unattractive. Critics complained of this, failing to see that dull unattractive people are all around us, and many people live with them. Henry could have indulged in colourful characters who were larger than life, the Fagins and Betsy Trotwoods, but Henry's families are ordinary — on the surface. The more we learn about them, the more extraordinary they become, though they always remain trapped by ordinary convention.

An immense cast is revealed. The central figures — Hetty, tamed by her husband's impatience; Richard, diminished by her anxiety to please him; Phillip, their difficult son — are surrounded by a galaxy of relations and friends and acquaintances: Aunt Theodora, too progressive for her own time; Uncle Hilary, who has done well overseas and returns with a dashing new horseless carriage; Hugh Turney, suffering from the then unmentionable disease of syphilis, whose gradual decline is shown without sentimentality but is moving nevertheless; the jolly vicar, Mr Mundy, cavorting on his sled when Blackheath is covered with snow at Christmas; Mona Monk, the pathetic maid who has been seduced by her father; the wistful courage of the poor-boy Cranmer, grateful for Phillip's attention — hundreds of characters, and none could be described as 'lesser', for Henry is devoted to them all. He was wise to wait until he knew that human frailty was just as attractive as heroism, and much the same in the end. As the story gradually unfolds and the characters spring into focus under his microscope, he records their ambitions and disappointments with equal compassion.

The background is completely convincing, as authentic as an early photograph, as if Henry had been there himself — which he had as a very small boy. The 'Chronicle' may lack the gusto of Dickens, but in the portrayal of a slice of life it is as truthful.

At the end of 1949, Henry was thankful to have the opportunity to embark on the 'Chronicle' at last. Though the process of writing was hard, it was all that mattered. Answering Thomas Olsen, a young reporter on the *Newcastle Evening World*, who had written to him for advice, Henry urged him to stick to journalism rather than move to the countryside as he intended:

> After a bit, a holiday that goes on being a holiday ceases to be anything like a holiday. I also believe very strongly that one does better work working against time or against other work. Force of circumstance is a splendid spur. Believe me, the trouble with most writers who for the time being are economically independent, is that their natural indolence tends to enslave them. I believe in work because only by work is play really play.

No one could deny Henry his industry. On his return to North Devon, as he contemplated the 'Chronicle', he felt the exhilaration of a traveller embarking on a long-awaited journey. 'After 20 years, I begin to see clear sky, to write my own books again,' he wrote to me at Cambridge. 'In the past, journalism irked and sapped. All bits and pieces, necessary to get money to live and support others. Now I must stop all that and concentrate on my own books.'

That year he was badly in need of money, so he had the necessary spur. He started optimistically, as he confided in a letter to my mother on 26 December asking us to tea on New Year's Day, and revealing his hopes for *The Dark Lantern*:

> There are a lot of potential readers (or were; many

must have died of natural causes!) who await this book ever since 1928 in fact, & I think it best for it to be kept entirely hidden until a week or two before publication — if it is to be published, one can't tell until it's completed. It's very difficult to do, all being imagined, all completely new to me, even the characters appear & grow as it proceeds — which is perhaps the proper condition for the completely free & untrammelled imagination. And this way, one understands & loves the characters as a mother her children, defects & all!

Within a year, this enthusiasm was shattered by the news from Collins that there would be no publication of *The Dark Lantern* in 1950, and possibly not in 1951, either.

Henry travelled to London shortly after Christmas 1950 with the much-revised manuscript and was told, 'Mr Collins is too busy to see you, very sorry, he has to catch a train.' Henry commented that the coincidence was ominous, and, sure enough, when he did find the time to read the manuscript, Collins told Henry he could cancel their contract if he wished; in other words he turned it down. Apparently the main trouble was an 'unattractive hero' in Richard Maddison.

Henry claimed that he paid back part of the advance and took the manuscript to Faber & Faber, his former publisher, where he was told that the directors were not in the friendliest of moods in view of what had happened in the past. They rejected it in their turn, even though the valued name of Williamson would have returned to the Faber imprint. Henry took the news bravely: 'Fabers,' he commented privately, 'have lost their touch. They think I have lost mine. An engine can lose tune so gradually that the driver is scarcely aware of it happening . . . . Well, they have missed a unique series, if I live to complete it!'

He needed every scrap of his self-confidence. By now his

financial situation was critical. At the end of the year his total earnings came to £165, but he managed to take three weeks' holiday in France, driving straight to Bungay in Norfolk afterwards where he read the manuscript chapter by chapter to Loetitia: 'She said it was a perfect book, the characters living & real, and even protested when I ameliorated some of the reactions of the hyper-nervous Richard. She said it was exciting, true to life, unexaggerated, and she could not see how the critics could have thought otherwise.'

His faith restored by her encouragement, Henry now sent the manuscript to Malcolm Elwin, the reader for Macdonald. It had been re-written twelve times. Elwin accepted the lengthy novel of 183,000 words at once, and the struggle for publication was over at last.

In those days publishers moved quickly, the book was printed in proof form within four days, and then:

> as Zero day approached, we sent a dozen copies round to famous authors, and I inscribed them. The subscription disappointed Macdonalds: their traveller conference reported, from all over the country, resistance to the book. The booksellers simply didn't want anything of HW. 'His readers don't like him any more.' M's had paid an advance on 10,000 copies; they subscribed 250 to Smiths, 360 to Boots, rest in proportion. (I suppose Smiths and Boots bought between them about 35,000 of a Priestley novel.) Anyway they didn't mind. Macs found what Faber had told me: public gone. As the advance was long ago spent on education, etc., HW wind up. Book awful; dull; hated writing it; boring etc., etc. Dull as concrete underground base of house. No one replied. Reviews negative, very few, 3, after the first fortnight out.

The bitter disillusionment was understandable; the truth, inescapable. The gap between his novels had been too long, and many of his readers had been unable to forgive him for that declaration to the 'great man across the Rhine'. Henry Williamson was out of fashion; indeed, one critic was to call the 'Chronicle' 'the most unfashionable novel of our time'. This set the pattern for the next twenty years of struggle and lack of recognition, and helps explain many of Henry's moods and actions during this period. Inevitably, Henry turned against the work which appeared to be doomed to oblivion, but at this low point he received a letter of encouragement from the writer Frank Swinnerton:

> I have read with enthusiasm; because the book is a classic in the classic manner. It has most of the things I like best — fun, insight, and beauty among them — and from the very first page sets up an enchantment by its most artful simplicity, which keeps going through the whole book in a most marvellous way. The writing is lovely. AB [Arnold Bennett] would have given you full marks, as I do. I am sure you will have great success with the book, now and onwards into the far distant future.

Henry was elated by Swinnerton's response, *amazed* and *shaken*: 'The past fortnight had been black depression; knowing I had failed before I started; local papers sent copy for review, didn't bother to do it; not one copy in local shop. One bookseller said, "Isn't your name Wilkinson?"'

With a fresh surge of optimism Henry started to write *Lucifer* as a separate book from the series. He had been working on it for years: 'Suddenly this nitwit saw what to do. He would turn Lucifer into a novel with PM as centre at once and not wait until 1980 to produce a genuine old period light lantern. And at once the thing leapt alive! I doted on it; I could splash about, I could say what I liked about PM from the start, because I was no longer restricted to a deadly monotone, a narrow form, a stifling vehicle.'

172

But he knew he was being false to himself. He returned to *Donkey Boy* in chronological sequence, as the second volume in the 'Chronicle', while *Lucifer Before Sunrise* finally became the fourteenth. Henry had been working on *Donkey Boy* at the same time as *Lucifer* and had finished 23,000 words: 'I am now at 1900. I like it, what is more. I never did the Lantern. It scared me .... You should not assume that these books are autobiographical,' he wrote to John Hanson. 'The grain of mustard seed maybe; but the tree therefrom is growth free from air, and possibly soil.' When he was 60,000 words into the book and still exuberant, he made the significant comment on the first volume: 'Of course I didn't mean my characters to be attractive; I hoped they would be interesting, i.e. book readable.'

This sense of well-being was short-lived, for his expectations were shattered once again with the publication of *Donkey Boy* at the end of 1952: 'Timid now, & morbidly sensitive: a feeling of being passé & no good. An ageing chorus girl in the back row. Reviewers have chucked it aside. Macdonalds say it hasn't sold at all.' Ten thousand copies had been printed but the book stopped selling at 4,000, leaving Henry wondering if he should repay half his £750 advance. Defiantly he quoted Loetitia's praise for *Donkey Boy*, 'says she's read it thrice, and thinks it beautiful'; but he added, 'I wish I knew if it was real, good, or vital.'

He persevered, he had no alternative, though he knew that it would be difficult to sustain the original freshness and that he would have to work even harder: 'It is the only way to get a book done, to live in it by excluding everything else.' This meant he had to live like a hermit, which was against his nature and virtually impossible; but it helps to explain his rage when he was interrupted. Writing wistfully to a friend about Ox's Cross, he said:

It is nice up here, but one lives in dread of being visited.

After digging an acre, clearing it, helping neighbours pitch hay, then writing hours at a stretch on top of it, or before it, visitors, all on holiday and relaxed (except certain psychopaths who drain one of blood) — no time to bathe or sail or do anything I would LIKE to do, it is sheer weariness, concealed, one hopes, to have to stand up to the egos of others. Fortunately, one's books are dud; no sales, no readers; so visitors are few and far, though nine came last week, three of them in a butcher's van from Ilfracombe, the best of the lot! They apparently approved of Devon books and funny bits. What is more they had four new ones from Smiths in the van, brought out for signature. I had not the heart to resist.

He was supported by Loetitia's encouragement and the perception of the few critics who recognized the value of the 'Chronicle' at once. Maurice Wiggin called the novels 'one of the few truly great achievements in twentieth-century fiction', and John Betjeman (in *The Daily Telegraph*) was one of the first to praise *The Dark Lantern*: 'There is magic in this book ... this excursion into a late Victorian suburb and merchant materialism is unexpected and it is as genuine and affectionate as it is accomplished.' George Painter reviewed the fourth volume, *How Dear is Life* (1954), in *The Listener*: 'Mr Williamson's prose is like sunlight and clean air; and then, when necessary, it has the taste of fear in the mouth, the terrible beauty of life on the edge of the abyss'; while John Middleton Murry, in his book on Katherine Mansfield, singled out *A Fox Under My Cloak*, which dealt with the Great War:

I do not know of any picture of the 1914–18 war which can be compared with it for sheer power of enduring in the reader's memory. In a queer way it is not terrible; it does not haunt so much as satisfy the imagination. It is human, it is humorous, it is pathetic, it is noble — and above all else it is beautiful. It is the work of a truly gifted artist, come at last, after much inward travail, to a mastery of his own self-disturbing powers and working on the grand scale.

Judging by the first five novels, Murry predicted, 'This will be in its entirety one of the most remarkable English novels of our time.'

With such belief to sustain him, Henry laboured over his epic for the next twenty years.

Was Murry's prediction fulfilled? Possibly Henry laboured too long and embraced too many volumes, for there is a slight falling-off as Henry grew older and tired, but that does not detract from the early perfection. Every reader will have his own opinion but, as we have seen, many were shocked by the fifteenth and final volume, *The Gale of the World*.

That book was unlucky from the start: publication was held up for months due to Henry's alterations to the galley-proofs, which were even more extensive than usual; then, after 3,000 copies had been printed and bound, a type transposition was discovered and they had to be scrapped. Finally, 6,000 copies were published in 1969, and Henry wrote with relief that 'during those years one had been visited by fear of failure at all levels, together with exaltation which at times arose to a point of feeling oneself to be in a glow, to be in levitation.' Francis King's review was less glowing: 'Even the weariest river winds somewhere safe to sea.'

The Gale of the World is barely recognizable as the work of the same man who wrote *The Dark Lantern* and *Donkey Boy* with their scrupulous discipline and impartiality. Compassion has been replaced by anger, and this at least commands respect as Henry goes raging into the dark night.

There is a feeling of bitter, weary frustration in Phillip's relationships with various women, and a sexual frankness which was alien to Henry's personal discretion on such matters. He was even accused of trying to be 'trendy', to use that wretched description of people who are trying to be something which they are not. One passage reveals just how far Henry has strayed, as Laura remembers an abortion:

> I'm no good anyway. No-one ever waited, made love so that I really wanted it. Or stayed afterwards. Perhaps she was a repressed homosexual, men unconsciously wanting revenge? What made female cats attack a eunuch tom-cat? Because it was a peeping tom, and if strong, pounced on other courting toms — scratched, bit them, likewise females. Out of spite? Am I like that, really? Wanting revenge, because my father raped me when I was a child, was it punishment for coming on him when he was frigging the nanny goat behind the hedge? If I wrote that, no-one would believe it. Mother found out and I had to sleep with Grannie ever afterwards....
>
> Was it when we started to walk upright? Animals are shapely, compared with women after twenty-five. Black brassières and French knickers — trap for John Thomas, Esquire — and finally cancer of the breast, from too much mauling. God, I am human bait, nothing more....

The fact that Henry retained his power to shock at the age of seventy-four cannot be denied him, but his readers did not expect him to write like this, while others detested the blatant support for Sir Oswald Mosley, disguised as Sir Hereward Birkin. Just as Henry did in the Savage Club, Phillip Maddison aired his political views in The Barbarians: 'Atrocities induce atrocities — all those civilians burned by our phosphorous bombs on German towns — all those Jews

burned in revenge.' It is the time of the Nuremberg trials
after the war and Phillip wonders aloud 'if, when the history
of this war ever comes to be written impartially, it will be
learned, for example, that the art treasures found in German
salt-mines were put there to be out of the way of Allied
bombing?'

Past images rise to the surface with the murkiness of a
dream. There is a sentimental reference to the altercation
with Windles (depicted as Billy) on the Norfolk farm at the
end of the war:

> [Phillip's] left eye, which had been stinging while he
> wrote the letter, was now sharply hurting. It had been
> like that, when he was tired, ever since Billy had driven
> his fist into it. Whenever he thought of his eldest son, it
> was as though he was speaking to Billy's image: Never
> worry, if you are near me, Boy Billy, it was all my own
> fault. We were both breaking down on the farm, the
> war was within us. I love you dearly, Boy Billy; I love
> you.

Henry tried to expunge the past by disposing of his characters (as if he knew that the real relationships would never
survive). He resorted to the usual expiation here, with
Billy's death in the Alps, just as Willie Maddison had to
drown in *The Pathway* and Barleybright fell to her death in a
mountaineering accident in *The Sun in the Sands*. In the
'Chronicle', Phillip's idealized first wife dies in childbirth.
Colin Wilson has commented that: 'Williamson seems to
have this obsessive need to insist that he lost the love of his
life through the cruelty of fate; in fact, the majority of his
close relationships with women seem to have been broken up
because he was an intolerable husband or lover, selfish, bad-
tempered and neurotic.'

Richard Maddison is allowed a natural death in *The Gale of
the World*, but the scene is macabre as Phillip tells him that his

grandson Billy is dead before him. As he leaves the hospital room, after an attempt at reconciliation, Phillip hears a groan of despair and returns to tell him with the utmost cruelty: 'Father, I know it's no consolation, but think of Billy, he and his crew had to bail out over the Alps, and Billy was held by his parachute on a crag and frozen to death. Your grandson was a brave boy, Father.' Richard Maddison turns his face to the wall, and Phillip hears his last words: 'I begin to see you are against me too, are you? Well, you must be on your way — I must not keep you.'

There are other passages where Henry recalls his own childhood with that objectivity which was both the pride of his writing and his personal hell. Phillip describes the death of his mother, Hetty:

> When she was dying I kissed her on the brow without emotion. After her burial I prayed to go down into the grave with her. At the same time I shouted within myself that she leave me alone. And in times of stress my thoughts of her have been impatient: that she was so afraid of my father, that she extended his nervousness: the result being that I grew up in fear of him and a coward.

Even at this late moment, Henry is searching for an alibi; but the mystery remains: an alibi for what? Surely not his own inadequacy? Significantly, in *Donkey Boy*, it is only the most intelligent of his relatives, Aunt Theodora, who really appreciates the talent that lies behind the mischief which exasperates his father. Perhaps if Henry had liked himself more, Phillip Maddison would have been more sympathetic to his readers. As it was, many of them could not stand him. Colin Wilson's opinion that Phillip was 'a most irritating person' was shared by many critics: 'So arrogant, so vain, so domineering,' Francis King; 'Maddison is his customary spikey, self-righteous self,' David Holloway; 'A suburban bank clerk,' John Davenport; 'Young as he is, naïve as he is, and to that extent forgivable, Phillip Maddison is also, at times, simply a bloody fool,' John Terraine; while George Painter and Bernard Bergonzi come close to describing Henry himself with their respective verdicts on Phillip Maddison — 'a divided man, sometimes cruel, cowardly and sinful, sometimes possessed of courage, kindness and insight,' and 'Phillip's character ... is complex: he is inconsequential and often light-hearted; at the same time he is remarkably lacking in self-confidence and plagued by anxieties and is liable, for the best of motives, to act in a foolishly rash or blundering manner.'

As I have mentioned, it was never Henry's intention to show Phillip as an attractive hero; he knew himself too well for that. With *The Gale of the World* he was writing the book he wished to write, not completing the 'Chronicle' as others expected. That he looked back in torment makes it strangely powerful though many people felt he went too far. Colin Wilson found it shocking:

> quite simply too personal; he is again scratching old sores and regurgitating old venom.... It rambles on, with a mixture of autobiography, fantasy and wish-fulfilment, leaving Phillip in the arms of the aristocratic Melissa Wilby. Phillip tells her: 'You have brought love to me, love that dissolves arrogance and hatred.' But you feel that nothing will ever dissolve Williamson's arrogance and hatred.

Yet this passion is the strength of the book. It reaches a climax with a violent storm, based on the Lynton flood disaster which Henry witnessed in 1952.

The 'Chronicle' comes full circle as Phillip is discovered alive and ready to start his own epic work with the help of Melissa:

> With you I shall be able to begin my chronicle! Do you

179

know, I'm glad I didn't write novels before. They
would probably have been angry and satirical if written
in the 'thirties. Now I think I can understand every kind
of man and woman. Particularly my father.

I shall start my chronicle in the mid-nineties, on a
spring night, with that reserved shy young man walking
up the hill at Wakenham. He was carrying his dark
lantern....'

Melissa comforts him. 'Weep no more old soldier,' she
whispers, and, as they walk romantically hand in hand along
the shore, Phillip rejoices in the love she has brought him —
'love that dissolves arrogance and hatred ... love by which
one can see all things as the sun sees them; without shadows.'
He holds up his arms crying, 'Oh my friends! My friends in
ancient sunlight!'

Henry completed the manuscript on the afternoon of
Sunday 11 February 1968 in his cottage at Ilfracombe, adding
a postscript as if he was reluctant to say goodbye to an old
friend:

I got up from my writing table overcome by emotion,
crying out words of grief and amazement while walking aimlessly about the rooms of the cottage empty
except for myself, disturbed by feelings of a lost freedom which also had been a tyranny during the two
decades now closed behind one.

Behind the tears were love and gratitude that one
had been born in England, that one had been privileged
to experience hardship that had burned away the selfish
dross of oneself, and thereby, perhaps, made one wor-
thy of an attempt to speak for those who had not come
back from the Western Front.

Everything in Henry's life stemmed from that Western
Front after which there could never be such innocence again,
though he searched for it always.

ELEVEN

Second marriage

HENRY HAD MARRIED his second wife, Christine Duffield, in 1949 and their son Harry was born on 12 May 1950. I remember Christine as unaffected and cheerful. She had considerable spirit, founding a school with her friend, Elizabeth Olive, with assistance from the Parents National Education Union. Renting a cottage at one end of Croyde beach, they coped with an average of twenty-five pupils at £30 a term. In the morning the children worked hard, but they were allowed to do much as they liked in the afternoon: playing games or going on nature rambles, swimming or dividing into armies. Harry Williamson loved it:

> There were so many activities; we had a band, I played bass drum, and there was not a feeling of school so much as organized fun. Subsequently, I learned that a disproportionately large number of children got good degrees, which suggests to me that a certain amount of interest and freedom is worth a lot more than severe discipline on its own which was the alternative in schooling at that time.

His rôle as the teacher's son was not as awkward as it might have been: 'Mother was very good at that and it made no difference. Probably she beat me harder than anyone else if they were naughty.'

Even Henry was pleased, writing to a friend in November 1955: 'We are fairly snug here. Christine teaches at Croyde, with Poody [*sic*]. Leaves 8.30 am, returns 4.30 pm. Bus. I usually meet them with the van. They love the work — 22 tots in a cottage school.'

In view of the demands that Henry made of those closest to him, it could be said that the breakdown of the second marriage was inevitable. But one cause of it might have been averted: the sheer weight of the 'Chronicle' material which began to press down on their lives. My father's easy gibe that Henry had dredged the material for his first-war novels from old copies of the *Illustrated London News* was unworthy. Henry of course took advantage of every source available to convey, convincingly and accurately, the rhythm of life in Edwardian England: and he succeeded. He had a remarkable ear for dialect (and even baby talk) and drew above all from his rich imagination; but extensive research into the period was essential, and indeed the sheer bulk of documents grew so alarmingly that Henry became quite desperate in his efforts to keep his papers under control. Needing extra space, he thought of buying a cottage in Appledore for £350, 'Near the pub where the BY [Bright Young] People once haunted, and E. Waugh wrote, in seclusion, *Vile Bodies*.'

Though little evidence is left, it is true that the Bright Young People came there in the early 1930s: old fishermen relate with relish how they rowed visitors to the yacht anchored in the estuary where the celebrated drug-addict, Brenda Dean Paul, swam naked; the village of Instow, opposite, enjoyed an élite invasion of wealthy lesbians in the summer; while Evelyn Waugh once stayed on Lundy Island for a holiday with friends (the legend persists that either Williamson or Waugh escaped through a pub window in Appledore to avoid a meeting, but this is a hearsay after fifty years). When Henry considered the cottage in 1953, he was saddened by the changes he found in the village of Appledore — 'Paper, Walls ice cream cartons, shrieking children. A polluted estuary; a £1 million electric-coal station erected just over the water on the snipe bogs that once were. The Burrows are a tank ground now.' He was remembering the estuary from halcyon days, when he was younger and the landscape fresher.

He thought of moving to Ireland to be near his old friend, Sir John Heygate, but decided he was 'too tired, too old, to pull up roots again'. So Henry bought a cottage in Ilfracombe, at Capstone Place near the harbour, 'on impulse' for the modest sum of £75, or so he claimed. Later he regretted this, complaining to a friend that the cottage was being gutted for re-building, but the workmen were letting him down: 'I am out of my depth with it.' At least the cottage took the overflow of documents, but these continued to increase with every book.

After a childhood which must have been more difficult than he suggests today, Harry Williamson speaks sympathetically of his father's troubles, acknowledging Henry's intrinsic decency:

> I have very warm memories of my early childhood; his relationship with my mother was fresh at that time and hadn't got to the problem area that occurred later. He was writing and one wouldn't see him for several days at a time, or briefly for a cup of tea, and then he'd go back to work — so it's not surprising I have no powerful memory of him during the first few years, though I do remember being scooped up and kissed and hugged. Father and mother had a delayed honeymoon in France, and as there was no room in the back of the Aston Martin I was sent to Gypsy in Norfolk. I don't remember too much except that it was great fun and she was very kind.

When did he realize that his father was famous? Harry

could remember to the day. 'I used to build guns when I was a kid, out of bits of aluminium tubing and cork and gunpowder which I stole when I was five or six, absolutely lethal really, and stuff them with paper and a bag of old tintacks.' One day, he was hiding behind the hedge ready to fire at strangers when a car stopped and a man got out. ' "What's that you've got?" I said, "A gun." "That's a nice toy." "It's not a toy," I told him indignantly, "it works." ' The visitor who had come to see his father was the second Earl Haig, son of the British Commander-in-Chief after 1915. Unlike many of his contemporaries, Henry appreciated the difficulties of the generals and did not condemn them (another example of his ability to see both sides of any argument). As for Harry, he thought, Hey! That's a very important man come to see my father, and realized that Henry was different. 'This was an impression I tried to fight because it seemed to attach a stigma and I was different enough as it was, living up here totally alone with no childhood friends I could speak of until I was about ten.'

Harry was at Millfield School when he realized that his parents were separating and he tried to find out exactly what was going on.

I considered it my *right* to understand what was happening to my parents. It all stemmed from the fact that my mother tried to re-organize Henry's life; she was fed up with boxes full of unopened letters and him swearing at his fans because they wrote too many letters and he was not able to deal with them, saying every day that he wanted a secretary, and then a secretary would come and he'd say, 'No, I don't want a secretary,' and she'd be fired, or else he'd try to get off with them, and my mother would be there, and there'd be a tremendous friction between the two women, obviously, what do you expect ... he was a bit like that.

We didn't have this house then [the new building at Ox's Cross], Henry used to work in the Hut and the studio, and there was the caravan where my mother used to cook and eat. Then we bought the house in Ilfracombe which rapidly became full of papers. By 1959 it was too confusing for her.

It seems surprising that Christine failed to realize when she married him that life with Henry would be complicated, but Harry points out that his father had only just returned from Norfolk and was starting life afresh, having thrown all his old papers away. 'I remember it being very tidy and ordered and gradually getting more confused as this enormous amount of research accumulated for the 'Chronicle', you've no idea, it kept on getting worse and worse.'

I asked Harry why they were unable to make allowances for his vital research. 'It's not as if he would finish a book and then throw all those papers away. He'd leave them out in case he needed to refer to them, five books later. This is logical but in the end it came to the point when he would spend hours searching for some references because his filing system wasn't together . . . among them would be old cheque stubs and press cuttings, the organization was falling to pieces.' At the same time, Henry had a vague idea where everything was in the hundreds of thousands of scattered papers, and a total reorganization might have been disastrous, apart from being a full-time job in itself.

Mentally exhausted, Henry wrote to friends for encouragement, comparing his troubles to those of writers before him:

I feel hesitant and ashamed of appearing once more as a fuddy duddy introvert-failure. I have been fighting this cowardly feeling, which is stronger than I've had it before. One needs constant reassurance and one in that condition is a BORE and a life-waster of others. Pit of

stomach like lead, etc. I have been reading Scott Fitzgerald's CRACK UP, in the new volume, and learn that
at 40 he was done-for, all books out of print, & fighting
alcoholism. Now he is an Alumni [*sic*] of Princeton,
every scrap is cared for, bless him; and Princeton.

Another time Henry referred to the 'icy yet kindly aloof-
ness' of Somerset Maugham — 'He has no illusions: he had a
disastrous early life, like so many writers.' Plainly Henry
was thinking of himself.

Inevitably, Henry blunted his frustration by finding fault
with those around him. In such cases, the cause of grievance
can be as insignificant as a slice of burnt toast: Christine's
offence was the installation of a gas fire in the caravan,
because the coal fire took two hours to light. To Henry this
was proof that her mind was 'unbalanced'. Harry Williamson
thought it reasonable: 'It's dangerous, sure, but people
do have gas fires in a caravan. In defence of my mother, it
may be illogical but in some ways it is convenient to put in a
gas fire and save yourself two hours lighting time, and not
particularly unbalanced.'

Amanda Allsop remembers an incident when Henry lost
his temper when she was a child on holiday, staying with the
family at the cottage in Ilfracombe: 'Christine had left the
milk out of the fridge so he screamed and shouted and poured
the milk away and screamed and shouted a bit more, and I do
remember feeling dreadfully sorry for Christine and thinking what a rotten life she had — I remember because it was
the first time in my selfish childhood that it occurred to me
that adults could have a bad time.'

This was the period when Henry confided in my mother
that he feared he was going mad.

The atmosphere was poisoned by the pressure of work.
While Christine and Harry slept in the caravan, Henry
stayed in the Hut writing into the night, but he started

emerging at dawn with his gun, firing over the top of the caravan as a summons to bring him his tea. It was a terrifying start to their day, to be woken by the blast of gunfire. Harry also remembers Henry's violence:

> I remember him beating up my mother, and bruises and screams, and I would come along and I would attack him and as soon as I attacked him he would start crying, and say 'What am I doing, that my son should have to stop me beating my wife?' Not verbatim, but words to that effect. It was like he was possessed by demons. That might be melodramatic, but there are all sorts of things we don't understand and I'm sure that's one of them. I think it was something to do with the pressure of war as well. It was something that he *met* in the war.

I wondered if Henry's experience in the First War had become the perennial alibi, but Harry Williamson is certain that it troubled him physically as well as mentally all his life. Apart from frequent pain and cramp in his toes, Henry suffered from the after-effects of mustard gas: he was left with a bad lung and one eye which watered constantly, so that he was forever removing his glasses to dab it with a handkerchief (this is referred to in the novels, although Harry stresses that they are not strictly autobiographical). Harry also remembers that whenever there was an explosion in the nearby slate quarry at night, Henry would wake up 'still dozy and cry out, "What's that! Has the bombardment started?"' — as if he were re-living his time in the trenches. Another time, when Harry was entertaining his friends by playing 'heavy rock-and-roll', Henry thought he heard gunfire, but that confusion is understandable.

Harry told me:

> The tragedy for my father was that for him the Edwardian period had produced a particular flowering of

beautiful people in England at the beginning of the century, and it was terrible to see them just wiped out. If there had been a war in 1966 when the post-war children had grown up in prosperity without any shadow of war, and they had suddenly been wiped out in a nuclear holocaust, imagine how we would feel if we had survived. It would remain with us for the rest of our lives.

It was torment for Henry but also for those around him. Christine finally left him in 1962 to teach in the Exmoor village of Exford, though she told her son later that she could never be sure if she had made the right decision: 'She was terribly worried. She was an insecure person, her mother was very Victorian and repressive, and having the corner-stone of her life pulled away, or having pulled herself away, she felt a strong Protestant sense of guilt.'

Henry went to Exford with the hope of winning her back — transformed, as Harry describes him, 'from the general-issimo into a romantic fool again'. But it was too late. By this time she was seeing the man she was later to marry, and there were the first signs of the disturbing illness to come. When she was found in the middle of the night wandering in her nightgown, she was taken to hospital in Exeter where they gave her electrical shock treatment for several months. Harry considered this unnecessary and believed it helped to destroy her memory: 'They told her, "It's for your own good, to forget the past," but they didn't take into account that it was erasing the present as well. She was terrified of it. She used to say to me, "Don't let them take me there again, it's so frightening."'

The uncertainty of the doctors must have been frightening as well. They diagnosed various illnesses but she became worse after 1966, with severe headaches, loss of appetite and balance, and a gradual loss of her strength until she was virtually bedridden. Just when the doctors had decided that she was suffering from multiple sclerosis, luck turned in her favour with a visit to an expert neurologist in Plymouth who discovered that a tumour had been forcing the two halves of her brain apart. 'It was a relief,' said her son, 'that finally they did *know* what was wrong with her. One prays that now she will be all right.'

An extremely delicate and intricate operation was needed, but the tumour was removed successfully. Indeed, as I saw for myself in Appledore in 1981, Christine's perseverance has been rewarded eventually by complete recovery. That dreadful chapter in her life is over at last. 'When you've been very near to dying, you realise how good life is. I think that happened to Henry too. He knew how lucky he was to be alive when so many of his friends were killed in the First War.'

Like so many who were close to Henry, and knew his unkindness, Christine remembers him affectionately today. Her Ingrid Bergman smile, which I remember so well, still lights up as she talks of Henry, and her illness — even though the two were not unconnected.

'I dearly loved the man. But he did drive me completely round the bend — perhaps I was too young.'

'Was he cruel?' I asked, as I had of Loetitia.

She hesitated, denied it, then laughed the thought away — 'Aren't all the best people cruel?' She defended him on the grounds of his 'terrible experience' in the battlefields of 1914-18. 'Then there was the severity of his father, who failed to understand that quick, sensitive boy. His father ticked him off in that stern Victorian way.'

As the Irish say, she knew 'the two days' with Henry, the best and the worst of times. 'In 1948 we lived in the Hut alone, drinking water from the well, and it was very lovely. Most evenings he would read aloud to me, from Scott Fitzgerald, or the latest chapter of the book he was working on.

She remembers reading 'The Flax of Dream' for the first time: 'I'd never read anything so beautiful in my life.' But she was too close to be in awe of Henry as a writer. 'Living with Willie [as she calls him], I was always so busy — making coffee, working in the garden — silly things! — that I didn't realise I was living with an English Tolstoy. I should have known.'

'Didn't you realize he was a great writer?'

'No! But Willie talked about Tolstoy in a very admiring way and *he did* realize he was quite a writer himself!'

Of his politics, she says, 'Henry was trying to be a European in the broadest sense — that's what a lot of publishers couldn't forgive.'

She asked then if I had ever seen a particular photograph (since mislaid) of Henry as a boy, 'very thin, with an enormous shock of hair and big black eyes'. She told me of the time his mother took him to Belgium when he was nine years old. They visited a convent, where the Mother Superior said, 'I can see you're a very good boy.' This made a great impression on Henry. 'There was a lot of the boy in him,' said Christine, describing his compulsion to play the clown when confronted by someone he did not wish to meet: 'It wasn't nasty, but it could be embarrassing.'

Although she would not got so far as to say so herself, I suspect that Henry resented Christine's separate career as schoolteacher. When, after three years, her friend Elizabeth had to move away and offered Christine the running of the school on her own, Henry did not encourage her ('I think he believed I was sillier than I am'). So the school was closed — and eight-year-old Harry announced, 'the happiest years of my life are over.'

'As a young man,' continued Christine, 'Henry was inspired; but, as he grew older, it became hard work to write.' She abandoned her next job within a year just to cope with the correspondence which arrived from all over the world.

Fortunately, an excellent faithful typist in Cornwall deciphered the hand-written manuscripts, with their spidery corrections, and put them into shape for the publisher. Nonetheless, it could have been a mistake for Christine to live so closely to Henry with so few separate interests of her own.

'I wouldn't like you to think that I ran away from Willie because I didn't love him, bless the man. Nor did I leave him for anyone else. It was simply that I couldn't stand any more.'

At first, Henry wrote to me about Christine with genuine grief:

> The drain via C's sad condition . . . 'why did you have me put away? I know now what hell is — it is insanity — and being drugged — & my head bursting, bursting, the top being pressed up — and I am locked in with many tragic people who have been here, in the ward, for 20 years. I tried to escape and they caught me and locked me in.'
>
> Poor soul — one has to reassure her, go to Exeter twice a week & give all one has to tell her — what I believe — that the shock treatment will reinforce her tired blood veins to the brain cells, & so no short-circuits will occur, & the strong film crossing with another & taking its place on the TV screen; oddly. So I thank God for my 'hallucination' which can go into words, words, words, & even provide a living & that of others.

Nonetheless, in spite of his extraordinary gift for seeing things from both sides, Henry was soon casting himself as the martyr. Meeting him at a party, Amanda Allsop gained the impression from him 'that he'd been generally ill-treated by those close to him (pa, Christine). A few unfinished sentences about heaven — sounds as if he's going through a

191

religious phase. Talked about Christ dying for us...
(obviously feels that Christ was ill-treated too — identifies
with him!)'

He was lucky to be so armour-plated in his selfishness, for
his guilt would have been appalling otherwise. 'I would
have guarded her when she most needed comfort,' he wrote
to me about Christine; but when she was with him he failed
to provide that comfort. Writing to Amanda Allsop on 30
December 1972, he was able to make the honest poignant
admission: '10 years and 8 days since Christine went away.
22 Dec 1962 — night of the Great Blizzard over England:
frost for 9 weeks. No-one has ever taken her place.'

Henry knew that another vital relationship had failed,
however hard he tried to explain it away. He knew he was
not an easy man to live with: when Loetitia had written to
him, 'You are a wonderful old boy,' he replied, 'I know what
I am.' The ability to see both sides could be turned against
himself, as he revealed in a passage from *The Golden Virgin*
(1957, the sixth 'Chronicle'), with lacerating self-awareness:
'There are insensitive men and sensitive men, and sometimes
the most sensitive are at times the most self-tortured, and
therefore torturing. Objects of hate are but our own chim-
erae. They arise from wounds within us. So we seek scape-
goats to void our hurts.'

By the beginning of the 1970s, Harry was twenty-one and
Henry had fewer responsibilities. He had tried to be a good
father, compensating for his relative neglect of Windles
(who had been given little formal education) by sending
Harry to the most expensive school in Britain. Later, at
Imperial College, Harry missed the glamour. When he
abandoned science for music, Henry was disappointed, describing him in a letter in 1972 as 'a sort of tramp'. On the
other hand, when Harry was charged with possession of

cannabis, 'Henry was right there!' The amount involved was smaller than the head of a match, and Harry believes it was planted. 'As soon as Henry realized that I wasn't a big drug smuggler or turning kids on to heroin, he was right behind me and paid my fine. He was very, very good. He tried to be a good father and worked very hard to send me to Millfield. He wanted to give me the best. Unfortunately, it was too good.' When I asked Harry Williamson if he loved his father, he was able to reply without hesitation, 'Yes, very much.'

If they were somewhat remote from each other by the early 1970s, it is understandable. Henry's writing days were over, whereas Harry was on the threshold of his career, struggling to establish himself as the successful musician he is today. Henry continued to use Ox's Cross as his base, but father and son led separate lives — and Henry knew loneliness.

TWELVE

Problems of friendship

HENRY HAD FREQUENTLY complained of loneliness before, but from the moment Christine left he had cause to. He wrote to me at the time:

> I'm alone and just can't cope with summer visitors, housekeeping, doing my own washing etc., etc., while shopping, cooking and mending moth-holes (joke).... Sleep little, awake 5 am to write (dope) or rather re-write, any time to 10-11 am. Then the field after some breakfast and mason the hut front or workshop gable (thick dollops of bitumen). Cut endless grass (2 acres) — the evening dope of TV. I fell asleep last night: & crawled at 11 pm to bed & slept, thank God....
>
> Well — I must have my 3rd bathe this summer, soon! I take Harry to school — he's had measles — tomorrow, & feel rather sad. I'm more fond of him than I thought — 'thought' being superficial dullness due to lack of proper food/sleep.

When he saw Rex Aylmer in Barnstaple, Henry sighed, 'I weigh two tons and am walking on eggs. I have really no friends left now.'

This was not altogether his fault, for many of his friends were dead by this time — friends such as Victor Yeates, who

had been at Colfe's School with him ('as a fellow-member of
the class usually known as the Special Slackers . . . we formed
an Owl Club and explored woods, fields and ponds'). Yeates
served in the Royal Flying Corps, recording 248 flying hours.
He 'strung some words together' afterwards and asked
Henry's advice, which was given generously, indeed Henry
found the flying scenes so powerful that he persuaded Yeates
to turn his experiences into a novel (*Winged Victory*), and
rewrote the final chapter himself when his friend was too ill
to do so. On its publication in 1934, Henry paid an anguished
visit to Reginald Pound at the *Daily Express*, begging him to
serialize. He quoted praise from T. E. Lawrence ('how fortunate the RAF has been to collar for itself one of the most
distinguished histories of the war'), but there was no serialization and fewer than 1,000 copies sold, although *Winged
Victory* has gained in reputation over the years since, largely
due to Henry's perseverence. Yeates did not live to see the
success of later editions, since he died from tuberculosis in
1935; but he recognized his debt to Henry with his dedication, 'To Henry Williamson at whose suggestion this book
was begun, and with whose encouragement & help it was
written and ended'. He could hardly have hoped for a better
friend, and Henry spoke to me about him in the 1970s, always
faithful to his memory.

The happiest memories of Harry Williamson's childhood
were the annual summer holidays with his mother and father
when they crossed the Irish Channel and made their way
slowly in their shooting-brake, with a tent, to Ballarena
twenty miles from Londonderry, where they stayed with
Henry's friend, Sir John Heygate. (Heygate's estate contained a private mountain, air-strip and railway station,
largely maintained by the salmon fishing in his private river:
once they netted 400 salmon at an average weight of 12 lbs
and flew them straight to Manchester.) Possibly Henry's
closest friend, it was Heygate who had helped Henry to

plaster the Georgeham institute sign with newspapers; Heygate who had accompanied Henry on the trip to Germany to the Nuremberg Rally to see Hitler; and Heygate who had once sprayed a car with bullets from his sub-machine gun in Piccadilly after an argument with Henry, apparently escaping arrest by the police. In 1955, Henry decided to move to Ireland, writing from there that he had no wish to return to North Devon, 'No friends left there'. However, the move proved too formidable and he returned, to even fewer friends than before. 'I feel sad, abandoned,' he told me, adding perceptively, 'abandoned to myself, perhaps *by* myself.'

Henry did not belong to a particular set of people with mutual interests, his friends were separate and varied. One of the closest was Sir Maurice Renshaw, who was seventeen when they first met at Instow, where the Renshaws had a family home. They became friends for life. Sir Maurice — one person who never abandoned him — is fiercely protective of Henry's reputation today; he received me with some suspicion as he recalled, with evident bitterness, that he had seldom seen Henry made so upset by anyone, man, woman or child, as he had been by my father when he abused him that afternoon in Barnstaple. The only time he had seen him so badly hurt was after Kenneth Allsop's questions on television, which were 'disgracefully personal'. I pointed out that Henry had forgiven Ken, and Sir Maurice replied: 'Well, he would, wouldn't he? Henry was that sort of chap. He excused your father saying he was suffering from his leg. I thought it very generous of him.'

Sir Maurice claimed that it was Henry's kindness which led so often to his disillusionment:

Willie [Williamson] had a tremendous amount of fantasy about him. He lived on fantasy. The reason he overestimated people right away was the force of his

own subjectivity — he wanted to like them, therefore
he did. All his geese were swans. But he did not have a
sufficiently objective view of himself.

Fundamentally he was so kind he projected his kindness on to other people. I remember him as a sweet man,
a good drinking companion and walking companion.
He had a hell of a life really, always writing against
time, meeting deadlines which were almost impossible
to cope with; when he did, he'd relax and be such fun!
He was a great one for buffoonery, given to showing
off — peacockery. He was a mercurial person: physically he looked like a Celt, but he was seized by the
Teutonic attitudes and virtues.

Sir Maurice suggests that Henry was never able to become
an integrated personality after the First War: 'so he attempted to write himself into an integrated state. He was a
ravaged soul since that war, it affected him very badly.' In
the first instance, Henry had been a friend of his mother,
Lady Renshaw, and her circle, who regarded writers with
some amusement: 'I sympathize with my elders, who
thought that scribblers were not our cup of tea, but we
tolerated Henry because he was fun, he was a sort of Peter
Pan who never grew up. He was a very good fellow.'

Though Henry was a faithful friend, he could be exasper-
ating, too, as we have seen. A rift had grown between
himself and Malcolm Elwin, a distinguished biographer in
his own right, who had been so helpful in encouraging
Macdonald to publish the 'Chronicle'. Henry appreciated his
support to begin with and, as I have mentioned earlier,
appointed him as his literary executor; but their close
personal and professional relationship came to an end in the
middle of the 1950s. Henry wrote to a friend:

There are, and remain, unhappy things here. I've tried
hard to get straight with the Elwins but he dismisses all

I say .... Our worlds are different; I fancy he, in his, has never been wrong. Even when he wrote that insensitive essay on Jefferies — 'The Essential Jefferies' — and got bad reviews he only said that reviewers were a lot of stupid low types etc. 'Sparrow to Eagle' the *Spectator* review was headed. His essay was crude and unkind; but he did not know this. I don't mind being barred his house — I never could talk to him — 'No!' he always interrupted and held forth at length on another tack.

I said I was probably the cause of hurt to his wife ... could we have a frank talk to clear the air. The prison door remains locked. Often at night, 3 am-5 am, I'd be on the rocks mentally; this man who hailed me as a great genius, do come & stay with us, an honour etc., etc., in 1943. One should, I suppose, never enter into a unilateral friendship based not on mutual liking of *persons*. However, it is, I hope, concluded now. What hurt was that I gave his step-daughter, when we thought, in 1946, that we were to be married, many unique photographs of myself when young — and when it was off in Dec 1946, she never returned them. Lately I wrote to him, under a strong feeling (she had married in 1952 and gone to Singapore), asking him when he saw her again, to try & get them returned. He said 'Somehow you have found out that she has just come here from Singapore' ['here' being a house on the shore of Putsborough Sands]. He went on to say that my letters & photographs had been 'destroyed'.... It seemed a little insensitive to me.

His request must have seemed as insensitive to Elwin, whose widow, Eve, remembers the events differently:

You are a brave man to try to follow the thin thread of fact leading through Henry's vast mazes of fabrication.

To change my metaphor, you must know of his propensity to chew over old bones for years, and then serve them up as splendid pasties. To my knowledge there was never any question of an engagement between Henry and Sue in 1946, she being then only sixteen and he just fifty. Certainly Malcolm never barred the house here to Henry, to be proved by their correspondence over all the years when Malcolm was helping Henry publish the endless volumes of *A Chronicle of Ancient Sunlight*, none of the early ones being unedited by Malcolm.

Even so there was an estrangement towards the end between Henry and her husband, and she adds: 'Anything I wrote about him would certainly be unprintable.'

Henry's partnership with the artist Charles Tunnicliffe also ended unhappily. Tunnicliffe realized he was the natural illustrator for *Tarka the Otter* and submitted several aquatints of an otter which encouraged Putnam to re-publish the book with wood engravings in 1932. Tunnicliffe's strong, unsentimental illustrations proved the perfect complement to the text, and Putnam continued with *The Old Stag*, *The Lone Swallows* and *The Peregrine's Saga*, launching the artist on a new phase in his career 'which he looked back upon ruefully' (according to his biographer Ian Niall, *Portrait of a Country Artist*, 1980), 'wishing he had nothing to do with a very difficult and sometimes disturbed man'.

Their first meeting was typical: as Tunnicliffe stepped off the train at Filleigh, Henry stepped into it with a cheerful wave of goodbye. His secretary took the artist to Shallowford where Mrs Williamson gave him dinner, but it was hardly the welcome he expected. When there was no sign of Henry the next morning, he posted a disgruntled note to his wife, 'It's now 11.30 or 12 o'clock and I haven't seen the great man yet!' When he did, 'the great man' played Wagner 'full blast', and though there was an instinctive, mutual admiration for the other man's work, Henry made Tunnicliffe conscious of his Cheshire accent and feel inferior generally. Tunnicliffe returned in the winter for a Meet of the Cheriton Otterhounds, and when the hunters waded into the river to rescue the remnants of an otter from the mouths of the hounds, Tunnicliffe ran forward with his camera to capture the moment while Henry yelled furiously from the bank, 'Get sketching, Tunnicliffe!'

Charles Tunnicliffe persevered, making twenty-four full-page engravings and a set of tailpieces. It would be hard to imagine an illustrator who could have enhanced the subject more brilliantly, adding his own viewpoint with the huntsmen shown as dark and menacing, rather than jovial, while 'Tarka crossing the Braunton Burrows at night' conveys an immense solitude.

Henry was delighted, but it was tactless of him to suggest that from now on Tunnicliffe should concentrate on illustrating Williamson alone — which would bring him fame, though he should not expect riches. This was all too true and became the real source of contention: while Henry gained in royalties and basked in the greater glory of the illustrations, Tunnicliffe received no more than his modest fee. Ian Niall records the deterioration in their relationship, which seems dismayingly familiar:

Williamson's own domestic situation was about as unstable as possible. He was involved in the calf love of a young girl over whom he had apparently lost his head. He burdened the Tunnicliffes with his torment over what the girl really felt, how her parents reacted, what would come of it all in the end. The burden was something the Tunnicliffes hadn't bargained for. Williamson wrote rather confused letters, jumping from one subject to another, telling them that his food

C. F. Tunnicliffe's frontispiece to the famous illustrated edition
of *Tarka the Otter*. The perfect match of writer and illustrator.
The Bodley Head

'Tarka crossing the Burrows on his way to the Estuary',
C. F. Tunnicliffe.   *The Bodley Head*

went sour in his mouth, his head ached. He thought of
killing himself. On another occasion he revealed how
he had suffered from the domination of others ever
since childhood, from his father, his schoolmaster,
editors, etc., all trying to mould him into their own
images. All this had been mental torture which had
come to a head in 1914-18, but still went on. But he then
switched to the matter of illustration, saying that a
hound Tunnicliffe had drawn would have to come out
because it was a bit too dramatic.

By 1935, the partnership was so strained that Henry began
his letters stiffly with 'Dear Tunnicliffe' instead of the
cordial 'Dear Tunny' as before; yet it was characteristic that
he protested to Mrs Tunnicliffe of feeling 'put down' when
he received a letter without any heading at all, remarking
that her husband must regret the association bitterly to
decapitate him in such a fashion. The bitterness was true:
Tunnicliffe had been furious over Henry's complaint that he
had studied a detail (the fin of a salmon) in one of the
illustrations for *Salar the Salmon* through a magnifying glass,
and found it wrong. Later Henry admitted his mistake and
pleaded that his sight was 'incompetent' after a week of
rewriting. Tunnicliffe was unable to forgive the slur and
sent an angry letter telling him exactly what he thought of
his criticism.

   I do find the illustrations for *Salar* less effective than some,
but I am prejudiced because Tunnicliffe supplied fifteen
magnificent, full-page scraperboards for my father's *Going
Fishing* (Country Life, 1942); the colour-plates for the special
edition of *Salar* were beautiful, but bland by comparison. Ian
Niall confirms that the Farson-Tunnicliffe collaboration
was entirely happy: 'When Farson saw the result he wrote
to say he had been filled with nostalgia for a particular
stream in Devon . . . . *Going Fishing* was always collected by

fishermen and indeed by a lot of people who never cast a fly in their lives. It was not only beautifully written but wonderfully interpreted by Tunnicliffe.'

The lesson Tunnicliffe learned from his collaboration with Henry was less happy: 'He must never again allow himself to become involved in the affairs of an author whose work he had to illustrate.' The colour edition of *Salar* proved a surprising failure, with only 140 copies sold, and when he was approached years later by an American publisher on a 'Best of Henry Williamson' project, Tunnicliffe declined: 'he had no taste for any of it. So far as he was concerned this was where he had come in. He didn't want to sit through it again, however chastened Williamson might have been after their earlier conflict.' To be fair to Henry, Tunnicliffe was strong-willed, too. And, from all I have heard of him, somewhat humourless.

Henry's subsequent collaboration with Barry Driscoll, who illustrated the Nonesuch edition of *Tarka*, published in 1964, was triumphant by comparison, though there was an equally bumpy beginning when Driscoll came to Ox's Cross.

Henry had taken an immediate liking to Driscoll when they met a few months earlier in the Studio Club in Swallow Street. 'I admired "The Flax of Dream" and was terribly impressed,' Barry Driscoll told me, 'but all Henry wanted to talk about was this extraordinary Swedish girl, and he asked me intimate questions of how one set about attracting young girls. I was pretty young and absolutely stunned!'

He was even more stunned when he received a phone call from Nonesuch informing him that Henry had insisted that Driscoll was the only illustrator he wanted, for Henry had not seen any of his work. But Henry had unusual perception and may have measured the man's talent in his imagination. His intuition was correct; Driscoll is one of the finest recorders of wild life, even if not yet so widely known as his predecessor, Tunnicliffe.

Feeling immensely privileged, Driscoll arrived at Ox's Cross with his wife, Kiffy, his son Guy, and his daughter Pippa. At four o'clock in the morning he was woken by an angry knocking and a rasping, peremptory voice demanding, 'Barry, Barry!' He found Henry glowering outside the caravan door: 'Milk. Have you any milk?'

'I've only just arrived, Henry,' Driscoll protested, 'we haven't had time to go shopping.'

'It's bloody nigh impossible to get milk in the West Country these days,' Henry continued, 'with all these outsiders invading the place, most of them Jews.'

He departed angrily, leaving Driscoll dismayed:

I thought, Oh no, not *already* — on my first day. Trying to get back to sleep I heard a Grasshopper Warbler. I'd never heard one before and thought, How marvellous to hear one in Henry's place. So the next morning I forgot the incident in the night-time and greeted Henry cheerfully, 'Good morning, Henry. Do you know, after you left I heard a Grasshopper Warbler.' Henry looked at me with absolute hatred. 'For Christ's sake!' he snapped, 'I hope you're not going to talk about bloody *animals* all the time.'

The situation improved after Henry kicked Driscoll's dog.

When he kicked Titus up the arse, I threatened to punch him if he ever did it again, and a new relationship dawned. Instead of treating me as a sycophant he gave me a certain respect and told me I had the freedom to enter his studio and look through his papers whenever I wished. I found a bad, wishy-washy watercolour postcard of a young SS officer, blond and handsome, with his hat off, grinning at the artist. On the other side was the inscription — 'Heinrich. You should be with us now.' — and the date, 1936. I closed the box. I didn't want to look any more.

203

Driscoll found it characteristic that the glass case in Henry's 'eyrie' above the studio contained his two favourite possessions: a British military cross and a swastika armband.

The mention of the military cross has produced a poignant postscript. Neither the *London Gazette* nor the Army Medals Office of the Ministry of Defence can trace the award of the military cross to Williamson. This was the reply I feared, but it was a shock all the same. At first I wondered if I should keep silent about the apparent deception, for it seemed that I had caught Henry out in the worst sort of lie — a false claim to courage. Then I realized that I could not remember Henry ever stating that he had been awarded the MC and that, far from boasting of personal courage in the First War, he had written constantly of his cowardice. The mere fact that he had such a medal in his possession would naturally have led people to assume that it was his own — rather than something awarded to another man and bought, say, at a sale. My hope is that it belonged to a friend of his, in which case possession would be wholly honourable.

But if it were to turn out that Henry had pretended that the medal was his own, received for gallantry, how much would the deception matter? Had he used the letters after his name, or made the claim in public — as countless bogus officers have done — the offence would be odious. But Henry was not a bogus officer and he had experienced the trenches. To have such a medal, which he admired, was surely an extension of a game — a form of harmless wishful thinking. Henry was a man who preferred to see things as they should have been: the uncharitable may call this deception, but it would be kinder, and I believe more accurate, to think of it as fantasy on a grand scale, a compensation for his inability to direct his life as he wished in his search for the 'sun without shadows'. Betty Allsop clearly remembers Henry denying that he was awarded the MC and telling the Allsops how much he would hate people to think that he was ever making that claim. Her view is that these relics from the war were nothing more nor less than nostalgic reminders.

To return to Barry Driscoll. A few days after his arrival, his mother-in-law came to stay in Georgeham:

> She thought Henry such a gentle man, not realizing what a monster he could be, and Henry decided she would grace some anniversary of the First World War. We sat there in the front pew of the Church in Ilfracombe, myself and my family, the Mayor in chains, and Henry. The rest of the pews were filled by veterans of the First War, Old Contemptibles proudly wearing their medals, who had spent the last two hours outside swapping stories of the marvellous time they'd had killing Fritz. And then the vicar stood up and introduced Henry as 'one of our greatest living writers and recorders of the Great War, one of your comrades'.
>
> Henry walked to the pulpit in an obviously sombre mood, somehow dressed completely in black, maybe some of it was his old Fascist uniform. Quite movingly he talked in his most sepulchral voice of the day when a young English soldier lay dying under the barbed wire with his hand outstretched to a young dying German soldier the other side, the Tommy crying 'Mother!', and the other calling 'Mütter!' By this time the old soldiers were terribly restless and looked at Henry in the most peculiar way afterwards, outside under the Union Jacks, as if they were thinking 'He's more of a bloody *German* than an Englishman!'

One night, Driscoll was asleep in the caravan when he was awoken by cries coming from the Hut:

> I thought, Christ! Henry's in trouble. I dragged on my trousers and ran across the field and fell across a saw-horse which hit me straight on the knees, landing me on

my back, winded. I managed to get up and ran to the window and there was Henry on the far side illuminated by the lamp-light, saint-like, hair standing on end, shaking his fist, and these weird, incredible cries. I wondered who was with him. When he disappeared, a great black shape filled the window. Then it moved aside and Henry reappeared, gesticulating. I was really scared; it seemed as if he was having a confrontation with the Devil and I hammered on the door calling out, 'Henry, are you all right?'

There was complete silence for a few moments, then he opened the door. 'Hullo, Barry, what brings you?' he asked in his calmest voice. 'Come on in, do sit down. Would you care for a little whisky?'

'I heard all these cries...' I stopped, suddenly realizing he did not want me to go on. Henry dismissed it, saying he had been reading a letter which he found particularly irritating. Later, I realized of course the black shadow was Henry himself when he moved round the other side of the oil lamp, but it was really terrifying.

It was a strange holiday, a sort of love-hate relationship, but I enjoyed it, and the children, Guy and Pippa, loved every moment, and Pippa loved Henry.

Pippa Driscoll was twelve years old at the time, and, as Loetitia has said, 'Henry loved people when they were young — up to the age of eleven or twelve'. Barry says that Henry deliberately set out to make Pippa fall in love with him:

In the mornings he'd come over in one of his quiet moods and he'd read *Scribbling Lark*. The kids loved it. Then he'd say to my wife or myself, could you spare Pippa a little? My wife, Kiffy, was niggled but not suspicious. To begin with, Henry told Pippa 'You remind me of Barleybright [the ideal companion of the novels]. At the end he'd say, 'You *are* Barley.' It could have ruined her life, this outrageous flattery! He'd say, 'I'd like to read you a passage and ask your opinion,' and he'd read aloud to her for two or three hours. 'Don't you want to come down to the beach with us?' we asked her. No, she preferred to stay with Henry. Such was his power that he got her to listen to the *entire* recording of *Tristan* without a word of complaint.

There were *no* sexual implications whatsoever, but Henry liked very pretty girls. He didn't force her, she was entranced.

Henry respected my wife, she could talk to him like nobody else I know. If he tried to bully her, she wouldn't have it. If he complained about his breakfast, she'd say get it yourself. He was living on his own at the time, but when Harry eventually turned up we picnicked below the old lighthouse overlooking the estuary one very hot day. Young Harry put his arms round Pippa and the two kids walked off in a romantic haze and you could see parts of their figures in the shimmering distance, like a mirage. I said to Henry, 'You're amazing. It really *is* the way you described it in *The Pathway*.' Henry was marvellous that day, playing the tom-toms on some old tin cans, dancing about like a wild savage. Did you ever see him compose? He lay down some distance away, his hands stiffly by his side, wearing those outrageous shorts that fell below his knees. He moved his hands onto his chest, talking to himself, testing the lines, then he stretched his arms aside in a Christ-like position. I'm sure he was engrossed and wasn't doing this for effect.

At night when he lit bonfires and told the kids terrible ghostly stories, he was magical. He described a strange dream he'd had years earlier, when he was standing in an army hut with a stage at the end of it and steps going up on either side. A marionette of Hitler marched up and strutted about a bit and walked down the stairs, and then this great red giant came out and clove off the puppet's head. The dream switched to a fire in a birch forest, with the marionette of Hitler laid upon it. And two days later, Henry said, he heard of the death of Hitler. The way he told it, my hair went up on the back of my neck. He was a brilliant actor. He'd speak very softly, with great portent, and suddenly he'd leap in the air with a great scream 'Aaagh!', and everyone leapt to their feet as well.

Henry's gift for dramatics has been confirmed by his son, Richard, who remembers how he would prance into a room wearing 'a funny wig', or throw bread and paper darts at people dining in a high-class restaurant, which made them roar with laughter, as children. On other occasions, as Father Brocard Sewell recalls, people were less amused by his practical jokes, such as the time he dented all the bowler hats hanging in the cloakroom of the Savage Club. But, as Richard Williamson adds, 'The problem with Henry was that he could switch moods just like that, and then he'd be depressed for weeks.'

Ironically, while Henry had disliked Tunnicliffe's habit of going to the local cinema to see Garbo instead of visiting the settings for *Tarka*, he had no wish to show these to Driscoll: 'I wanted to see all those places but he gave me the impression he *loathed* animals. He'd never take the work seriously, just joked all the time about Charcoal the Water Hotter, as he called him.' Driscoll was also disappointed that Henry had revised *Tarka* yet again, ostensibly for the seventeenth time, and found that the prose had become turgid in comparison to the freshness of the first edition. Even so, in spite of Henry's indifference to the work and the moments of cantankerousness, Barry Driscoll remembers the collaboration with affection: 'Don't get the wrong impression, I *loved* Henry'. And Geraldine Norman, who had been listening to us, confirmed, 'The way you've both been talking, he was a *great* man.'

If visitors expected Henry to be a 'cuddly' personality because he wrote about otters, they were in for a shock; but, with the passage of time, the 'difficult' side of his nature seems less important. Was he really so difficult?

Amanda Allsop remembers a dinner party when Henry sat next to her uncle and talked continually about Hitler — 'and I don't believe Henry did not know he was Jewish, it's the sort of thing he did.' But she adds:

> Do you know, I honestly believe that if I hadn't been told so often what an appallingly difficult man he was, I think I would have been unaware that he wasn't the most wonderful, charming and enchanting person. Everything he said seemed to be sparked with genius — most of it was. I don't think he ever got angry with me — I think I would have remembered — and perhaps to me he was an ideal father who was nicer than mine because mine got cross with me.

Of course Henry could be difficult, and few who knew him well would deny it, certainly not Loetitia Williamson. When I called him that in the *Sunday Telegraph Magazine*, one person took exception and complained in the local paper. I was relieved when this was followed by a letter from the painter Edward Ford, who wrote that Henry had produced my article in an Ilfracombe pub and showed it around with obvious pleasure. Henry was difficult in his own way — perhaps 'quirky' would be a better word — with a singularly 'individual' humour which many people failed to understand. 'My Norfolk years destroyed what confidence I ever had,' he wrote to me plaintively after his return to Devon;

but he belied this at once by continuing, 'That is why I am a weevil in a nut, or a deevil in a hut.'

At times that 'deevil' was taken too seriously. I would not have wished him otherwise, and am glad he did not become submissive in old age, resorting to that smiling stoicism which so many elderly people assume in order to ingratiate. Far from cringing, Henry became more cantankerous.

Difficult or not, Henry retained his physical attaction to a startling degree even in his late seventies, and Barry Driscoll remembers how athletic he was at that age: 'I had dinner with him and Ken Allsop at the Renaissance Club and we left to look for a drink afterwards. As we walked along search-ing for a taxi, Ken said, "Look, he moves like a young man."' Henry always had a presence and now his shock of white hair gave him grandeur too. His sexual appeal was still strong and it was noticed in newspaper offices not only that Henry headed for the youngest and prettiest secretaries but that they clustered around him. Meeting him at a West Country Writers' Conference in Barnstaple, Denys Val Baker noted that Henry behaved 'pretty outrageously'. At later conferences:

> Henry would invariably appear with some gorgeous young creature on his arm, and it never seemed sur-prising only inevitable. I can remember quite seriously hesitating about bringing my own very pretty eighteen-year-old daughter to meet Henry even when he was in his seventies, knowing for sure that he would probably have swept her giddily off her feet with his incredible old-world blend of passion and romanticism.

When I interviewed him for television shortly after Christine had left him, Henry arrived at the Wembley Studios with the young novelist, Ann Quinn, whose first

novel *Berg* had offended some people with its liberal scatter-
ing of four-letter words. Henry had defended it in 1964 as 'an
innocent allegory or moral-tale sprung from an impulse
similar to that which impelled Hardy's phrase, "If way to
the better there be it exacts a full look at the worst."' Far
from being jealous of younger writers, as one newspaper
claimed after his death, Henry was always generous with his
encouragement. Personally he found *Berg* 'sordid', but he
saw the promise and 'a talent of rarity and grace'. He may
have been prejudiced in her favour, for Ann Quinn was gay,
outspoken and vital, a gust of fresh air to revive the master
writer.

Henry was in good form all that day, relishing the
attention of the cameras and acting up accordingly. Describing his performance in *The Observer*, Maurice Richardson
wrote of him as:

> An odd time-defying character. He made a curiously
> mixed, mainly pleasing impression, with a strong aura
> from the 1920s. One moment he suggested an old-style
> Fitzroy Tavern squatter; the next one of those unfor-
> tunate ex-officers, post-World War One, whose
> chicken farms were always getting flooded. A gentle
> disposition, to go with the animalian empathy of those
> Otter and Salmon books was much in evidence.... I
> found him especially fascinating on the subject of his
> own political baboonery. His explanation of his unhap-
> piest enthusiasm was that Hitler was really the great
> pacifist *manqué* destroyed by an Achilles heel of fear ...
> Even so, I switched off, convinced that he — William-
> son — would never willingly hurt a fly, not even in a
> paroxysm of pacifism.

Plainly Henry enjoyed showing off in front of Ann Quinn,
and when the elderly chauffeur reported back after driving
them to the West End, he did so with dazed admiration: 'In

all my years of driving, I've never known the likes of what that old gentleman got up to in the back seat with that young lady!'

Though Henry is often thought of as a recluse, 'the hermit of Ox's Cross', there were times when he craved for company, finding it in a series of flirtations which bordered on fantasy and may not have been realized. After his death, Sue Caron, described by the *News of the World* as the editress of 'several erotic magazines' and author of 'hundreds of pornographic articles', claimed that Henry met her when she was eighteen and he was sixty-seven, and showered her with as many as ten letters a day. Calling her 'Foxey', 'My little tinkerbell fairy', and 'My little Falcon', he declared 'I love you like a bottle of good wine . . . I love you in my arms, I want you always near me, with me in the flesh; but also I seem to know my pattern and my fate.' The last words suggest the element of wishful fantasy.

It is remarkable and not at all pathetic that Henry should seek out romance as he did, at an age when most men would have abandoned the search. If the 'affair' proved unsatisfactory, he did not complain. Writing to me in 1971 on New Year's Eve, when Henry liked to send end-of-the-year letters, he referred to another relationship (after references to Scott Fitzgerald and Hemingway, which revealed an interest in modern American literature I had not expected):

Thank you for your kind letter. I was late at Muggeridge's, & not seeing the old boy there, decided he'd dropt the idea of a summer walk with me on the Chains of Exmoor. It would have been fun — one refers of course to Malcom M. I didn't like the B'ple pub, ill-bred young men press around the bar & don't consider old men waiting to order a drink. (At the same time, one should always remember the 1st sentence of the Great Gatsby — that immortal book. And a FIRST novel by that dear man. Oddly it recalls the Sun Also Rises (Cape in England called it FIESTA) surely the best (and 1st) book by that great bear of a man.) Only memory is in rays, like one's life — not a word written since 5 August 1971, when that girl that you kindly asked to your house with me — suddenly left as secretary. A queer case: she used me to desert her (married) 'boy friend' (aged 41) to get him to divorce his wife (their marriage washed out) and live with her. He said to her when she left PORLOCK for Ilfracombe — 'Are you going to destroy HW as you have destroyed me?' (I hear they are now together again) And wish her luck — She'd had previous bad luck, poor girl. with affectionate regards for 1972 & onwards, dear Dan, from Henry.

I think Ronald Duncan best summed up Henry's effect on women: 'Women did fall for Henry very easily. He gave women the sense that he needed them.'

THIRTEEN

Changes at Ox's Cross

BY NOW OX'S CROSS was a strange conglomeration of buildings. There was the simple Hut which symbolized Henry (built with the help of friends in the 1920s); the slightly larger studio with the loft; the permanent caravan; and Harry's lorry (painted in psychedelic patterns) which served as a movable home. The strangest addition was the large new building which loomed over the field like an Ibsenish symbol of gigantic loneliness, the empty home of the master writer. It was built for the benefit of Henry's trust, as an investment: 'It cost me £25,000,' he told me, 'the end of my cash.' It was hard to remember that in the 1920s he had paid £125 for the entire field.

Henry was lucky to be living in the same place fifty years on, surrounded by trees he had planted himself. He belonged in the Hut and the nearby studio; yet, because they lacked electricity and a telephone, he spent more and more time in the cottage at Ilfracombe, where he did not belong at all. He seemed even less suited to the new house. The design was certainly impressive: virtually one immensely high room, which might have been useful to a muralist or a sculptor on a grand scale, but, even in its unfinished state, was clearly inappropriate to a writer. There was a sort of minstrel's gallery, and the smaller rooms took little advantage of the panoramic views towards the estuary. Today it has a happier atmosphere now that it is lived in by Harry and his family, with ample space for recording sessions; but, as far as Henry was concerned, I felt it was an aberration. He never stayed there, though he told me of his hope that it might become the Henry Williamson Museum. The only point in turning a writer's home into a museum is to show how he lived or to display the details of his trade (letters, notebooks and first editions): the house is unsuitable for either purpose.

Writing in 1955, before the new house was built, Henry confided his hope that his son Richard would live at Ox's Cross, praising his 'remarkable powers and balance and penetration' as a writer and naturalist in the same tradition: 'He shall have my old Hut. And this field, when I am dead. I should not like to think of it becoming a motel or a tea-house park. But that doesn't avail — all is vanity.'

At the time of writing, the future of Ox's Cross is uncertain: Harry Williamson lives there and works in the new house, while Richard continues as a Nature Warden near Chichester. The Trustees hope to keep Ox's Cross in the family and to preserve the simple wooden Hut as the perfect memorial. It was good to learn in 1981 that they have granted a lease to the Henry Williamson Society, which has launched a fund to preserve it.

Meanwhile the wealth of Henry's papers and letters are protected by his son Richard, who acts as Henry's literary executor with his wife Anne. I was worried about their safety during Henry's last years, when he spoke of objects being lost or stolen. He referred constantly to a loose brick in the Hut which provided a hiding place where he concealed his keys and money, but it was hardly a secret as he revealed it to everyone. Whenever he said that money had been lost or stolen, it invariably turned up again, but the scare was alarming. He *had* been burgled in November 1972, though he only realized it the following March when the police searched

215

a house in Barnstaple and recovered the following objects which they traced to Henry:

Copper kettle	Watch
Hunting horn	American hip-flask
Beer warmer	Stud box
Cigarette case	Seven half-crown coins
Bottle opener	Quantity of foreign coins
Pair of spectacles	Green canvas knapsack

When Henry went to the police station to identify his property, which he valued modestly at £50, he recognized one of the policemen. As a boy of sixteen, Brian Kingshott had dared to introduce himself in the ice-cream parlour in Barnstaple, revealing that he hoped to write a book himself one day. Henry had given him a pencil saying, 'Now you have a pencil all you need is paper and then you can write your book because until the first word is written it will remain an ambitious dream.'

Brian Kingshott was surprised after such a long interval (in his case, largely spent at sea as a radio officer in the Merchant Navy), that Henry not only remembered him but asked about the book:

I had to admit I had not yet written and he admonished me: 'Everyone thinks they can write a book and perhaps they can. But who will ever know, for it must be committed to paper. No one can read what is in your head however good it is.' I told him I had an idea, but I wasn't sure how to go about it. He replied: 'You probably never will be. You must write, rewrite and probably rewrite again and still it will not be right. You must have an overwhelming desire to write and when you reach that stage nothing will stop you. You must put it on paper, first one word then another then another, then you are writing. One word of advice: it

will never be exactly as you want it no matter how
many times you rewrite it but don't give up and don't
throw away any notes. Do not be so critical that on
rewriting you lose your original theme. It may never be
published but you will never regret doing it; of course,
if it is published, you can say, I did that. Have faith, for
you don't know what you can do until you try.

Wise advice, which belies the slur that Henry was grudging
to up-and-coming writers, as we also saw in Henry's
reaction to Ann Quinn's *Berg*. Though it is not yet
published, Brian Kingshott's book about the Merchant Navy
has been written, and he says this was due to Henry's
encouragement.

To my regret, I seldom talked to Henry about books or
writing, though he had plenty of this from other people. I
saw so much of him in his final years in North Devon that I
failed to appreciate how lucky I was in his company, and
though I felt increasing sympathy towards him I was often
exasperated by the interruptions as I struggled to make my
living by my own writing. I am glad to think I never used this
as an excuse to him, nor inflicted anything I had written on
him. One afternoon I was disarmed to discover he had been
sitting outside in the porch, waiting patiently until he knew I
had finished typing, which proved he understood my problems, too.

Towards the end of his life, his conversation was so
sporadic that it would be a distortion to assemble his
thoughts into an orderly sequence. I have chosen some
random notes from my 1975 Diary, starting with May:

May 3rd: . . . Henry has received a letter from a girl: 'I
phoned her at 10 at night and she had run upstairs in her
nightie and asks *me* to stop!' Also, a doting letter from a
22-year-old girl in Aberdeen who is 'lonely but
affectionate and genuine'. He says, 'I'm going back-

wards all the time. The children are superb, the only trouble is their father isn't.'

May 4th: . . . Henry disrupts the day effectively as we go to the King's Arms in Georgeham which is full and lively at 1.30. HW says his brief-case has vanished, making everyone feel guilty. We go on, as planned, to Ox's Cross, where Carol (Harry Williamson's girl friend at the time) provides deliciously rough home-made brown bread, sardines, butter & cheese. We've brought two bottles of wine. A hunt for the damned brief-case. Found! Now I wonder if HW had really lost it. Interesting 1st World War stories: Henry saluting the Germans as he goes to carry back a wounded Tommy, draped over the wire. The German captain points: 'Take him!' the firing ceases. Apparently H.W. nearly got gonged.

May 5th: . . . H.W. descends at lunchtime: 'Sorry I'm late', though I wasn't expecting him. Hear the 1st War story again, but this time it is not HW himself who performed such bravery, but a Corporal, a boy of nine stone, killed the following day — 'Or he would have received the VC.'

More of a 'solitary' than ever, Henry harked back to the memories of war which were lodged in his mind. As I listened to them, his description of the war as 'beautiful' became more comprehensible: a terrible beauty, but a higher experience than most of us will know. Visiting the trenches myself in 1961, seeing those cemeteries of identical crosses, I felt a deep sense of melancholy because of the knowledge of what had gone before; but visitors to the front a few months after the Armistice of November 1919 were astonished by the fields of crops planted by the French farmers up to the edge of the trenches, already tall and luxuriant from the human fertilizer buried underneath. And these visitors exclaimed how strangely beautiful it was.

It was the perseverance of man which inspired Henry, rather than the bloodshed which haunts us today, and this made him aware of a deeper purpose in life than he might have had otherwise. In this sense it was almost a religious experience, which only increased his feeling that it was his duty to record the finer aspects of life: 'What impertinence for any man to deny God in all things alive on the earth!' he exclaimed.

My notes continue:

May 5th: ... An evening of incomparable beauty, no wonder HW has written that this is 'the loveliest bay in the West Country'. A glistening silver sea, Baggy a strange black shape jutting into it. Surprising sight: skymen like immense birds jump off Baggy and fly down to the beach. Bassey catches two small rabbits on walk: her tongue bleeding and eyes scratched, but happy. If there is reincarnation, I'd like to come back as one of my own dogs, none of this human-being nonsense. I return from walk to find HW waiting.

May 6th: HW yet again, just as I have started *Transplant* [the first draft of a novel finally published in 1981]. I typed the first two words, literally, when down the lane he comes, heralded by Blacky's furious barking. She hates him and I am beginning to do so, too, at such moments. Endless stories: Switzerland — Sophie (?) she was either 27 or 58, but she was in love with him! When he leaves, my heart sinks as he smiles: 'All right if I drop in on you some time?' ...

May 24th: 2 visits from HW. Oh God! Twice in one day! ...

May 29th: Henry phones from Ilfracombe to say his

car's out of action. Thank God. But no such luck. Only ½ an hour later, he appears having parked elsewhere, so no warning. At his worst. Complains he is tired of people dropping in on 'the famous Henry Williamson'. For once, I tell him I am trying to write my novel.

'But you shouldn't.'

'Shouldn't write it?'

'No, shouldn't discuss things while you're writing.'

'But you called to discuss the programme [our television interview to celebrate his eightieth birthday] while I *was* writing.'

May 30th: After walking with the dogs to collect the papers at the end of the beach, and feeding the hens who are now laying 4 eggs a day, dogs bark and there is Henry motionless, standing in the doorway. 8.30 am.

'I think we'd better cancel it,' he said.

'All right,' I said.

Well, it was bound to happen. Upsetting nevertheless.

Polish floor. Just finished... HENRY!! Apologises: 'We must never quarrell...'

I am writing this now as he sits opposite in the sun — half asleep. At least I think he is. Earlier, the familiar mention of the OM only this time it was H. G. Wells at the Savage Club who told him he deserved it. Talking of the Full Moon he says: 'I feel awfully inspired when I see a shadow on a shadow.'

If this is madness there is method in it. But I am not sure what he means!

To my sorrow, as I have said, I failed to realize how much Henry was looking forward to our television programme. It was intended as a form of tribute to his eightieth birthday, and it may have led him to anticipate greater recognition on 1 December. And why not? With the British respect for longevity, when any eighty-year-old is regarded with wry affection, there was every reason to expect attention, especially as it was overdue. Henry would have been less than human if he had not been excited by the prospect and I suspect he was being disingenuous when he wrote to me in April, 'I did hope that 1 December would be kept dark: but what's the odds?'

I doubt if Henry bothered about popularity, for he knew he had his faithful followers, even though they had diminished since the notorious declaration to 'the great man across the Rhine'. Before he started the 'Chronicle', he had written to me at Cambridge: '... I have never been popular and now at last realize that I shall never be while I am alive. I know why, too. Feelings should all have been used objectively. Such work therefore, if masterly, is unexceptionable [*sic*].' I do not think he believed this, for he was embarking on his life's work, but after the 'Chronicle' was finished his disillusionment was complete.

Harry Williamson spoke to me about this: 'He knew he was writing stuff that wouldn't be acceptable. Henry told me, "You're going to have to wait until the year 2000, if the world lasts that long, before anyone accepts any of these books as unbiased history of the first and second wars." This is how he regarded them, as objective history, he told me that many times.'

I asked Harry if his father was desperately disappointed by the lack of appreciation of the 'Chronicle':

No, he knew the books would not be recognized until the end of the century because people are so conditioned. And this is true, go into a village shop and buy ten different boys' comics and we're still fighting the Germans. They're either small, mean and cunning, or big, stupid, ugly Krauts and Huns, there isn't a mention of the Russians! It's crazy conditioning, when the kids around here play games, the Germans are always the

221

'baddies', and we're supposed to be in the Common Market with them! I think it is crazy.

With the general apathy towards the 'Chronicle', and the particular antipathy for *The Gale of the World*, Henry must indeed have felt he was writing for posterity. But although he had abandoned any thoughts of popularity, I believe he cared desperately for recognition, particularly in the literary world to which be belonged.

This was one reason why he had always relished his visits to London, with parties arranged by his daughter, Margaret Bream, and conversation at the Savage Club. He liked to feel in the swim of things. Once he astonished Angus Wilson by appearing unexpectedly at the British Museum Reading Room to express his admiration for *Hemlock and After*. In this he was paying a literary courtesy call, making himself known as well. In turn, Sir Angus has written to me expressing his admiration for *Dandelion Days* and *The Dream of Fair Women*, as well as for *Tarka* and *Salar*, with the familiar reservation: 'Of course, his war years caused his politics but one has to say thank God not every soldier went the same way.' Again the falling shadow of the First War and his sympathy towards the Germans, for which he forfeited the respect of so many of his fellow-writers. Surely they would forgive him on his eightieth birthday? Unwittingly, my television film encouraged him to think so.

Henry was an excellent performer on film, if seldom used — no doubt because his politics intervened again, prejudicing producers against him. But he was dismayed by his performance on our first appearance together, in a programme called *The Writers*, for TWW (now HTV) in the 1960s. As I had no books to my credit then (my first was published in 1972), I protested that I would be appearing under false pretences; but the producer explained that Leslie Thomas had dropped out, so I accepted as a stop-gap, grateful to appear with Henry. At least my previous experience of television proved an advantage during the recording and Henry wrote to me expansively a few days later:

> I've been telling people that you know how to 'face' the TV camera & I don't. You cut across the screen with a ¾ profile, the best angle, while I, like a toad in the hole, squinted at an unseen point somewhere below my boots. As though writhing like some low-down snake-in-a-pit. But, truly, you were good — clear, concise, direct, poised — while I (it seemed) was squirming.

This was generous to me but unfair to himself, though his awareness of 'angles' proved how ready he was to learn the tricks of the television trade.

The Writers recording became known between us as the 'Cardiff Adventure'. When the recording was finished, with the usual post-programme euphoria, I led Henry and a mutual friend, Bob Benson, to the dockland of Tiger Bay and a promised treat — dinner at the Windsor Hotel. This unlikely spot contained one of the great French restaurants outside France — or at least, it had done once. The moment we passed through the Snakepit bar, I sensed that something terrible had happened. Everything had changed: not a dark corner or a simple space left unmolested. Worst of all, the food had 'gone contemporary'. After a dreadful meal, I headed for the bar to drown my disappointment, while Henry and Bob Benson had a pointless but furious argument about the First War.

Fortunately, in contrast to the bleating note in so many of his letters ('one is neurotic, a worrying type') — which conveyed one aspect of the man, but far from the whole — Henry had a glorious capacity for comedy, which restored the balance. He was fun. After our meal at the Windsor, he began by entertaining the customers, who had remained

223

much the same from the old days of the Snakepit and offset the glare. Everyone cheered and laughed, until he paid too much attention to a young half-caste, who complained when her lover appeared — a black man of such proportions that he had to stoop in order to get inside the room. Thinking it was Benson who had thrust a hand up his girlfriend's skirt (for it could hardly have been the distinguished, grey-haired gentleman beside him) the black man raised a massive fist, to be stopped by the girl in time as she explained the mistake. Whereupon Henry disarmed everyone by dancing the can-can on the top of the new formica bar. From then on the evening deteriorated. 'I enjoyed it all,' wrote Henry afterwards. 'My only regret is lack of restraint & bad manners shouting at your friend & being horribly egocentric & rude.'

Later television appearances were less traumatic. The BBC did a profile directed by Patrick Garland, for whom Henry had nothing but praise, especially when he discovered after reading several passages aloud and asking whether they should start filming, that the cameras had been rolling discreetly all the time. There was also the outstanding documentary, *The Vanishing Hedgerows*, directed by David Cobham for BBC 2, which won the Silver Nymph Award at the Monaco Television Festival: 'I knew my stuff, that's all,' said Henry, and he did. (Later, David Cobham made the feature film of *Tarka the Otter*, learning of Henry's death as he finished shooting the sequence of Tarka's final battle in the estuary of the two rivers.)

Now it was my turn again. We started filming on Monday 9 June 1975, when the director, Jeff Milland, and the crew arrived from HTV headquarters in Bristol. We filmed over three days: in the Hut; reading aloud from his books at the end of Baggy Point; walking across the Braunton Burrows in the perfect warmth of early summer to the site of the old lighthouse overlooking the estuary, where we picnicked by the breakwaters. Williamson weather and Williamson landscape. Henry was helpful throughout, though he looked sad and vulnerable in the final film.

As the year continued, he seemed uncertain if the filming was over, leaving a wistful message in my diary for 13 October when I was out: 'Forgive a crude visit: only sea and waves and uniform sun greet the wanderer who must return at once. . . . This is the 3rd time when I broke off work of writing to attend to the expectant broadcast. It is not here, alas; & I must leave at once for inland ways.' Plainly, he was confused.

One evening he arrived at the Grey House with his son John and his grandson, a well-mannered and intelligent boy. Understandably, Henry was proud to show them off, but I have seldom seen him in such a state of ebullience. At one point in his rapid conversation he referred to a girl who drowned herself because of him, and I wondered if he was thinking of Ann Quinn, although her suicide had nothing to do with him; but it seemed possible that he was confusing her, somehow, with Willie Maddison who had 'drowned' in the estuary. When he spoke of the girl's passionate attraction to him, I tried to change the subject. He went on to tell us excitedly of a visit he had made to the bank that morning, an incident which was plainly incredible. At first the teller had refused to let him withdraw any money; then Henry suggested the sale of a new short story in return, and the clerk asked him to read it aloud. When Henry finished, the clerk hesitated, saying it was not one of his best stories but he was prepared to advance the money all the same. To confound the fantasy, Henry produced a green plastic wallet supplied by the bank which seemed stuffed with crisp new notes.

Already, I had been told of an incident in a Barnstaple café where Henry produced and dropped money with utter recklessness, surrounded by envious, watchful eyes. And I knew of the wandering, battered, brown leather brief-case, though it usually turned up again.

I began to accept that his mind was becoming erratic and that he was liable to forget something within an hour. It was at this time that he made the visit I have already mentioned in my Introduction: he arrived one evening with the cheerful explanation that he thought it was time that he looked in, and I did not tell him that he had called at the Grey House that morning. Another day, he demanded: 'Are you expectings guests?'

'No,' I replied, slightly surprised. 'Why?'

'Most people seem to be expecting guests when I call on them nowadays,' he sighed.

More and more his mind stuck on the First War, repeating his experience of the Christmas truce and other acts of heroism, on both sides of the wire. A letter he sent me from Capstone Place, starting, 'I am in a wearied condition...' was dated *1918*. With a poignant pleasure, he quoted constantly from A. E. Housman's 'Epitaph On An Army of Mercenaries':

> These, in the day when heaven was falling,
> The hour when earth's foundations fled,
> Followed their mercenary calling
> And took their wages and are dead.

In the circumstances, it alarmed me to realize that he was looking forward to his eightieth birthday with quite such expectation.

The day before his birthday, 30 November, the *Sunday Telegraph Magazine* published my article 'Recognizing Henry Williamson', and then for the first time I appreciated the extent of the loyalty still felt by his readers. Journalists know that most features disappear without a ripple (unless, like 'Never Trust Your Cat', they are calculated to provoke a bulging postbag).

But there is the rare occasion when people write out of

sympathy, as they did then, for Henry. I received close on fifty letters from strangers expressing their love for his books and their admiration for the man. I have no idea how many letters Henry received, but he opened his battered brief-case shortly afterwards, revealing a bundle of un-opened envelopes. The letters I received were not concerned with the correspondents themselves, which is usually the case, but were straightforward, unpretentious letters of gratitude for the pleasure gained from Henry's books. One man wrote: 'I believe he came close to holding the key to life itself.' I can think of no contemporary writer who would have commanded such a response at the time, with the possible exception of J. B. Priestley.

The great day arrived on 1 December 1975 — and it went. I have mentioned in my Introduction that his sons travelled to Barnstaple to celebrate his birthday at a dinner held in the Imperial Hotel, and he told me about this with great pleasure. But that was all. No tribute in the Sunday papers, apart from mine; not even the freedom of Barnstaple, which I assumed he would be given though I over-estimated civic pride. Above all, no public honour; this was mean-spirited and will be seen as such one day.

It was not for lack of trying. Attempts had been made, mainly by Victor Bonham-Carter, the secretary of the Royal Literary Fund, who included Henry in the names he recommended for a Civil List Pension when he went to Downing Street in 1970. This was rejected on the reasonable grounds that Henry was not in actual need; so Bonham-Carter wrote to Kenneth Allsop in March that same year asking for a letter of appreciation which he could forward, 'in order that Henry may be considered for an Honour, which some of us feel is long overdue'. Ken replied saying how delighted he would be to see Henry's last 'rather wintry years warmed by a formal recognition,' and enclosed his letter of support:

I personally believe that Henry's creative scale is that of a genius. One uses the word sparingly, and in this case it doesn't imply a belief in his total and sublime perfection as a writer. I mean it in the sense that his work has always been distinguished by the intensity of vision of an artist with a purpose beyond and separate from that of merely earning a living.

I think I can be objective about expressing this judgement of him, because in fact his political philosophy could hardly be more distant from my personal outlook on man and society. So it is in spite of this that my admiration for his prose and for that rare trueness of devotion to his craft is unqualified. He will, I am certain, eventually be acknowledged to be one of the great writers of this age: it would be good if some of that acknowledgement could be accorded him while he is still living and aware of it.

In spite of their efforts, the campaign came to nothing, and Victor Bonham-Carter concluded ruefully when he wrote to me on 9 December 1980: 'As to the Honour, I think his pro-Hitler stance was never forgotten, I have no proof of this, but I assumed it to be the case.'

An ironic footnote concerns another 'Honour' that never was — a public house in Georgeham to be called the Williamson Inn. 'Did I tell you,' he wrote to a friend on his fifty-seventh birthday, 'that the brewers next spring are giving a party in glebe field, all welcome, on day of renaming the King's Arms? It is to be the Williamson Inn.... One Saturday in May probably. An honour. We are keeping it dark until the week before the ceremony.' Perhaps it was wishful thinking then, but I believe there will be a Williamson Inn — in the twenty-first century.

*   *   *

Henry must have felt a void of disappointment when his eightieth birthday was over. He was worried by an impending operation for piles when he came to see me for the last time, though he seemed confused and worried over the date. It is not exactly clear what happened, but it seems that he arrived at the North Devon Infirmary on the right day but had been given a card with the wrong appointment.

Harry Williamson believes that what followed was totally unnecessary: 'He was still trying to work, bumbling around the place pretty harmlessly, parking his car on double-yellow lines occasionally, that was about the extent of his illness. He was suffering from piles and for some reason he thought he had to go into hospital to have something done, so he admitted himself.' There was a terrible sequence of misunderstanding, with the nurses telling him he had made a mistake and Henry unable to understand what was happening. By the time he realized he was not supposed to be there, they had taken his clothes away. Harry continues:

> Being a very strong sort of person, he didn't want to stay in there, but they wouldn't give him his clothes back so he left in his pyjamas in the middle of the night trying to find his car. He was wandering around the High Street when the police found him and said, 'What are you doing?', and he said, 'I'm looking for my car', and there he was in his pyjamas.
>
> I know from a conventional, normal society point of view that it is a crazy thing to do, but it's not that crazy. If you were walking around in your own car-park with your pyjamas on they couldn't arrest you, but they took him away, to hospital. He protested forcibly, volubly, he was very fit — and about two days before that he'd been up here at Ox's Cross splitting wood with a seven-pound axe, he was fit, you know. So he resisted, and so

they said, 'We'll have to tranquillize him,' and they gave him a massive dose of tranquillizers.

Harry discovered all this later. At the time he assumed Henry was staying at the cottage at Capstone Place, but when he had not heard from his father for two days, he began to worry. Then Margaret telephoned to ask if he knew that Henry had been taken to the hospital in Ilfracombe.

'I went down to see him and I walked into the room and there were three or four elderly gentlemen in the room and I couldn't recognize which one was Henry.'

FOURTEEN

'Summer come again!!'

HENRY HAD CHANGED in four days. As Harry says: 'It didn't look like him at all. He looked like some mummified Viking . . . very tall, cheek-bones sunken, staring eyes . . . all the flesh gone from his face . . . his whole vitality had been drained. And quite honestly I put it down to tranquillizers.' But Henry recovered sufficiently to greet members of his family who came to see him in hospital later, even exclaiming to one of his sons: 'What a wonderful coat! What is it? A hundred per cent mouse?'

When he was well enough to leave, he spent several weeks with his son Richard at West Dean Woods near Chichester, until the police found him wandering about the fields at night. It was decided then to send him to Twyford Abbey, on the outskirts of London, where he could be properly cared for.

Visitors to the abbey were shocked when they saw him. Peter Gibbs, who had known Henry since his Georgeham childhood days, found it difficult to make contact. He went into the room first to see if Henry had any clothes on, and when Mrs Gibbs followed, she found it 'rather dreadful, he was haggard and vacant. We chatted but it was very difficult for he didn't answer.' Ronald Duncan, who sent a friend to visit reported afterwards that, 'Henry never asked how I was, never spoke about anything except the Somme.' On another occasion Henry beckoned a visitor outside, holding on to his trousers in case they fell to his ankles, so thin had he become. As they walked the grounds he looked at his companion's face and there was a brief recognition in his eyes, and then it faded.

Another lifelong friend was so distressed by their last meeting that it upsets him to remember it even now:

> This person was not the Henry I knew but a vacant clown, as if another person had taken his place and all that was left was the shell. He ran at the double everywhere in his nightgown and whenever he came across the monk in the quadrangle who sat in a sort of reception room, Henry came to attention in a whimsical way, saluted, and then crossed himself. The kindly monk said 'We don't know what goes on inside that old head of yours, Henry', and tapped him affectionately on the forehead, but Henry made no reply. He never spoke to us.'

His wife added: 'Henry's trouble was that he didn't know fact from fantasy. He'd played at it so often that it got him in the end, so he couldn't tell one from the other.'

Henry suffered all the degradation of senility, sharing the room with other men who were incontinent. On one occasion, he was found naked on the platform of the local station as if he were trying to escape. Where to? Did he loathe restraint so desperately?

Little is gained by investigating this last phase of his life further; but this was the sweltering summer of 1976 and there were times when I wished he could have walked at the end of Baggy Point and fallen over the cliff to the rocks below. He was such a wild spirit it was painful to think of him enclosed. I had no idea how closely Henry's thoughts had wandered in the same direction.

Henry on the signpost at Ox's Cross, gazing across Braunton
Burrows towards the estuary, c.1950. My favourite photograph.
Daniel Farson

Baggy Point, at the corner of Putsborough Sands, where Henry's
footsteps would have been the only man–made marks when he arrived
there in the summer of 1914. A magical spot, I remember my father
pointing to it and saying 'this is the perfect place for journey's end.'
Daniel Farson

According to Harry, Henry spoke about death often, though he did not fear it. He had conquered that fear at the end of the First War, when he was lying on an operating table and felt as if he were flying through the sky. He told Harry:

> I was attached by this tiny silver cord and I was so happy to be flying, I wanted to fly away and away and away. And then suddenly I thought, But if I break that cord I won't be able to come back to my body, I looked down and the cord was getting thinner and thinner, and there were all these buildings and I could see the trees and through them the operating theatre, and the men who were operating on me, in terrific detail . . . everything was transparent.

He told Harry that at this point he still had a choice, he was so close to death he could have died, or he could come back. Harry says: 'He knew he had work to do, that he had responsibility, and that experience made him realize that he'd been born for a purpose, so he came back and got on with it. This was something he wasn't very public about.' Towards the end, he told Harry at Ox's Cross, 'I want to go out on Baggy Point at a very low tide and climb as far out on the rocks as I can and go to sleep in the sunshine and be washed off and drift out to sea.'

Harry saw his father again at Twyford Abbey, and there were times when Henry knew him, but it sounds as if Henry's spirit had departed already:

> It was as if the tranquillizers had removed the network that held the spirit of his body. You would talk and if you looked into his eyes you could see that a bit of him was there but most of him was a thousand miles away in some other dimension as if he was talking to someone else, one of his old friends like Hardy, or even someone

in the 16th century. It's amazing when people get senile because if you forget about the conventions and try to look into where they are, they're in worlds which an average person finds it very difficult to reach. He would sit me in a chair and walk round me talking about lots of different things at once. But then he had amazing moments of very great precision and lucidity when he asked about the field and the house and my family and knew everything, and then suddenly in the middle of a story he'd drift away.

There was one person he always recognized on her regular visits several times a week — his daughter Margaret Bream. On their last meeting he put his hand over hers and said, 'My heart is broken.' Then he removed it gently, and Margaret felt that he wished to make the final journey on his own.

Henry died on 13 August 1977. Windles, his eldest son, returned from Canada and attended the funeral at Georgeham a few days later. Henry's body was laid to rest in the graveyard near the stream, only a few yards from Skirr Cottage where he had been happy.

Henry did not have the easiest of lives, but then, tranquility was not a luxury he expected. As Richard Williamson said, he had 'too much to do, he was like a pressure cooker'. When he felt himself slipping away on that operating table, he knew it was his duty to return: grandiose thinking perhaps, but he was convinced that his writing mattered more than anything or anyone. This might be the selfishness of genius, but as far as he was concerned he had no choice. At the end of their traumatic television interview he told Kenneth Allsop: 'When I look into some of the pages of *Tarka* or *Salar the Salmon*, or the others, I think However did I write that? And then I remember, it wrote itself. The feeling comes when you feel inspired. And I would say that it is no conceit on my part because I believe I am a trustee of the gift that was inborn with me...' Referring to the gift of writers like Keats or Burns, he described it as 'a very beautiful thing', and he knew he had it.

Henry was never the same after his experiences in the First War — perhaps, like other ex-soldiers, never entirely sane either. There was a Colonel Clitheroe, DSO, of the Life Guards, who erected a signpost outside the gates of Hotham Hall in Yorkshire, where it stands to this day: 'To Ypres 347 miles. In defending the Salient our casualties were 90,000 killed; 71,000 missing; 410,000 wounded.' The memory of that war never left this man; inside the grounds you can find the tombstone to his horse: 'To the memory of a Gallant Horse. Bred in Holderness and Hunted Here. He landed in France 15 August 1914. Mons. Le Cateau. Aisne. Ypres. The Somme. Cambre. He knew them all and now Lies Here.' Some people may laugh at such sentiments; Henry would have understood.

In this sense Henry belonged to his time, the years surrounding the 1914-1918 war. He became increasingly solitary as his contemporaries died.

Shocked beyond recovery by his experience of the Christmas truce, with its realization that both armies believed they were fighting for 'the right', Henry veered in the opposite direction from the majority of his fellow-writers by becoming pro-German instead of pro-Soviet, and he never came back. Not once did he recant or make the easy apology which would have gained him instant forgiveness. He remained true to his beliefs, and in this respect he was more of a patriot than most. I have no reason to doubt his repeated assurance to me that if England had been invaded he would have taken up his pitchfork to defend his land, though it would have been a terrible choice if he had come face to face with a young soldier in German uniform in a second war. Always tolerant, he was not anti-semitic as people believed. (I heard him rebuke someone who *was*: 'You are wrong to talk about them like that. The Jews are a good and talented people.') But he sometimes provoked, for sheer devilment.

He held his views rigidly, but he was far from a narrow man. His taste in books ranged from his beloved Jefferies, Francis Thompson and John Cowper Powys, to the prose of Shelley, the great works of Trollope and the modern American writers Hemingway and Scott Fitzgerald. He gained vast pleasure from music, with favourite pieces by Delius, Debussy, Ravel, and, of course, above all, Wagner. A dozen books could be written about Henry Williamson and every one would be different. His span was so wide that this book could have swollen to ten times its length, and I had to control it from doing so. Ironically, in striving to see as the sun without shadows, he was constantly in the shadows himself, a grievance-collector even when none existed. Writing to me when he barely knew me, he lamented about his Hut: 'It is sunny up here in the field; but the hut is in the shade; and so cold. Where can one go? What do? IT'S CURSED IN HERE. A summer shed; not a winter place. NO SUN. The god of the golden sun; and perchance songlight is like sunlight and darkens the countenance of the soul.' This is interesting in retrospect, although it cannot have impressed me much then. Henry had his elfin moods as my father suggested. If I had to sum up in a single word, I should choose 'compassionate' — a rare, radiant quality, which shines out from the fifty books which followed *The Beautiful Years*.

No one could accuse Henry of self-satisfaction: he could always sympathize with the other person's point of view. There is a marvellous passage from 'London Children and Wild Flowers', an article first published in the *English Review*, which Father Brocard Sewell quoted at the Cheltenham Festival of Literature in 1980 when he gave a talk on

'Henry Williamson: Old Soldier'. Henry describes a visit to the countryside and his dismay one Sunday in May 1920 as he thought of the land after an invasion by hundreds of London trippers:

> The paths were beaten into mire by the passing and repassing of a thousand feet, acres of bluebells had been uprooted and taken away, many trampled and crushed, or gathered and carelessly cast on the paths. The apple blossom was stripped from the trees... the blooms were gone, a whole spring-life of them, carried away by the people who had come from Walworth, Shoreditch, and Woolwich.

Henry walked unhappily to the tram terminus for the journey back, and there he saw the Londoners clutching their emblems of spring:

> ... children wriggled and chattered, holding in their arms great bunches of bluebells with their sappy stalks gleaming white where the sun had not stained them; boys with purple-dusty grass bennets and girls with lilac-coloured cuckoo flowers and drooping buttercups.... I looked at the transfigured faces of the children — old or young they were all children — who breathed in the smoke and worked in the shadow, and saw that the beauty of the wild flowers had passed into their eyes; although the woods were ravaged, the spoiling and pillaging had not been in vain....

Henry was filled with ecstasy. It takes a great naturalist to know that people come first.

A Service of Thanksgiving for Henry Williamson was given at noon on 1 December 1977 at St Martin-in-the-Fields. A friend of mine remarked that 'Thanksgiving' seemed a curious word to apply to someone recently dead, but this is exactly what it was: a celebration for a writer who gave others extra happiness, if not always to those closest to him, or to himself.

It was a happy crowded occasion. Loetitia Williamson, who had remained loyal throughout and was the first to be remembered in Henry's will, was the most beloved person present. The secretary-companion who had shared their lives in the 1930s-1940s was there, but Christine was too ill to make the journey.

Amanda Allsop read stanzas from Shelley's 'Adonais' and the poet, Ted Hughes, gave his Tribute: 'We have come together today to remember the extraordinary vitality, and the long life — productive and energetic almost to the very end — and the genius, of an extraordinary man.' He described Henry's 'miraculous ear for dialect, full of wit and drama. And he was always different, mercurial, emotional, outrageous, amusing. But in one thing he was constant, and constantly attractive. He was untamed, and he was free.' Referring to the 'demon' which gave Henry his bad hours, Hughes explained that this was 'the powerhouse of his writing':

> it connected him to the dark world of the elements. It was the beast on his back that drove him. It was also Tarka — still wild, alert, open to everything, ready for anything. It was what pulsed through the best of his writing and it was genuinely him. And for that, I, for one, loved him.

Richard Williamson, who admits that his father 'tended to think of himself first', adds: 'we've forgotten all these things. He was a good man.' The bitterness has faded.

My own memory of Henry has grown brighter in the writing of this book. As I have said, I understand him better now, and like him more. I am glad that I dared the unforgivable on one of his last visits in 1975, asking him to sign my copy of *Tarka*, which he did with a smile and great sweetness:

> This book, gladly signed, for Daniel Farson.
> Literary gent of a breed like unto my own.
> At Vention, a sunny evening, sky bright and,
> at last, it is Summer come again!!

Index

Index

The Lone Swallows, 29, 39–40, 137, 199
Lucifer Before Sunrise, 93–4, 172–3

Macdonalds (publishers), 125, 144, 171, 173, 197
Mais, S.P.B., 79
Manchester, 17
Mansfield, Katherine, 174
Martin, Kingsley, 140
Mary, Princess Royal, 14
Masefield, John, x, 1, 58
Maugham, Somerset, 4, 5, 60, 133, 186
Milland, Jeff, 224
Millfield School, 91, 184, 193
Mitford, Unity, 101, 103
Monaco Television Festival, 224
Morrison, Herbert, 101
Morte Point, 88–9
Mortimore, Roger, 166
Mosley, Lady Diana, 101, 102–3, 109, 158
Mosley, Sir Oswald, 105, 108, 113, 115; HW's support for, 6, 97, 101–4, 111, 149, 176; interned during war, 109; on HW, 118–19, 154, 156, 157–8
Muggeridge, Malcolm, 103, 212
Munich, 96–7
Murry, John Middleton, 72–3, 119–20, 128, 174–5

National Front, 92
Nazism, 15, 91–102
New York, 65–6
Newcastle Evening World, 169
News of the World, 212
Niall, Ian, 199, 200–2
Nonesuch Press, 202
Norfolk, 10, 43; HW's farm in, 105–9, 113–14, 121–2
Norfolk Constabulary, 110–11, 112–13
Norman, Geraldine, 209
North Devon Infirmary, 229

Nuremberg rallies, 93, 96, 113, 196

The Observer, 211
The Old Stag, 133, 199
Olive, Elizabeth, 181, 190
Olsen, Thomas, 169
On Foot in Devon, 88–9
Orgill, Douglas, 100
Owl Club, 38–9, 52
Ox's Cross, 38–9, 52–5, 64, 109, 113, 122, 214–15

Painter, George, 174, 179
Panorama (magazine), 88, 125, 136
Parents National Education Union, 181
Pascal, Gabriel, 27
The Pathway, 21, 41, 60–1, 69–74, 80, 93, 165, 177, 207
The Patriot's Progress, 18–19, 165
Paul, Brenda Dean, 182
Pearson's Magazine, 47
The Peregrine's Saga and Other Stories, 37–8, 81, 199
Personal Choice (TV programme), 159–61
The Phasian Bird, 139
Picture Post, 136–7
The Pleasure Ground, 106–7
Plomley, Roy, 22
Pope, Michael, 22
Porter, Eric, 114
Pound, Reginald, 195
Powell, Anthony, 5
Powys, John Cowper, 236
Priestley, J.B., 77, 80, 171, 227
Pritchett, Sir Victor, 5
Proust, Marcel, 5, 165
Purser, Philip, 114
Putnam (publishers), 47, 52, 199
Putsborough Sands, 26

Quinn, Ann, 210–12, 217, 225

Raphael, Frederic, 114–17
Ravel, Maurice, 236

Index

COUNTRY CLASSICS

This popular series of quality paperbacks includes famous classics and forgotten masterpieces of writing about the countryside and rural subjects. The books are all produced in a 216 x 135mm format with beautiful colour covers. Selected titles are available in hardback.

Adventures Among Birds
W. H. Hudson

W. H. Hudson was one of the great field naturalists and ornithologists of the last century. In this book, he describes incidents and adventures watching birds across England, from wild geese in Norfolk to goldfinches in Dorset.

'This enchanting book is about the time before motorways and about the pure joy of having ears and eyes.'

EDWARD BLISHON,
Pick of the Paperbacks,
Radio 4

Paperback £3.95
Hardback £8.95

Country Tales
H. E. Bates

The best of H. E. Bates's much-loved stories about the countryside gathered together in one volume. The book contains 25 tales set in the remote hamlets, villages and market towns of England in the 1910s, 20s and 30s.

Every story is available only in this edition, which includes such classics as 'The Black Boxer', 'The Woman Who Had Imagination' and 'Harvest Moon'.

£4.95

Paperback only

The Country House-Wife's Garden
William Lawson

The first book ever written on gardening for women, a delightful pot-pourri of hints and gardening lore written in the seventeenth century by a Yorkshire parson. A perfect gift for the gardener.

Introduced by Rosemary Verey.

'This is an enchanting book.'

ALAN MELVILLE, Popular Gardening

Paperback £2.50
Hardback £4.95

The Essential Gilbert White of Selborne

The first popular selection from all of White's writings. A perfect introduction for the newcomer to White and Selborne.

Illustrated with wood engravings by Eric Ravilious.

Paperback £4.95
Hardback £8.95
384pp

Gypsy Folk Tales
John Sampson (Ed.)

Nothing brings us closer to the spirit of Romany life than these strange, haunting tales of poor country folk, beggars and travellers in a land of giants and dragons, great mansions, hovels, enchanted castles, witchcraft and magic.

'His great collections of folk-tales are treasure-houses of quaint expressions and beautiful turns of phrase.'

WALTER STARKIE

Paperback only £3.50

Life in a Devon Village
Henry Williamson

An enchanting memoir of village life in the Twenties. A companion volume to *Village Tales*.

'A welcome reprint ... Williamson is still our best nature writer since Richard Jefferies.'

BRIAN JACKMAN, The Sunday Times

Paperback £3.95
Hardback £8.95

Memoirs of a Surrey Labourer
George Bourne

'*There's writing for you.*'   HENRY WILLIAMSON

Paperback only £4.95

The Old Farm
Thomas Hennell

A fascinating record of traditional farms and farming methods, it presents a vivid portrait of old-fashioned country life and lore, from the dialects of the shepherds to cider-making, straw-plaiting and charcoal-burning, from weather-forecasting to mole-catching.

Paperback only £3.95

Sweet Thames Run Softly
Robert Gibbings

The story of a summer journey by rowing boat from the source of the Thames to London. Illustrated throughout with the author's own wood engravings.

'For the soul's refreshment read and keep this book. It is wise, kindly and full of lovely things.'

Sunday Times

'An intoxicating book, almost Edwardian in spirit.'

ANDREW LANGLEY, Daily Telegraph

'An enchanting experience ... there is only one other in the compendium of Thames literature which is deserving of inclusion in the same class — the immortal Three Men in a Boat.'

SENEX, Oxford Times

Paperback only £3.95

ORDER FORM

COUNTRY CLASSICS

	Hardback	Paperback
___ ADVENTURES AMONG BIRDS	£8.95	£3.95
___ THE COUNTRY HOUSE-WIFE'S GARDEN		£2.50
___ COUNTRY TALES	—	£4.95
___ THE ESSENTIAL GILBERT WHITE	£8.95	£4.95
___ GYPSY FOLK TALES	—	£3.50
___ LIFE IN A DEVON VILLAGE	£8.95	£3.95
___ MEMOIRS OF A SURREY LABOURER	—	£4.95
___ THE OLD FARM	—	£3.95
___ SWEET THAMES RUN SOFTLY	—	£3.95

If you cannot find these titles in your bookshop, they can be obtained directly from the publisher. Indicate the number of copies required and fill in the form below (in block letters please):

NAME ....

ADDRESS ....

....

....

Send to Robinson Publishing Cash Sales, P.O. Box 11, Falmouth, Cornwall TR10 9EN. Please enclose cheque or postal order to the value of the cover price plus: In UK only – 55p for the first book, 22p for the second book, and 14p for each additional book to a maximum £1.75. BFPO and Eire – 55p for the first book, 22p for the second book, and 14p for the next seven books and 8p for each book thereafter. Overseas – £1.25 for the first book, 31p per copy for each additional book.

Whilst every effort is made to keep prices low, it is sometimes necessary to increase prices at short notice. Robinson Publishing reserve the right to show on covers, and charge, new retail prices which may differ from those advertised in text or elsewhere.